2

# CONTEMPORARY AUTHORS

## 1945 TO THE PRESENT

THE BRITANNICA GUIDE TO AUTHORS

# CONTEMPORARY AUTHORS

## 1945 TO THE PRESENT

EDITED BY ADAM AUGUSTYN, ASSISTANT MANAGER AND ASSISTANT EDITOR, LITERATURE

**Britannica®**
Educational Publishing

IN ASSOCIATION WITH

**ROSEN**
EDUCATIONAL SERVICES

Published in 2014 by Britannica Educational Publishing
(a trademark of Encyclopædia Britannica, Inc.)
in association with Rosen Educational Services, LLC
29 East 21st Street, New York, NY 10010.

Distributed exclusively by Rosen Educational Services.
For a listing of additional Britannica Educational Publishing titles, call toll free (800) 237-9932.

First Edition

Britannica Educational Publishing
J.E. Luebering: Director, Core Reference Group
Adam Augustyn: Assistant Manager, Core Reference Group
Marilyn L. Barton: Senior Coordinator, Production Control
Steven Bosco: Director, Editorial Technologies
Lisa S. Braucher: Senior Producer and Data Editor
Jennifer Sale, Product Coordinator
Kathy Nakamura: Manager, Media Acquisition

Rosen Educational Services
Hope Lourie Killcoyne: Executive Editor
Nelson Sá: Art Director
Cindy Reiman: Photography Manager
Karen Huang: Photo Researcher
Brian Garvey: Designer
Introduction by Joseph Kampff

**Library of Congress Cataloging-in-Publication Data**

Contemporary authors: 1945 to the present/edited by: Adam Augustyn. —First edition.
    pages cm
"In association with Britannica Educational Publishing, Rosen Educational Services."
Includes bibliographical references and index.
ISBN 978-1-62275-003-0 (library binding)
1. Authors—20th century—Biography. 2. Literature, Modern—20th century—
History and criticism. 3. Authorship—History—20th century. I. Augustyn, Adam, 1979–
editor of compilation.
PN451.C623 2013
808'.045—dc23
[B]

                                                                                2013002674

*Manufactured in the United States of America*

# CONTENTS

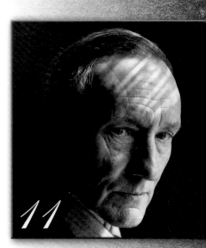

11

13

43

*61*

*91*

*114*

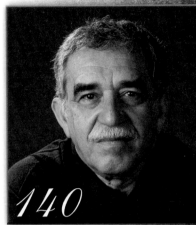

*140*

*148*

*168*

201

212

218

# INTRODUCTION

*Toni Morrison, 2008.* Francois Guillot/AFP/Getty Images

U nlike earlier periods of literary history such as the Enlightenment, Romanticism, and Modernism, which have established defining characteristics and took place over generally agreed-upon timespans, the period of literary production following World War II and up to today is still developing. While one can state with certainty that Voltaire was a principle figure of the Enlightenment, that William Wordsworth and Samuel Taylor Coleridge set out the basic program of English Romanticism in their *Lyrical Ballads*, and that James

Joyce's *Ulysses* is an exemplary Modernist text, it is with less confidence that one can situate the work of, for example, Toni Morrison in literary history. With contemporary and near-contemporary authors, we do not have the critical distance afforded by the passage of time from which to assess their works. While Toni Morrison is recognized today as one of the most important authors of the late-twentieth century—she won the Nobel Prize in Literature in 1993—it is impossible to say whether her work will be as highly valued one hundred years from now. Major literary awards often provide some assurance of an author's enduring significance, but they are no guarantee: tastes change frequently and sometimes inexplicably. Then there is the question of placing contemporary authors' works within specific contexts.

Perhaps owing to globalization and the development of mass media after World War II, the widely acclaimed authors of this period represent an unprecedented range of nationalities, genres, traditions, and worldviews. Morrison, for example, may be understood as working within (and reworking) such diverse traditions as American slave narrative, politically engaged African American writing, magical realism, Southern Gothic, and postmodernism. While earlier periods in literary history tend to be relatively precise in their geographies and genres, some prominent features of post-1945 literature are its cosmopolitanism and diversity. *Contemporary Authors: 1945 to the Present* reflects the expansiveness of contemporary literature by providing in-depth and authoritative biographical, contextual, bibliographical, and other critical information on authors from as far afield as Turkey, Japan, and Nigeria, working in a wide variety of genres such as experimental theatre, science fiction, Beat poetry, graphic novels, and children's literature. This volume is an invaluable asset for students, researchers, and casual readers who want a better understanding of the varied authors of the recent past and today.

One of the first writers profiled in this book is notable for having published only one novel during his lifetime. The American author Ralph Ellison (1914–94) published *Invisible Man* in 1952. Since its appearance, Ellison's novel has been enormously influential and well received, winning the prestigious National Book Award in 1953. Ellison's exploration of racial injustice, alienation, labor exploitation, and the effects of social invisibility experienced by marginalized people continues to resonate with many readers today. Ellison studied music at the Tuskegee Normal and Industrial Institute before leaving the American South for New York City in 1936. At the time, New York was a hotbed of African American political and cultural activity, but Ellison was criticized by his fellow black authors for his treatment of his writings as primarily works of art rather than instruments of social change. Regarded as an important innovator of American prose, Ellison taught creative writing and lectured on African-American culture at numerous American universities until his death. His second novel, Juneteenth, was published posthumously in 1999.

Allen Ginsberg (1926–97) was a major figure of the Beat movement in the United States. The Beats were fascinated by the possibilities they saw in drugs, jazz music, sex, and Zen Buddhism for liberation from conventional American life in the 1950s. Their experimentation and rebelliousness carried over into their literary productions. Ginsberg's father was a poet as well as an English teacher, and his mother suffered from psychological disorders for which she was committed to a psychiatric hospital for a number of years before her death. Ginsberg later treats his relationship with his mother in one of his most important works, *Kaddish* (a Jewish prayer for the dead), which he published in 1961. Readers will most likely recognize Ginsberg, however, from his long poem *Howl*, which begins with a powerful evocation of the Beats' dissatisfaction with the time:

> *I saw the best minds of my generation destroyed*
> *by madness, starving hysterical naked, dragging them-*
> *selves through the negro streets at dawn looking for an*
> *angry fix,*

While attending Columbia University, Ginsberg met a number of people who would become important figures in the Beat movement, such as Jack Kerouac (1922–69)—whose sprawling novel *On the Road* is considered probably the most important work of Beat literature.

In novels such as *The Bluest Eye*, *Tar Baby*, and *Jazz*, Toni Morrison (1931– ) picks up many of the motifs of Ellison's *Invisible Man*. Like Ellison, she attended a historically black college (Howard University) in the South before moving to the northeastern United States, where she earned a master's in English at Cornell University in 1955. Always deeply concerned with the black experience in the United States, Morrison eventually returned to Howard, where she taught from 1957 to 1964. After working as a fiction editor for a number of years, Morrison published her first novel, *The Bluest Eye*, in 1970. The novel portrays the subtle yet powerfully destructive effects the desire for an impossible standard of white beauty has on the psyche of its young black protagonist.

Morrison's most successful and highly regarded novel, *Beloved*, was published in 1987 and won the Pulitzer Prize a year later. *Beloved* is a fictionalized retelling of the true story of an escaped slave who killed her child to prevent her from being taken back into slavery. Dedicated to the "sixty million or more" who died in the American slave trade, the novel reminds readers that the spectre of slavery still haunts the American political, social, economic, and psychic landscape. In addition to her success as an author, Morrison is an influential literary scholar.

Aside from the notoriously reclusive J.D. Salinger, of all the authors in this volume, perhaps the least can be said for certain about the personal life of Thomas Pynchon (1937– ). Unlike many other writers of his generation, Pynchon has unswervingly refused to engage with the media, and there are very few photographs of him in circulation. Pynchon studied English at Cornell University, served in the U.S. Navy, and worked as a technical writer at Boeing Company before turning to fiction writing full-time. He wrote one of the most important novels of the late-twentieth century, *Gravity's Rainbow* (1973). *Gravity's Rainbow*, which won the National Book Award in 1974, is a long, elaborate novel that attempts to catalogue in intricate prose the dystopian facets of the post-World War II world in encyclopedic detail. Pynchon's paranoid and darkly humourous fictions have inspired many writers who followed him, notably David Foster Wallace (1962–2008), whose extraordinary 1996 novel *Infinite Jest* matches Pynchon's fictions in its ambitious postmodern take on contemporary American life.

Of the same generation as Pynchon, the English playwright Harold Pinter (1930–2008) is also notable for the difficulty of his works. Pinter was born to working-class parents in London and briefly studied acting at the Royal Academy of Dramatic Art. Pinter's first full-length play, the absurdist comedy *The Birthday Party*, baffled the audience at its premier in 1958 but has since become one of his most performed and anthologized works. The play exhibits many of Pinter's signature techniques such as sparse production; fragmented, frequently incoherent dialogue; and extended periods of silence. Pinter achieved critical acclaim with his second full-length play, *The Caregiver*, and would go on to write many successful works for the stage, television, and film. Among his many accolades, Pinter was awarded the Nobel Prize for Literature in 2005 and made a chevalier of the French Legion of Honour in 2007.

The Canadian author Margret Atwood (1939– ) is remarkable for her ability to expertly negotiate a wide range of subject matter while working in a variety of genres, exploring feminist and gender issues in novels such as *Surfacing* and *The Handmaid's Tale* and the implications of genetic engineering in the dystopic, speculative fictions of *Oryx and Crake* and *After the Flood*. Atwood's father was a scientist, and she spent much of her youth with him in Northern Canada while he did research. Her early encounters with science spurred her interest in science fiction and had a profound effect on her work. Atwood began writing seriously while she was a teenager, and she earned a master's in English from Radcliffe College in Massachusetts in 1962. In addition to her success as a novelist, Atwood has published many short-story and poetry collections and a number of nonfiction works, including *In Other Worlds: SF and the Human Imagination*, in which she elucidates the distinctions between the many subgenres—such as speculative fiction and fantasy—that fall into the category of science fiction.

Murakami Haruki (1949– ) is one of the most internationally acclaimed and widely translated novelists to come out of Japan. His 1987 novel *Noruwei no mori* (*Norwegian Wood*)—a best-seller in Japan that established him as one of that country's greatest literary stars—is a coming-of-age story set in Tokyo that explores themes of traumatic loss and Japanese identity around the time of the student protests in the late 1960s. His other important works include the experimental Sekai no owari to hadoboirudo wandarando (*Hard-Boiled Wonderland and the End of the World*) and the massive tome *1Q84*, which follows two characters as they traverse an alternate reality of their own creation. Fascinated by American popular culture, Murakami has published his translations of works by authors such as Raymond Carver, Ursula K. Le Guin, and J.D. Salinger in Japan.

Although he was one of the most celebrated South American writers of his generation, Roberto Bolaño (1953–2003) did not have any of his works translated into English during his lifetime. His 1998 novel *Los detectives salvajes* was a tremendous success in the United States when it finally appeared in translation as *The Savage Detectives* in 2007. Bolaño was born in Santiago, Chili, but frequently moved around the country as a child until his family settled down for a time in Mexico City in 1968. There, he became dedicated to leftist causes and began to write politically charged poetry. As an adult, Bolaño moved to Spain, where he wrote incessantly, turning to novels later in life, until he died of liver failure at age 50. What many critics consider to be his masterpiece, *2066*—an enormous novel of over 1,100 pages divided into five sections—was published posthumously a year later. The book features many of the signature characteristics of Bolaño's writing style: shifting narrative perspectives, loosely fictionalized retellings of real-world events, and incredibly detailed descriptive language.

The Harry Potter series of children's books by British author J.K. Rowling (1965– ) have proved enormously popular with young people and adults alike. Rowling begin work on the Harry Potter stories soon after graduating from college in the late 1980s. Before the publication of *Harry Potter and the Philosopher's Stone* in 1997 (released in the U.S. and elsewhere as Harry Potter and the Sorcerer's Stone), Rowling was supplementing her income from teaching with government assistance. The novel was an instant hit, receiving a number of prestigious children's book awards. Since then, all seven books in the series about the adventures of a boy wizard have been best-sellers, the stories have been adapted into commercially successful films, and the Harry Potter series has become beloved by a generation of young readers around the world. Today, Rowling—who made her entrance into adult fiction with her 2012 novel *The Casual Vacancy*—is one of England's most successful novelists.

The son of two Holocaust survivors, Art Spiegelman (1948– ) was born in Stockholm, Sweden, before his family came to the United States in 1951. Raised in Queens, New York, Spiegelman began drawing edgy cartoons at an early age, and studied art at the High School of Art and Design in Manhattan. Spiegelman studied briefly at New York State's Binghamton University, where he got involved in the underground comics scene, but left soon after his mother's suicide in 1968. Spiegelman's critically acclaimed graphic novels of his father's experiences in the concentration camp and his own struggle with survivor's guilt in *Maus I: A Survivor's Tale: My Father Bleeds History* and *Maus II: A Survivor's Tale: And Here My Troubles Began* helped to garner a wider audience for graphic novels in the 1980s and 1990s. *Maus* earned a "Special Award" Pulitzer Prize in 1992, and has been translated into more than 20 languages. In response to the World Trade Center attack on September 11, 2001, Spiegelman published *In the Shadow of No Towers*, a series of large-format comic strips documenting his own attempts to cope with the traumatic shock of the attack.

*Contemporary Authors: 1945 to the Present* includes entries on more than 150 authors from around the world. These exceptional writers often engage critically with the most important events of our time while expanding the boundaries of literary expression. Writing in a wide array of languages, styles, and genres—sometimes within a single work—the authors represented in this volume reflect the far-ranging diversity and complexity of contemporary life. This volume not only presents an indispensable key to the lives and works of the most important authors of the recent past and today, it also provides a solid foundation for understanding the literature of the future.

# AVROM SUTZKEVER

(b. July 15, 1913, Smorgon, White Russia, Russian Empire [now
Smarhon, Belarus]—d. January 20, 2010, Tel Aviv–Yafo, Israel)

Avrom (or Abraham) Sutzkever was a Yiddish-language
poet whose works chronicle his childhood in Siberia,
his life in the Vilna (Vilnius) ghetto during World War II,
and his escape to join Jewish partisans. After the Holocaust
he became a major figure in Yiddish letters in Israel and
throughout the world.

In 1915 Sutzkever and his family fled their home in
White Russia to Siberia to escape World War I; they
returned to the region in 1920 and lived near Vilna, where
Sutzkever later studied literary criticism at the University
of Vilna. He began writing poetry in Hebrew around 1927.
He was influenced by intellectual thought at the Yiddish
Scientific Institute (what would later become the YIVO
Institute for Jewish Research) and became associated with
Yung Vilne ("Young Vilna"), a group of aspiring Yiddish
writers living in Vilna. A poet who celebrated nature,
beauty, and language, Sutzkever was artistically and ideo-
logically at odds with this group, whose work reflected a
more urban, leftist orientation.

Early in his career Sutzkever contributed to the
American Modernist poetry journal *In zikh* ("In Oneself"
or "Introspection"). His first published collection, *Lider*
(1937; "Songs"), received critical acclaim, praised for its
innovative imagery, language, and form. His collection
*Valdiks* (1940; "Sylvan") celebrates nature. *Di festung* (1945;
"The Fortress") reflects his experiences as a member of
the ghetto resistance movement in Belorussia (Belarus)

and his service with Jewish partisans during World War II. Sutzkever was also a central cultural figure in the Vilna ghetto, where he organized and inspired revues, exhibitions, lectures, and poetry readings during the war. He was a member of the "Paper Brigade," a group of Jewish intellectuals chosen to select Jewish cultural artifacts to be sent to the Institute for the Investigation of the Jewish Question, founded by Nazi ideologist Alfred Rosenberg; the remainder was sold for pulp. Both during and immediately after the war, Sutzkever led the effort to save for the Jews whatever could be rescued, first from the Nazis and then from the Soviets. His efforts were not in vain; thousands of volumes and documents survived and were eventually reclaimed in the 1990s by the YIVO Institute for Jewish Research.

Sutzkever returned to Poland in 1946 and then lived briefly in France and the Netherlands. In 1946 he testified at the Nürnberg trials, and in 1947 he settled in Palestine (later Israel), where from 1949 to 1995 he edited *Di goldene keyt* ("The Golden Chain"), a Yiddish literary journal.

The prose volume *Fun Vilner geto* (1946; "From the Vilna Ghetto"), the poetry collections *Lider fun geto* (1946; "Songs from the Ghetto"), *Geheymshtot* (1948; "Secret City"), and *Yidishe gas* (1948; "Jewish Street"), and the volume of prose poetry *Griner akvaryum* (1975; "Green Aquarium") are all based on his experiences during World War II. *Sibir* (1953; *Siberia*) recalls his early childhood. Sutzkever's other collections of poetry include *In midber Sinai* (1957; *In the Sinai Desert*), *Di fidlroyz* (1974; *The Fiddle Rose: Poems 1970–1972*), and *Fun alte un yunge ksavyadn* (1982; *Laughter Beneath the Forest: Poems from Old and New Manuscripts*). *Burnt Pearls: Ghetto Poems of Abraham Sutzkever* (1981), *A. Sutzkever: Selected Poetry and Prose* (1991), and *Beneath the Trees* (2003) are collections of his work in English translation.

# ROBERTSON DAVIES

(b. August 28, 1913, Thamesville, Ontario, Canada —
d. December 2, 1995, Orangeville, Ontario)

The novelist and playwright William Robertson Davies is known for producing works that offer penetrating observations on Canadian provincialism and prudery.

Educated in England at the University of Oxford, Davies had training in acting, directing, and stage management as a member of the Old Vic Repertory Company. He edited the Peterborough *Examiner* (1942–63), a newspaper owned by his family, and taught English at the University of Toronto (1960–81; emeritus thereafter).

Davies's early reputation was based on the plays *Eros at Breakfast* (1949) and *At My Heart's Core* (1950), which are satires on Canadian standards and values. He also published collections of humorous essays, such as *The Diary of Samuel Marchbanks* (1947); *The Table Talk of Samuel Marchbanks* (1949), in which an irascible old bachelor's opinions highlight the problems of sustaining culture in Canada; and *Samuel Marchbanks' Almanack* (1967). Davies's three trilogies of novels secured his reputation as Canada's foremost man of letters. Known as a traditional storyteller, he was a master of imaginative writing and wicked wit. The Salterton trilogy consists of *Tempest-Tost* (1951), *Leaven of Malice* (1954), and *A Mixture of Frailties* (1958), all of which are comedies of manners set in the fictional provincial Canadian university town of Salterton. Even better known are the novels of the Deptford trilogy, consisting of *Fifth Business* (1970), *The Manticore* (1972), and *World of Wonders* (1975). These books examine the intersecting lives of three men from the small Canadian town of Deptford and interweave Davies's moral concerns with bits of arcane lore and his enduring interest in Jungian psychotherapy. The Cornish trilogy, titled after the surname of the novels' protagonists, consists of *The Rebel Angels* (1981), *What's Bred in the Bone* (1985), and *The Lyre of Orpheus* (1988); these novels satirize the art world, grand opera, and other aspects of high culture in Canada. *Murther & Walking Spirits* (1991) was written from the perspective of a dead man. *The Cunning Man* (1994), set in Toronto, spans the 20th century through the memoirs of a doctor; characters from Davies's earlier works also appear in this novel. His later nonfiction included *The Mirror of Nature* (1983).

Davies was primarily concerned with the moral conflicts of characters in small Canadian towns. In the course of his narratives he wittily satirized bourgeois provincialism, explored the relation between mysticism and art, and affirmed the possibilities for self-knowledge through Jungian philosophy.

# *CLAUDE SIMON*

(b. October 10, 1913, Tananarive [now Antananarivo], Madagascar— d. July 6, 2005, Paris, France)

Claude Simon was a writer whose works are among the most authentic representatives of the French *nouveau roman* ("new novel") that emerged in the 1950s. He was awarded the Nobel Prize for Literature in 1985.

The son of a cavalry officer who was killed in World War I, Simon was raised by his mother in Perpignan, France. After studies at Paris, Oxford, and Cambridge, he traveled widely and then fought in World War II. He was captured by the Germans in May 1940, escaped, and joined the French Resistance, managing to complete

4

his first novel, *Le Tricheur* (1945; "The Trickster"), during the war years. Later he settled in his hometown in southern France, where he bought a vineyard and produced wine.

In *Le Vent* (1957; *The Wind*) Simon defined his goals: to challenge the fragmentation of his time and to rediscover the permanence of objects and people, evidenced by their survival through the upheavals of contemporary history. He treated the turmoil of the Spanish Civil War in *La Corde raide* (1947; "The Taut Rope") and *Le Sacre du printemps* (1954; "The Rite of Spring") and the 1940 collapse of France in *Le Tricheur*. Four novels—*L'Herbe* (1958; *The Grass*), *La Route des Flandres* (1960; *The Flanders Road*), *La Palace* (1962; *The Palace*), and *Histoire* (1967)—constitute a cycle containing recurring characters and events. Many critics consider these novels, especially *La Route des Flandres*, to be his most important work. Later novels include *La Bataille de Pharsale* (1969; *The Battle of Pharsalus*), *Triptyque* (1973; *Triptych*), *Les Géorgiques* (1981; *The Georgics*), and *Le Tramway* (2001; *The Trolley*).

Simon's style is a mixture of narration and stream of consciousness, lacking all punctuation and heavy with 1,000-word sentences. Through such masses of words, Simon attempted to capture the very progression of life. His novels remain readable despite their seeming chaos.

# *Vasco Pratolini*

(b. October 19, 1913, Florence, Italy—d. January 12, 1991, Rome)

The Italian short-story writer and novelist Vasco Pratolini is known particularly for compassionate portraits of the Florentine poor during the Fascist era. He is considered a major figure in Italian Neorealism.

Pratolini was reared in Florence, the setting of nearly all his fiction, in a poor family. He held various jobs until his health failed. His illness forced his confinement in a sanatorium from 1935 to 1937. He had no formal education but was an incessant reader, and during his confinement he began to write.

Pratolini went to Rome, where he met the novelist Elio Vittorini, who introduced him into literary circles and became a close friend. Like Vittorini, Pratolini rejected fascism; the Fascist government shut down Pratolini's literary magazine, *Campo di Marte* ("Field of Mars"), within nine months of its founding in 1939.

His first important novel, *Il quartiere* (1944; *The Naked Streets*), offers a vivid, exciting portrait of a gang of Florentine adolescents. *Cronaca familiare* (1947; *Two Brothers*) is a tender story of Pratolini's dead brother. *Cronache di poveri amanti* (1947; *A Tale of Poor Lovers*), which has been called one of the finest works of Italian Neorealism, became an immediate best-seller and won two international literary prizes. The novel gives a panoramic view of the Florentine poor at the time of the Fascist triumph in 1925–26. *Un eroe del nostro tempo* (1949; *A Hero of Today*, or, *A Hero of Our Time*) attacks fascism.

Between 1955 and 1966 Pratolini published three novels under the general title *Una storia italiana* ("An Italian Story"), covering the period from 1875 to 1945. The first, *Metello* (1955), considered the finest of the three, follows its working-class hero through the labour disputes after 1875 and climaxes with a successful building masons' strike in 1902. The second, *Lo scialo* (1960; "The Waste"), depicts the lassitude of the lower classes between 1902 and the mid-1920s preparatory to the Fascist takeover. The final volume, *Allegoria e derisione* (1966; "Allegory and Derision"), deals with the triumph and fall of Fascism, focusing on the moral and intellectual conflicts of the Florentine intelligentsia.

# *ARNO SCHMIDT*

(b. January 18, 1914, Hamburg-Hamm, Germany—d. June 3, 1979, Celle)

A rno Schmidt was a novelist, translator, and critic whose experimental prose established him as the preeminent Modernist of 20th-century German literature. With roots in both German Romanticism and Expressionism, he attempted to develop modern prose forms that correspond more closely to the workings of the conscious and subconscious mind and to revitalize a literary language that he considered debased by Nazism and war.

Born the son of a policeman in the working-class suburb of Hamburg-Hamm, Schmidt moved with his sister and mother back to his parents' hometown of Lauban in Silesia after the death of his father in 1928. He graduated from *Gymnasium* (a secondary school that prepares students for higher education) in 1933 and briefly attended a commercial school in nearby Görlitz; for the next seven years he worked as an accountant at a textile factory. In 1937 he married. Drafted into the army in 1940, he served in the artillery at a flak base in Norway until the end of the war. After being held as a prisoner of war for eight months, he worked briefly as an interpreter for the British military police. His home in Lauban and, more importantly for him, his library had been lost in the war, and he and his wife were officially classified as Displaced Persons. In 1946 they found refuge in a one-room apartment in Cordingen in Lower Saxony. From there he launched his literary career with a series of novellas, beginning with *Leviathan* (1949; Eng. trans. *Leviathan*), in which a doomed attempt to escape a bombing raid in a commandeered train reflects the plight of humankind as the plaything of a malicious God.

Schmidt continued to search for a home, moving from one cramped apartment to another in Lower Saxony, Rhine Hessia, the Saarland, and Darmstadt. His works during these years include a triptych of short novels dealing with war and its aftermath: *Brand's Haide* (1951; *Brand's Heath*), *Aus dem Leben eines Fauns* (1953; *Scenes from the Life of a Faun*), and *Schwarze Spiegel* (1951; *Dark Mirrors*). He also wrote a biography of Friedrich, baron de La Motte Fouqué, a popular 19th-century German writer (1958); two volumes of literary criticism; eight more novellas, including *Seelandschaft mit Pocahontas* (1955; *Lake Scenery with Pocahontas*), a bittersweet love story that almost landed him in court on charges of pornography and blasphemy; *Das steinerne Herz* (1956; *The Stony Heart*), a novel critical of postwar politics and society in both East and West Germany; and *Die Gelehrtenrepublik* (1957; translated as *The Egghead Republic* [1979] and *Republica Intelligentsia* [1994]), a dystopian science-fiction novel that satirizes East-West relations and remains his most popular work. To supplement his meagre income he translated both best-sellers and classics from the English. Over the next two decades he would translate works by James Fenimore Cooper, Wilkie Collins, Edward Bulwer-Lytton, and Edgar Allan Poe.

In 1958 Schmidt moved to the village of Bargfeld near Celle in the Lüneburg Heath. Over the next 20 years, until his death in 1979, he wrote some of the landmarks of postwar German literature. In *Kaff auch Mare Crisium* (1960; *Boondocks/Moondocks*), a novel set on the German heath and on the Moon in the wake of nuclear war, he began to push the limits of experimentation with orthography and punctuation. The influence of James Joyce and Sigmund Freud are apparent in both a collection of short stories,

*Kühe in Halbtrauer* (1964; *Country Matters*), and, most especially, in *Zettels Traum* (1970; *Bottom's Dream*)—a three-columned, more than 1,300-page, photo-offset typescript, centring on the mind and works of Poe. It was then that Schmidt developed his theory of "etyms," the small units of language that betray subconscious desires. Two further works on the same grand scale are the "novella-comedy" *Die Schule der Atheisten* (1972; *School for Atheists*) and *Abend mit Goldrand* (1975; *Evening Edged in Gold*), a dream-scape that has as its focal point Hiëronymus Bosch's *Garden of Earthly Delights* and that has come to be regarded as his finest and most mature work.

Schmidt was a man of vast autodidactic learning and Rabelaisian humour. Though complex and sometimes daunting, his works are enriched by inventive language

*Arno Schmidt.* © AP Images

9

and imbued with a profound commitment to humanity's intellectual achievements.

# WILLIAM S. BURROUGHS

(b. February 5, 1914, St. Louis, Missouri, U.S.—
d. August 2, 1997, Lawrence, Kansas)

William Seward Burroughs was an American writer of experimental novels that evoke, in deliberately erratic prose, a nightmarish, sometimes wildly humorous world. His sexual explicitness (he was an avowed and outspoken homosexual) and the frankness with which he dealt with his experiences as a drug addict won him a following among writers of the Beat movement.

Burroughs was the grandson of the inventor of the Burroughs adding machine and grew up in St. Louis in comfortable circumstances, graduating from Harvard University in 1936 and continuing study there in archaeology and ethnology. Having tired of the academic world, he then held a variety of jobs. In 1943 Burroughs moved to New York City, where he became friends with Jack Kerouac and Allen Ginsberg, two writers who would become principal figures in the Beat movement. Burroughs first took morphine about 1944, and he soon became addicted to heroin. That year Lucien Carr, a member of Burroughs's social circle, killed a man whom Carr claimed had made sexual advances toward him. Before turning himself in to the police, Carr confessed to Burroughs and Kerouac, who were both arrested as material witnesses. They were later released on bail, and neither man was charged with a crime; Carr was convicted of manslaughter but was later

*William S. Burroughs, 1976.* Juergen Vollmer/Redferns /Getty Images

pardoned. In 1945 Burroughs and Kerouac collaborated on a fictionalized retelling of those events entitled *And the Hippos Were Boiled in Their Tanks*. Rejected by publishers at the time, it was not published until 2008.

In 1949 he moved with his second wife to Mexico, where in 1951 he accidentally shot and killed her in a drunken prank. Fleeing Mexico, he wandered through the Amazon region of South America, continuing his experiments with drugs, a period of his life detailed in *The Yage Letters,* his correspondence with Ginsberg written in 1953 but not published until 1963. Between travels he lived in London, Paris, Tangier, and New York City but in 1981 settled in Lawrence, Kansas.

He used the pen name William Lee in his first published book, *Junkie: Confessions of an Unredeemed Drug Addict* (1953, reissued as *Junky* in 1977), an account of the addict's life. *The Naked Lunch* (Paris, 1959; U.S. title, *Naked Lunch*, 1962; film 1991) was completed after his treatment for drug addiction. All forms of addiction, according to Burroughs, are counterproductive for writing, and the only gain to his own work from his 15 years as an addict came from the knowledge he acquired of the bizarre, carnival milieu in which the drug taker is preyed upon as victim. The grotesqueness of this world is vividly satirized in *Naked Lunch*, which also is much preoccupied with homosexuality and police persecution. In the novels that followed—among them *The Soft Machine* (1961), *The Wild Boys* (1971), *Exterminator!* (1973), *Cities of the Red Night* (1981), *Place of Dead Roads* (1983), *Queer* (1985), *The Western Lands* (1987), and *My Education: A Book of Dreams* (1995)— Burroughs further experimented with the structure of the novel. *Burroughs* (1983), by filmmaker Howard Brookner, is a documentary on the artist's life.

# RALPH ELLISON

(b. March 1, 1914, Oklahoma City, Oklahoma, U.S.—
d. April 16, 1994, New York, New York)

The American writer Ralph Ellison won eminence with his first novel (and the only one published during his lifetime), *Invisible Man* (1952).

Ellison left Tuskegee Normal and Industrial Institute (now Tuskegee University) in 1936 after three years' study of music and moved to New York City. There he befriended Richard Wright, the Harlem editor of the Communist *Daily Worker* and soon to become one of the most influential African American writers of the 20th century, who encouraged Ellison to try his hand at writing. In 1937 Ellison began contributing short stories, reviews, and essays to various periodicals. He worked on the Federal Writers' Project from 1938 to 1942, which he followed with a stint as the managing editor of *The Negro Quarterly* for just under a year.

Following service in World War II, he produced *Invisible Man*, which won the 1953 National Book Award for fiction. The story is a bildungsroman that tells of a naive and idealistic (and, significantly, nameless) Southern black youth who goes to Harlem, joins the fight against white oppression, and ends up ignored by his fellow blacks as well as by whites. The novel won praise for its stylistic innovations in infusing classic literary motifs with modern black speech and culture, while providing a thoroughly unique take on the construction of contemporary African American identity. However, Ellison's treatment of his novel as first and foremost a work of art—as opposed to a primarily polemical work—led to some complaints from his fellow black novelists at the time that he was not sufficiently devoted to social

*Ralph Ellison, 1952.* Encyclopædia Britannica, Inc.

change. After *Invisible Man* appeared, Ellison published only two collections of essays: *Shadow and Act* (1964) and *Going to the Territory* (1986). He lectured widely on black culture, folklore, and creative writing and taught at various American colleges and universities. *Flying Home, and Other Stories* was published posthumously in 1996. He left a second novel unfinished at his death; it was published, in a much-shortened form, as *Juneteenth* in 1999.

# OCTAVIO PAZ

(b. March 31, 1914, Mexico City, Mexico—
d. April 19, 1998, Mexico City)

The Mexican poet, writer, and diplomat Octavio Paz is recognized as one of the major Latin American writers of the 20th century. He received the Nobel Prize for Literature in 1990.

Paz's family was ruined financially by the Mexican Civil War, and he grew up in straitened circumstances. Nonetheless, he had access to the excellent library that had been stocked by his grandfather, a politically active liberal intellectual who had himself been a writer. Paz was educated at a Roman Catholic school and at the University of Mexico. He published his first book of poetry, *Luna silvestre* ("Forest Moon"), in 1933 at age 19. In 1937 the young poet visited Spain, where he identified strongly with the Republican cause in the Spanish Civil War. His reflection on that experience, *Bajo tu clara sombra y otros poemas* ("Beneath Your Clear Shadow and Other Poems"), was published in Spain in 1937 and revealed him as a writer of real promise. Before returning home Paz visited Paris, where Surrealism and its adherents exerted a profound influence on him.

Back in Mexico, Paz founded and edited several important literary reviews, including *Taller* ("Workshop") from 1938 to 1941 and *El hijo pródigo* ("The Prodigal Son"), which he cofounded in 1943. His major poetic publications included *No pasaran!* (1937; "They Shall Not Pass!"), *Libertad bajo palabra* (1949; "Freedom Under Parole"), *¿Águila o sol?* (1951; *Eagle or Sun?*), and *Piedra de sol* (1957; *The Sun Stone*). In the same period, he produced prose volumes of essays and literary criticism, including *El laberinto de la soledad* (1950; *The Labyrinth of Solitude*), an influential essay in which he analyzes the character, history, and culture of Mexico; and *El arco y la lira* (1956; *The Bow and the Lyre*) and *Las peras del olmo* (1957; "The Pears of the Elm"), which are studies of contemporary Spanish American poetry.

Paz entered Mexico's diplomatic corps in 1945, after having lived for two years in San Francisco and New York, and served in a variety of assignments, including one as Mexico's ambassador to India from 1962 to 1968; in the latter year he resigned in protest over Mexico's brutal treatment of student radicals that year. From 1971 to 1976 Paz edited *Plural*, and in 1976 he founded *Vuelta*, which continued to be published until his death in 1998; both were reviews of literature and politics.

His poetry after 1962 includes *Blanco* (1967; Eng. trans. *Blanco*), influenced by Stéphane Mallarmé's poetry and John Cage's theories on music; *Ladera este* (1971; "East Slope"), which is suffused with Paz's understanding of East Indian myths; *Hijos del aire* (1979; *Airborn*), sonnet sequences created by Paz and the poet Charles Tomlinson building on each other's lines; and *Árbol adentro* (1987; *A Tree Within*), in which many of the poems are based on works by artists such as Marcel Duchamp and Robert Rauschenberg. An English-language selection, *The Collected Poems of Octavio Paz, 1957–1987*, was published in 1987.

His later prose works, some originally in English, include *Conjunciones y disyunciones* (1969; *Conjunctions and Disjunctions*), a discussion of the world's cultural attitudes; *El mono gramático* (1974; *The Monkey Grammarian*), a meditation on language; and *Tiempo nublado* (1983; "Cloudy Weather," translated as *One Earth, Four or Five Worlds: Reflections on Contemporary History*), a study of international politics with emphasis on the relationship between the United States and Latin America.

Paz was influenced in turn by Marxism, Surrealism, existentialism, Buddhism, and Hinduism. In the poetry of his maturity, he used a rich flow of surrealistic imagery in dealing with metaphysical questions. As one critic said, he explored the zones of modern culture outside the marketplace, and his most prominent theme was the human ability to overcome existential solitude through erotic love and artistic creativity. In addition to the Nobel Prize, Paz received numerous other awards, including the Cervantes Prize, the most prestigious Spanish-language accolade. The 15-volume *Obras completas de Octavio Paz* ("Complete Works of Octavio Paz") was published from 1994 to 2004.

# MARGUERITE DURAS

(b. April 4, 1914, Gia Dinh, Cochinchina [Vietnam] — d. March 3, 1996, Paris, France)

The French novelist, screenwriter, scenarist, playwright, and film director Marguerite Duras (a pseudonym of Marguerite Donnadieu) is internationally known for her screenplays of *Hiroshima mon amour* (1959) and *India Song* (1975). The novel *L'Amant* (1984; *The Lover*; film 1992) won the prestigious Prix Goncourt in 1984.

Duras spent most of her childhood in Indochina, but at the age of 17 she moved to France to study at the University of Paris, Sorbonne, from which she received *licences* in law and politics. She favoured leftist causes and for 10 years was a member of the Communist Party. She began writing in 1942. *Un Barrage contre le Pacifique* (1950; *The Sea Wall*), her third published novel and first success, dealt semiautobiographically with a poor French family in Indochina. Her next successes, *Le Marin de Gibraltar* (1952; *The Sailor from Gibraltar*) and *Moderato cantabile* (1958), were more lyrical and complex and more given to dialogue.

This splendid instinct for dialogue led Duras to produce the original screenplay for Alain Resnais's critically acclaimed film *Hiroshima mon amour*, about a brief love affair in postwar Hiroshima between a Japanese businessman and a French actress. She directed as well as wrote the 1975 film adaptation of her play *India Song*, which offers a static, moody portrayal of the wife of the French ambassador in Calcutta and her several lovers. Some of her screenplays were adaptations of her own novels and short stories.

Duras turned regularly to a more abstract and synthetic mode, with fewer characters, less plot and narrative, and fewer of the other elements of traditional fiction. The semiautobiographical story of *L'Amant*, about a French teenage girl's love affair with a Chinese man 12 years her senior, was revised in the novel *L'Amant de la Chine du Nord* (1991; *The North China Lover*). Among her other novels were *L'Après-midi de Monsieur Andesmas* (1962; *The Afternoon of Monsieur Andesmas*), *Le Ravissement de Lol V. Stein* (1964; *The Ravishing of Lol Stein*), *Détruire, dit-elle* (1969; *Destroy, She Said*), *L'Amour* (1971; "Love"), *L'Été 80* (1980; "Summer 80"), and *La Pluie d'été* (1990; *Summer Rain*). Collections of her plays were included in *Théâtre I* (1965), *Théâtre II* (1968), and *Théâtre III* (1984).

# JULIO CORTÁZAR

(b. August 26, 1914, Brussels, Belgium—
d. February 12, 1984, Paris, France)

The Argentine novelist and short-story writer Julio Cortázar combined existential questioning with experimental writing techniques in his works.

Cortázar was the son of Argentine parents and was educated in Argentina, where he taught secondary school and worked as a translator. *Bestiario* (1951; "Bestiary"), his first short-story collection, was published the year he moved to Paris, an act motivated by dissatisfaction with the increasingly corrupt and oppressive presidency of Juan Perón, as well as what he saw as the general stagnation of the Argentine middle class. Cortázar remained in Paris, where he received French citizenship in 1981, though he kept his Argentine citizenship as well. He also traveled widely.

Another collection of short stories, *Final del juego* (1956; "End of the Game"), was followed by *Las armas secretas* (1958; "Secret Weapons"). Some of those stories were translated into English as *End of the Game, and Other Stories* (1967). The main character of *El perseguidor* ("The Pursuer"), one of the stories in *Las armas secretas*, embodies many of the traits of Cortázar's later characters. The metaphysical anguish that he feels in his search for artistic perfection and in his failure to come to grips with the passage of time, coupled with his rejection of 20th-century values, was among Cortázar's central preoccupations. Another story, *Las babas del diablo* (1958; "The Devil's Drivel"), served as the basis for Michelangelo Antonioni's motion picture *Blow-up* (1966). Cortázar's masterpiece,

*Rayuela* (1963; *Hopscotch*), is an open-ended novel, or anti-novel; the reader is invited to rearrange the different parts of the novel according to a plan prescribed by the author. A series of playful and humorous stories written between 1952 and 1959 were published in *Historias de cronopios y de famas* (1962; *Cronopios and Famas*). His other works include *Todos los fuegos el fuego* (1966; *All Fires the Fire*) and *Libro de Manuel* (1973; *A Manual for Manuel*).

# JOHN BERRYMAN

(b. October 25, 1914, McAlester, Oklahoma, U.S.—
d. January 7, 1972, Minneapolis, Minnesota)

John Berryman was an American poet whose importance was assured by the publication in 1956 of the long poem *Homage to Mistress Bradstreet*.

Berryman was brought up a strict Roman Catholic in the small Oklahoma town of Anadarko, moving at 10 with his family to Tampa, Florida. When the boy was 12, his father killed himself. Berryman attended a private school in Connecticut and graduated from Columbia University, where he was influenced by his teacher, the poet Mark Van Doren. After study at the University of Cambridge in 1938, Berryman returned to the U.S. to teach at Wayne State University, Detroit, beginning a career that included posts at Harvard, Princeton, and the University of Minnesota.He began to publish in little magazines during the late 1930s, and in 1940 *Five Young American Poets* contained 20 of his poems. Two other volumes of poetry—*Poems* (1942) and *The Dispossessed* (1948)—followed. A richly erotic autobiographical sequence about a love affair, *Berryman's Sonnets*, appeared in 1967. Berryman was a versatile man of letters: "The Lovers" appeared in *The Best American Short Stories of 1946*, and his story "The Imaginary Jew" (1945) is often anthologized. His biography of Stephen Crane was published in 1950.

*Homage to Mistress Bradstreet* is a monologue that pays tribute to Anne Bradstreet, the first American woman poet: sometimes her voice is heard, sometimes Berryman's, and throughout a loving and intimate grasp of the details of American history is manifest. His new technical daring was also evident in *77 Dream Songs* (1964), augmented to form a sequence of 385 "Dream Songs" by *His Toy, His Dream, His Rest* (1968). Berryman's work bears some relation to the "confessional" school of poetry that flourished among many of his contemporaries, but in his case bursts of humour sporadically light up the troubled interior landscape. This autobiographical note continued to be sounded in *Love & Fame* (1970), in which he conveys much in a deceptively offhand manner.

Berryman committed suicide by jumping from a bridge onto the ice of the Mississippi River. *Recovery*, an account of his struggle against alcoholism, was published in 1973.

# DYLAN THOMAS

(b. October 27, 1914, Swansea, Glamorgan [now in Swansea], Wales —
d. November 9, 1953, New York, New York, U.S.)

Dylan Thomas was a Welsh poet and prose writer whose work is known for its comic exuberance, rhapsodic lilt, and pathos. His personal life, especially his reckless bouts of drinking (he died of an overdose of alcohol), was notorious.

Thomas spent his childhood in southwestern Wales. His father taught English at the Swansea grammar school, which in due course the boy attended. Because Dylan's mother was a farmer's daughter, he had a country home he could go to when on holiday. His poem "Fern Hill" (1946) describes its joys.

Although he edited the school magazine, contributing poetry and prose to it, Thomas did badly at school since he was always intellectually lazy with regard to any subject that did not directly concern him. His practical knowledge of English poetry was enormous, however. He had begun writing poems at a very early age, and scholars have shown that the bulk of his poetic output was completed, at least in embryonic form, by the time he moved to London at the age of 21. At age 16 he left school to work as a reporter on the *South Wales Evening Post*.

Thomas's first book, *18 Poems*, appeared in 1934, and it announced a strikingly new and individual, if not always comprehensible, voice in English poetry. His original style was further developed in *Twenty-Five Poems* (1936) and *The Map of Love* (1939). Thomas's work, in its overtly emotional impact, its insistence on the importance of sound and rhythm, its primitivism, and the tensions between its biblical echoes and its sexual imagery, owed more to his Welsh background than to the prevailing taste in English literature for grim social commentary. Therein lay its originality. The poetry written up to 1939 is concerned with introspective, obsessive, sexual, and religious currents of feeling; and Thomas seems to be arguing rhetorically with himself on the subjects of sex and death, sin and redemption, the natural processes, creation and decay. The writing shows prodigious energy, but the final effect is sometimes obscure or diffuse.

Thomas basically made London his home for some 10 years from about 1936. In 1937 he married the Irishwoman Caitlin Macnamara, with whom he had two sons and a daughter. He had become famous in literary circles, was sociable, and was very poor, with a wife and growing family to support. His attempts to make money with the British Broadcasting Corporation (BBC) and as a film script-writer were not sufficiently remunerative. He wrote film scripts during World War II, having been excused from military service owing to a lung condition. Unfortunately, he was totally lacking in any sort of business acumen. He fell badly behind with his income tax returns, and what money he managed to make was snatched from him, at source, by the British Exchequer. He took to drinking more heavily and to borrowing from richer friends. Still, he continued to work, though in his maturity the composition of his poems became an ever-slower and more painstaking business.

The poems collected in *Deaths and Entrances* (1946) show a greater lucidity and confirm Thomas as a religious poet. This book reveals an advance in sympathy and understanding due, in part, to the impact of World War II and to the deepening harmony between the poet and his Welsh environment, for he writes generally in a mood of reconciliation and acceptance. He often adopts a bardic tone and is a true romantic in claiming a high, almost priest-like function for the poet. He also makes extensive use of Christian myth and symbolism and often sounds a note of formal ritual and incantation in his poems. The re-creation of childhood experience produces a visionary, mystical poetry in which the landscapes of youth and infancy assume the holiness of the first Eden ("Poem in October," "Fern Hill"); for Thomas, childhood, with its intimations of immortality, is a state of innocence and grace. But the rhapsodic lilt and music of the later verse derives from a complex technical discipline, so that Thomas's absorption in his craft produces verbal harmonies that are unique in English poetry.

Meanwhile the London or London-based atmosphere became increasingly dangerous and uncongenial both to Thomas and to his wife. As early as 1946 he was talking of emigrating to the United States, and in 1947 he had what would seem to be a nervous breakdown but refused psychiatric assistance. He moved to Oxford, where he was given a cottage by the distinguished historian A.J.P. Taylor. His trips to London, however, principally in connection with his BBC work, were grueling, exhausting, and increasingly alcoholic. In 1949 Taylor's wife financed the purchase of a cottage, the Boat House, Laugharne, and Thomas returned to Wales. In the following year his first American tour was arranged, and for a while it seemed as if a happy compromise had been arranged between American money and Welsh tranquillity.

The prose that Thomas wrote is linked with his development as a poet, and his first stories, included in *The Map of Love* and *A Prospect of the Sea* (1955), are a by-product of the early poetry. But in *Portrait of the Artist as a Young Dog* (1940), the half-mythical Welsh landscapes of the early stories have been replaced by realistically and humorously observed scenes. A poet's growing consciousness of himself, of the real seriousness hidden behind his mask of comedy, and of the world around him is presented with that characteristic blend of humour and pathos that is later given such lively expression in his "play for voices," *Under Milk Wood* (1954). This play, which evokes the lives of the inhabitants of a small Welsh town, shows Thomas's full powers as an artist in comedy; it is richly imaginative in language, dramatic in characterization, and fertile in comic invention.

*Under Milk Wood* was presented at the Poetry Center in New York City in 1953, and its final version was broadcast by the BBC in 1954. In 1952 Thomas published his *Collected Poems*, which exhibited the deeper insight and superb craftsmanship of a major 20th-century English poet. The volume was an immediate success on both sides of the Atlantic. But, because of the insistence of the British government's tax department, his monetary difficulties persisted. He coped with his exhausting American tours by indulging in reckless drinking bouts. There were far too many people who seem to have derived pleasure from making the famous poet drunk. His personal despair mounted, his marriage was in peril, and at last, while in New York City and far from his Welsh home, he took such an overdose of hard liquor that he died.

# $S$AUL $B$ELLOW

(b. June 10, 1915, Lachine, near Montreal, Quebec, Canada —
d. April 5, 2005, Brookline, Massachusetts, U.S.)

$S$aul Bellow was an American novelist whose characterizations of modern urban man, disaffected by society but not destroyed in spirit, earned him the Nobel Prize for Literature in 1976. Brought up in a Jewish household and fluent in Yiddish—which influenced his energetic English style—he was representative of the Jewish American writers whose works became central to American literature after World War II.

Bellow's parents emigrated in 1913 from Russia to Montreal. When he was nine they moved to Chicago. He attended the University of Chicago and Northwestern University (B.S., 1937) and afterward combined writing with a teaching career at various universities, including the University of Minnesota, Princeton University, New York University, Bard College, the University of Chicago, and Boston University.

Bellow won a reputation among a small group of readers with his first two novels, *Dangling Man* (1944), a story in diary form of a man waiting to be inducted into the army, and *The Victim* (1947), a subtle study of the relationship between a Jew and a Gentile, each of whom becomes the other's victim. *The Adventures of Augie March* (1953) brought wider acclaim and won a National Book Award (1954). It is a picaresque story of a poor Jewish youth from Chicago, his progress—sometimes highly comic—through the world of the 20th century, and his attempts to make sense of it. In this novel Bellow employed for the first time a loose, breezy style in conscious revolt against the preoccupation of writers of that time with perfection of form.

*Henderson the Rain King* (1959) continued the approach of *The Adventures of Augie March*—that is, a roguish protagonist going from one adventure to the next—in its tale of an eccentric American millionaire on a quest in Africa. *Seize the Day* (1956), a novella, is a unique treatment of a failure in a society where the only success is success. He also wrote a volume of short stories, *Mosby's Memoirs* (1968), and *To Jerusalem and Back* (1976) about a trip to Israel.

In his later novels and novellas—*Herzog* (1964; National Book Award, 1965), *Mr. Sammler's Planet* (1970; National Book Award, 1971), *Humboldt's Gift* (1975; Pulitzer Prize, 1976), *The Dean's December* (1982), *More Die of Heartbreak* (1987), *A Theft* (1989), *The Bellarosa Connection* (1989), and *The Actual* (1997)—Bellow arrived at his most characteristic vein. The heroes of these works are often Jewish intellectuals whose interior monologues range from the sublime to the absurd. At the same time, their surrounding world, peopled by energetic and incorrigible realists, acts as a corrective to their intellectual speculations. It is this combination of cultural sophistication and the wisdom of the streets that constitutes Bellow's greatest originality. In *Ravelstein* (2000) he presented a fictional version of the life of teacher and philosopher Allan Bloom. Five years after Bellow's death, more than 700 of his letters, edited by Benjamin Taylor, were published in *Saul Bellow: Letters* (2010).

# *Arthur Miller*

(b. October 17, 1915, New York, New York, U.S.—
d. February 10, 2005, Roxbury, Connecticut)

The American playwright Arthur Miller combined social awareness with a searching concern for his characters' inner lives. He is best known for *Death of a Salesman* (1949).

Miller was shaped by the Great Depression, which spelled financial ruin for his father, a small manufacturer, and demonstrated to the young Miller the insecurity of modern existence. After graduation from high school he worked in a warehouse. With the money he earned he attended the University of Michigan (B.A., 1938), where he began to write plays. His first public success was with *Focus* (1945; film 1962 [made-for-television]), a novel about anti-Semitism. *All My Sons* (1947; film 1948), a drama about a manufacturer of faulty war materials that strongly reflects the influence of Henrik Ibsen, was his first important play. *Death of a Salesman* became one of the most famous American plays of its period. It is the tragedy of Willy Loman, a small man destroyed by false values that are in large part the values of his society. Miller received a Pulitzer Prize for the play, which was later adapted for the screen (1951 and several made-for-television versions).

*Playwright Arthur Miller with his wife, actress Marilyn Monroe, London, 1956.* Fox Photos/Hulton Archive/Getty Images

*The Crucible* (1953; film 1957, 1967 [made-for-television], 1996) was based on the witchcraft trials in Salem, Massachusetts, in 1692, a period Miller considered relevant to the 1950s, when investigation of subversive activities was widespread. In 1956, when Miller was called before the House Un-American Activities Committee, he refused to name people he had seen 10 years earlier at an alleged communist writers' meeting. He was convicted of contempt but appealed and won.

*A Memory of Two Mondays* and another short play, *A View from the Bridge* (a story of an Italian-American longshoreman whose passion for his niece destroys him), were staged on the same bill in 1955. *After the Fall* (1964; film 1974 [made-for-television]) is concerned with failure in human relationships and its consequences. *The Price* (1968) continued Miller's exploration of the theme of guilt and responsibility to oneself and to others by examining the strained relationship between two brothers. He directed the London production of the play in 1969. *The Archbishop's Ceiling*, produced in Washington, D.C., in 1977, dealt with the Soviet treatment of dissident writers. *The American Clock*, a series of dramatic vignettes based on American author and historian Studs Terkel's *Hard Times* (about the Great Depression), was produced at the 1980 American Spoleto Festival in Charleston, South Carolina. Later plays include *The Ride Down Mount Morgan* (1991), *Mr. Peters' Connections* (1998), and *Resurrection Blues* (2002).

Miller also wrote a screenplay, *The Misfits* (1961), for his second wife, the actress Marilyn Monroe (1926–62); they were married from 1956 to 1961. The filming of *The Misfits* served as the basis for the play *Finishing the Picture* (2004). *I Don't Need You Any More*, a collection of his short stories, appeared in 1967 and a collection of theatre essays in 1977. His autobiography, *Timebends*, was published in 1987. In 2001 Miller received the Japan Art Association's Praemium Imperiale prize for theatre/film.

# *H*UBERT *O*GUNDE

(b. 1916, Ososa, near Ijebu-Ode, Nigeria—
d. April 4, 1990, London, England)

The Nigerian playwright, actor, theatre manager, and musician Hubert Ogunde was a pioneer in the field of Nigerian folk opera (drama in which music and dancing play a significant role). He was the founder of the Ogunde Concert Party (1945), the first professional theatrical company in Nigeria. Often regarded as the father of Nigerian theatre, Ogunde sought to reawaken interest in his country's indigenous culture.

Ogunde's first folk opera, *The Garden of Eden and the Throne of God*, was performed with success in 1944 while he was still a member of the Nigerian Police Force. It was produced under the patronage of an African Protestant sect, and it mixed biblical themes with the traditions of Yoruba dance-drama. His popularity was established throughout Nigeria by his timely play *Strike and Hunger* (performed 1946), which dramatized the general strike of 1945. In 1946 the name of Ogunde's group was changed to the African Music Research Party, and in 1947 it became the Ogunde Theatre Company. Many of Ogunde's early plays were attacks on colonialism, while those of his later works with political themes deplored interparty strife and government corruption within Nigeria. Yoruba theatre became secularized through his careful blending of astute political or social satire with elements of music hall routines and slapstick.

Ogunde's most famous play, *Yoruba Ronu* (performed 1964; "Yorubas, Think!"), was such a biting attack on the premier of Nigeria's Western region that his company was banned from the region—the first instance in post-independence Nigeria of literary censorship. The ban was lifted in 1966 by Nigeria's new military government, and in that same year the Ogunde Dance Company was formed. *Otito Koro* (performed 1965; "Truth is Bitter") also satirizes political events in western Nigeria in 1963. An earlier play produced in 1946, *The Tiger's Empire*, also marked the first instance in Yoruban theatre that women were billed to appear in a play as professional artists in their own right.

Ogunde's technique was to sketch out the basic situation and plot, and then write down and rehearse only the songs of his plays. The dialogue was improvised, thus allowing the actors to adjust to their audience. The plays produced by his company usually reflected the prevailing political climate and interpreted for audiences the major issues and the aspirations of those in power. His company performed with equal ease in remote villages and in metropolitan centres of Nigeria (as well as throughout West Africa). Many of Ogunde's later folk operas were basically popular musicals featuring jazzy rhythms, fashionable dance routines, and contemporary satire. Through this format, he set an example for a successful commercial theatre and prepared audiences all over Nigeria for his followers. During the 1960s and '70s his plays became an important part of the urban pop culture of West Africa.

# BEVERLY CLEARY

(b. April 12, 1916, McMinnville, Oregon, U.S.)

Beverly Cleary is an American children's writer whose award-winning books are lively, humorous portrayals of problems and events faced in real life by school-aged girls and boys.

Beverly Bunn lived on a farm near Yamhill, Oregon, before moving to Portland—the setting of many of her books—when she was six. She was educated at the University of California, Berkeley, where she earned a B.A. in 1938, and at the University of Washington, where she took a second degree in library science the following year. From 1939 to 1940 she was a children's librarian at the public library in Yakima, Washington. In 1940 she eloped with Clarence T. Cleary. Their twin children later became models for her fictional fourth-grader twins, Mitch and Amy. After serving as the post librarian at the U.S. Army Hospital in Oakland, California, from 1942 to 1945, Cleary became a full-time writer for young people.

In 1950 her first book, *Henry Huggins*, was published, and, ever since, middle-grade schoolchildren have enjoyed reading about the adventures of its eponymous hero and his friends, including Beezus and Ramona Quimby, on Klickitat Street, a real street near Cleary's childhood home in Portland. Cleary's books realistically portray ordinary children in search of fun and friendship. Her adventurous and mischievous characters attempt to find reasonable solutions to the problems that they confront, such as an unsympathetic teacher or the discovery of a stray dog. Cleary was praised for treating children's concerns with both seriousness and gentle humour. Among the perennial favourites are *The Mouse and the Motorcycle* (1965), *Runaway Ralph* (1970), and the Ramona series, whose notable titles include *Ramona the Pest* (1968), *Ramona and Her Father* (1977), and *Ramona Quimby, Age 8* (1981).

Cleary, the recipient of many awards, won a Newbery Medal (for the most distinguished American children's book of the previous year) in 1984 for *Dear Mr. Henshaw* (1983), an epistolary novel about a boy who copes with his parents' divorce by writing to his favourite author. She also had several of her works adapted for television, and in 2010 *Ramona and Beezus*, a film adaptation that draws from several titles of the Ramona series, was released. In addition to more than 35 works of fiction for children and young adults, Cleary also published the volumes of memoirs *A Girl from Yamhill* (1988) and *My Own Two Feet* (1995).

# CAMILO JOSÉ CELA

(b. May 11, 1916, Iria Flavia, Spain—d. January 17, 2002, Madrid)

The Spanish writer Camilo José Cela Trulock won the Nobel Prize for Literature in 1989. He is perhaps best known for his novel *La familia de Pascual Duarte* (1942; *The Family of Pascual Duarte*) and is considered to have given new life to Spanish literature. His literary production—primarily novels, short narratives, and travel diaries—is characterized by experimentation and innovation in form and content. Cela is also credited by some critics with having established the narrative style known as tremendismo, a tendency to emphasize violence and grotesque imagery.

Cela attended the University of Madrid before and after the Spanish Civil War (1936–39), during which he served with Franco's army. His first novel, *Pascual Duarte*, established his European reputation. Traditional in form, it was both a popular and a critical success. His second novel, *La colmena* (1951; *The Hive*), with its fragmented chronology and large cast of characters, is an innovative and perceptive story of postwar Madrid. It solidified Cela's critical and popular reputation. Another of his better-known avant-garde novels, *San Camilo, 1936* (1969), is one continuous stream of consciousness. His later novels include *Cristo versus Arizona* (1988; "Christ Versus Arizona") and the Galician trilogy—*Mazurca para dos muertos* (1983; *Mazurka for Two Dead People*), *La cruz de San Andrés* (1994; "St. Andrew's Cross"), and *Madera de boj* (1999; *Boxwood*).

Cela's acute powers of observation and skill in colourful description also are apparent in his travel books, based on his trips through rural Spain and his visits to Latin American countries. The most noted of these are *Viaje a la Alcarría* (1948; *Journey to the Alcarría*), *Del Miño al Bidasoa* (1952; "From the Miño to the Bidasoa"), and *Judíos, moros y cristianos* (1956; "Jews, Moors, and Christians"). He retraced the itinerary of his first travel book for *Nuevo viaje a la Alcarría* (1986). Among his numerous short narratives are *Esas nubes que pasan* (1945; "The Passing Clouds") and the four works included in the collection *El molino de viento, y otras novelas cortas* (1956; "The Windmill and Other Short

Fiction"). Cela also wrote essays, poetry, and memoirs and in his later years made frequent television appearances.

In 1955 Cela settled in Majorca, where he founded a well-respected literary review, *Papeles de Son Armadans* (1956–79), and published books. He began in 1968 to publish his multivolume *Diccionario secreto*, a compilation of "unprintable" but well-known words and phrases. He became a member of the Spanish Academy in 1957.

# WALKER PERCY

(b. May 28, 1916, Birmingham, Alabama, U.S.—
d. May 10, 1990, Covington, Louisiana)

Walker Percy was an American novelist who wrote of the New South transformed by industry and technology.

Orphaned in late childhood after his father, a lawyer, committed suicide and his mother died in an automobile accident, Percy went with his brothers to live with their father's cousin, a bachelor and lawyer, in Greenville, Mississippi. Percy studied at the University of North Carolina (B.A., 1937) and Columbia University (M.D., 1941) and, while working as a pathologist at Bellevue Hospital, New York City, contracted tuberculosis, compelling him to rest at an upstate New York sanatorium. While recovering, he read widely, was attracted to the works of European existentialists, and decided on a career in writing. He also converted to Roman Catholicism.

During the 1950s, Percy wrote articles for philosophical, literary, and psychiatric journals, and not until 1961 was his first novel published, *The Moviegoer*, an existentialist work in which a jaded stockbroker seeks escape from the real world through frequent viewings of movies, where he finds at least a simulacrum of a search for meaning. *The Moviegoer* won a National Book Award and introduced Percy's concept of "Malaise," a disease of despair born of the rootless modern world. Other fiction included *The Last Gentleman* (1966); *Love in the Ruins: The Adventures of a Bad Catholic at a Time near the End of the World* (1971), a science-fiction novel that brings a lighter comic touch to Percy's treatment of "Malaise"; *Lancelot* (1977), an allegory of the King Arthur legend told through the reflections of a wife-murderer in a mental institution; *The Second Coming* (1980); and *The Thanatos Syndrome* (1987). He also wrote such nonfiction as *The Message in the Bottle* (1975), a sophisticated philosophical treatment of semantics, and *Lost in the Cosmos: The Last Self-Help Book* (1985), an offbeat amalgam of a self-help-book parody and a philosophical treatise.

# *ANNE HÉBERT*

(b. August 1, 1916, Sainte-Catherine-de-Fossambault, Quebec, Canada—d. January 22, 2000, Montreal, Quebec)

The French Canadian poet, novelist, and playwright Anne Hébert is noted as an original literary stylist. She lived most of her adult life in Paris.

Hébert spent her early years largely confined to her family's country home. In her youth she was encouraged to write by her father, who was a well-known poet and literary critic, and by her poet cousin, Hector de Saint-Denys Garneau. She published her first poems, later collected in *Les Songes en équilibre* (1942; "Dreams in Equilibrium"), in literary journals. This volume—which she did not include in her later collection *Oeuvres poétique* (1993; "Poetic Works")—was an apprentice work, somewhat romantic and traditional, though technically skilled. It gave little indication of the powerful writer who was to emerge. During this period of her life, she also wrote for television, radio, and the theatre. Her first book of prose, *Le Torrent* (1950; *The Torrent*), is a collection of violent stories centring on a young boy damaged by his brutal mother. It was followed by a second poetry collection, *Le Tombeau des rois* (1953; *The Tomb of the Kings*), which more clearly reveals her inner anguish and intensity of purpose. Quebec publishers became wary of her work, so aided by a gift from the Royal Society of Canada she moved to Paris to find a more sympathetic audience. After publishing *Poèmes* (1960), which included the poems of *Le Tombeau des rois*, *Mystère de la parole* ("The Mystery of the Words"), and a significant essay on poetry and for which she won her first Governor General's Award, she turned chiefly to fiction.

Her eight novels, six of which are set in the rural Quebec of her childhood, are psychological examinations of violence, rebellion, and the quest for personal freedom. Perhaps her best work, *Kamouraska* (1970; Eng. trans. *Kamouraska*; film 1973), is a tightly woven masterpiece of suspense that won France's Prix de Libraires. *Les Enfants du sabbat* (1975; *Children of the Black Sabbath*), which won Hébert a second Governor General's Award, is a tale of witchcraft and sorcery. The supernatural was a theme to which she would return. In *Héloïse* (1980; Eng. trans. *Heloise*), for example, the protagonist is a vampire. In *Les Fous de Bassan* (1982; *In the Shadow of the Wind*; film 1987), which won France's Prix Fémina, one of the narrators is a murdered teenage girl. The novel *L'Enfant chargé de songes* (1992; *Burden of Dreams*) won her a third Governor General's Award. Also in 1992, Hébert saw the publication of her first volume of poetry in more than a decade, *Le Jour n'a d'égal que la nuit* (*Day Has No Equal but Night*). She returned from France to reside in Montreal in 1997. Her last novel, *Un Habit de lumière* (*A Suit of Light*), was published in 1999.

# ROALD DAHL

(b. September 13, 1916, Llandaff, Wales —
d. November 23, 1990, Oxford, England)

The British writer Roald Dahl was a popular author of ingenious, irreverent children's books.

Following his graduation from Repton, a renowned British public school, in 1932, Dahl avoided a university education and joined an expedition to Newfoundland. He worked from 1937 to 1939 in Dar es Salaam, Tanganyika (now in Tanzania), but he enlisted in the Royal Air Force (RAF) when World War II broke out. Flying as a fighter pilot, he was seriously injured in a crash landing in Libya. He served with his squadron in Greece and then in Syria before doing a stint (1942–43) as assistant air attaché in Washington, D.C. (during which time he also served as a spy for the British government). There the novelist C.S. Forester encouraged him to write about his most exciting RAF adventures, which were published by the *Saturday Evening Post*.

Dahl's first book, *The Gremlins* (1943), was written for Walt Disney but was largely unsuccessful. His service in the RAF influenced his first story collection, *Over to You: Ten Stories of Flyers and Flying* (1946), a series of military tales that was warmly received by critics but did not sell well. He achieved best-seller status with *Someone like You* (1953; rev. ed. 1961), a collection of macabre stories for adults, which was followed by *Kiss, Kiss* (1959), which focused on stormy romantic relationships.

Dahl then turned primarily to writing the children's books that would give him lasting fame. Unlike most other books aimed at a young audience, Dahl's works had a darkly comic nature, frequently including gruesome violence and death. His villains were often malevolent adults who imperiled precocious and noble child protagonists. *James and the Giant Peach* (1961; film 1996), written for his own children, was a popular success, as was *Charlie and the Chocolate Factory* (1964), which was made into the films *Willy Wonka and the Chocolate Factory* (1971) and *Charlie and the Chocolate Factory* (2005). His other works for young readers include *Fantastic Mr. Fox* (1970; film 2009), *Charlie and the Great Glass Elevator* (1972), *The Enormous Crocodile* (1978), *The BFG* (1982), *The Witches* (1983), and *Matilda* (1988; film 1996).

Dahl also wrote several scripts for movies, among them *You Only Live Twice* (1967) and *Chitty Chitty Bang Bang* (1968). His autobiography, *Boy: Tales of Childhood*, was published in 1984.

# *ANTONIO BUERO VALLEJO*

(b. September 29, 1916, Guadalajara, Spain—
d. April 29, 2000, Madrid)

Antonio Buero Vallejo was a playwright who is considered the most important Spanish dramatist of the post-World War II generation.

Buero Vallejo studied art in Madrid and Guadalajara from 1934 to 1936. During the Civil War (1936–39), he served as a medical orderly in the Spanish Republican Army. After the war, he was condemned to death by the Nationalists, but the sentence was commuted to imprisonment. He was held in prison for more than six years.

During the 1940s and '50s, a period known as the "years of silence" in Spain because of the repressive nature of Francisco Franco's regime, Buero Vallejo managed to give a voice to the downtrodden. He won national notice in 1949 with his play *Historia de una escalera* (1950; *History of a Stairway*), for which he was awarded the Lope de Vega, an important literary prize. The play portrays the frustrations of apartment house tenants in a slum in Madrid. His one-act play produced in the same year, *Palabras en la arena* ("Words in the Sand"), which had for its theme adultery and the need for mercy, won the Amigos de los Quinteros Prize; many of his subsequent plays also earned Spanish literary awards. In *En la ardiente oscuridad* (1951; *In the Burning Darkness*), his second full-length play, a home for the blind stands as a metaphor for society. *La tejedora de sueños* (1952; *The Dream Weaver*, 1967) is based on mythology, and *Irene; o, el tesoro* (1954; "Irene; or, The Treasure") on the fantastic. His basic theme is the yearning for human happiness and the obstacles that frustrate its attainment. In *Hoy es fiesta* (1956; *Today's a Holiday*), Buero Vallejo returned to the slums of Madrid for his ironic and realistic material. His realism echoes the style of Arthur Miller. Buero Vallejo's later writing shows the influence of the German experimental dramatist Bertolt Brecht, whose works he translated.

Buero Vallejo's historical plays were carefully researched. They include *Un soñador para un pueblo* (1958; "A Dreamer for the Nation"), which deals with the failure to modernize Spain under Charles III, *Las meninas* (1960; "The Ladies-in-Waiting"), which is about the court painter Velázquez, and *El concierto de San Ovidio* (1962; *The Concert at Saint Ovide*), which is set in Paris during the French Revolution. *El tragaluz* (1967; *The Basement Window*) deals with the Spanish Civil War. Later works include *El sueño de la razón* (1970; *The Sleep of Reason*) and *La doble historia del Doctor Valmy* (1970; "The Double Life of Doctor Valmy").

In 1971 Buero Vallejo was elected to the Spanish Academy.

# PETER WEISS

(b. November 8, 1916, Nowawes, near Potsdam, Germany— d. May 10, 1982, Stockholm, Sweden)

Peter Weiss was a German dramatist and novelist whose plays achieved widespread success in both Europe and the United States in the 1960s.

The son of a textile manufacturer who was Jewish by origin but Christian by conversion, Weiss was brought up a Lutheran. In 1934 he and his family were forced into exile by Nazi persecution. He lived in England, Switzerland, and Czechoslovakia before settling, in 1939, in Sweden. He painted and made films (which showed the influence of the Surrealists) and also illustrated a Swedish edition of the *Thousand and One Nights*. Later he turned to fiction and drama. His early works were in Swedish, but by 1950 he had decided to publish in German. His initial literary influence was the novelist Franz Kafka, whose dreamlike world of subtle menace and frustration impressed Weiss. An important later influence was the American writer Henry Miller.

Weiss's *Die Verfolgung und Ermordung Jean Paul Marats, dargestellt durch die Schauspielgruppe des Hospizes zu Charenton unter Anleitung des Herrn de Sade* (*The Persecution and Assassination of Jean-Paul Marat as Performed by the Inmates of the Asylum of Charenton Under the Direction of the Marquis de Sade,* usually referred to as *Marat/Sade*) pits the ideals of individualism and of revolution against each other in a setting in which madness and reason seem inseparable. The play was first performed in West Berlin in 1964 and received a celebrated staging in New York City in 1965 by Peter Brook, who filmed it in 1967. *Die Ermittlung* (1965; *The Investigation*) is a documentary drama re-creating the Frankfurt trials of the men who carried out mass murders at Auschwitz; at the same time, it attacks later German hypocrisy over the existence of concentration camps and investigates the root causes of aggression. Weiss's other plays include documentary dramas attacking Portuguese imperialism in Angola, *Gesang vom lusitanischen Popanz* (1967; *The Song of the Lusitanian Bogey*); and American policy in the Vietnam War, *Viet Nam Diskurs* (1968; *Discourse on Viet Nam*).

Weiss wrote three autobiographical novels: *Der Schatten des Körpers des Kutschers* (1960; "The Shadow of the Body of the Coachman"), *Abschied von den Eltern* (1961; *The Leavetaking*), and *Fluchtpunkt* (1962; *Exile*). He won a number of literary awards, including the Charles Veillon Prize for *Fluchtpunkt* in 1963 and the Georg Büchner Prize in 1982. He was also a member of Gruppe 47, an association of German-speaking writers formed after World War II.

# CARSON McCULLERS

(b. February 19, 1917, Columbus, Georgia, U.S.—d. September 29, 1967, Nyack, New York)

Carson McCullers was an American writer of novels and stories that depict the inner lives of lonely people.

At age 17 Lula Carson Smith, whose father was a modestly successful jeweler in Columbus, Georgia, went to New York City to study at Columbia and New York Universities, and in 1937 she married Reeves McCullers, a writer whom she had met in Georgia and with whom she was to have a long and complicated relationship. They divorced in 1940 after he was found to have forged some of her royalty checks but remarried in 1945. Her life after that was clouded by pain, illness, and tragedy. She fell in love at least twice with women who did not reciprocate her feelings and once with a man who also interested her husband. Repeated strokes incapacitated her for long periods, and partial paralysis confined McCullers to a wheelchair in her later years.

Her achievement as a writer—a career that was successfully launched by her first novel, *The Heart Is a Lonely Hunter* (1940; film 1968)—was the outgrowth of her own character and lonely suffering. The novel concerns four inhabitants of a small town in Georgia—an adolescent girl with a passion to study music, an unsuccessful socialist agitator, a black physician struggling to maintain his personal dignity, and a widower who owns a café. *Reflections in a Golden Eye* (1941; film 1967), a shorter work set in a Southern army post that chronicles the unhappy life of a captain (a latent homosexual) and his wife (a nymphomaniac), confirmed McCullers's earlier success.

During the 1940s McCullers met American playwright Tennessee Williams, and they became friends. Williams encouraged her to make a play of her novel *The Member of the Wedding* (1946), a sensitive portrayal of a lonely adolescent whose attachment to her brother precipitates a crisis at his wedding. The novel proved to be her most popular work, and it was equally successful as a play, heralded by some as a new form of American theatre because of its emphasis on character interaction and psychology. The Broadway version ran for more than a year and was made into a movie in 1952.

McCullers's fictional characters endure various physical and psychological handicaps that complicate their natural but often bizarre searches for compassion. Her novels and stories demonstrate a Southern Gothic embrace of the eccentric and combine examinations of relationships between people, reflections on such subjects as the inherent incompatibility of the lover and the beloved, and a profound sense of the human longing to connect with others. She felt her characters powerfully, once stating that "I live with the people I create and it has always made my essential loneliness less keen." Her other works include *The Ballad of the Sad Café* (1951), the drama *The Square Root of Wonderful* (1958), and the novel *Clock Without Hands* (1961). Her *Collected Stories* appeared in 1987, and *Illumination and Night Glare: The Unfinished Autobiography of Carson McCullers*, segmented and with large textual gaps, was published in 1999.

# *Anthony Burgess*

(b. February 25, 1917, Manchester, England—
d. November 22, 1993, London)

John Anthony Burgess Wilson was an English novelist, critic, and man of letters whose fictional explorations of modern dilemmas combine wit, moral earnestness, and a note of the bizarre.

Trained in English literature and phonetics, Burgess taught in the extramural department of Birmingham University (1946–50), worked for the Ministry of Education (1948–50), and was an English instructor at Banbury Grammar School (1950–54). He then served as education officer in Malaya and Borneo (1954–59), where he wrote three novels with a Malayan setting.

Back in England he became a full-time and prolific professional writer. Under the pseudonym Anthony

Burgess he wrote the novels *The Wanting Seed* (1962), an antiutopian view of an overpopulated world, and *Honey for the Bears* (1963). As Joseph Kell he wrote *One Hand Clapping* (1961) and *Inside Mr. Enderby* (1963).

*A Clockwork Orange* (1962; film 1971) made Burgess's reputation as a novelist of comic and mordant power. The novel is written in a teenage argot of Burgess's invention, combining elements from British and American slang, Russian, and other sources. It examines society's unsuccessful attempt to psychologically "rehabilitate" an incurably violent juvenile delinquent. Other novels include *The Eve of Saint Venus* (1964) and *Enderby Outside* (1968). The latter is part of a series of humorous novels centred around the lyric poet F.X. Enderby, whom many critics have seen as a stand-in for Burgess himself. His later works include *Earthly Powers* (1980), *The End of the World News* (1983), *The Kingdom of the Wicked* (1985), *Any Old Iron* (1989), and *A Dead Man in Deptford* (1993). In his novels Burgess combined linguistic ingenuity and witty erudition with picaresque plots, bizarre story premises, and sharp social satire. Although his vision of modern society is a pessimistic one, his fiction is generally comic.

*Anthony Burgess, 1968.* **Marvin Lichtner/Time & Life Pictures/ Getty Images**

Burgess was the author of more than 50 books. In addition to novels and short stories, he was known for his works of literary criticism, including *Here Comes Everybody: An Introduction to James Joyce for the Ordinary Reader* (1965). He wrote television scripts, did translations for the stage, and wrote biographies of William Shakespeare, D.H. Lawrence, and Ernest Hemingway. Burgess also produced dozens of musical compositions, including choral works and orchestral pieces. He wrote a two-volume autobiography, *Little Wilson and Big God: Being the First Part of the Confessions of Anthony Burgess* (1987) and *You've Had Your Time: Being the Second Part of the Confessions of Anthony Burgess* (1990).

# ROBERT LOWELL, JR.

(b. March 1, 1917, Boston, Massachusetts, U.S.—
d. September 12, 1977, New York, New York)

The American poet Robert Lowell, Jr., is noted for his complex autobiographical poetry.

Lowell grew up in Boston. The famed 19th-century man of letters James Russell Lowell was his great-granduncle. Although he turned away from his Puritan heritage—largely because he was repelled by what he felt was the high value it placed on the accumulation of money—he continued to be fascinated by it, and it forms the subject of many of his poems. Lowell attended Harvard University, but, after falling under the influence of the Southern formalist school of poetry, he transferred to Kenyon College in Gambier, Ohio, where he studied with John Crowe Ransom, a leading exponent of the Fugitives (an influential group of young American poets formed after World War I), and began a lifelong friendship with Randall Jarrell, one of the shrewdest literary critics of the 20th century. Lowell graduated in 1940 and that year married the novelist Jean Stafford and converted temporarily to Roman Catholicism.

During World War II, Lowell was sentenced, for conscientious objection, to a year and a day in the federal penitentiary at Danbury, Connecticut, and he served five months of his sentence. His poem "In the Cage" from *Lord Weary's Castle* (1946) comments on this experience, as does in greater detail "Memories of West Street and Lepke" in *Life Studies* (1959). His first volume of poems, *Land of Unlikeness* (1944), deals with a world in crisis and the hunger for spiritual security. *Lord Weary's Castle*, which won the Pulitzer Prize in 1947, exhibits greater variety and command. It contains two of his most praised poems: "The Quaker Graveyard in Nantucket," elegizing Lowell's cousin Warren Winslow, lost at sea during World War II, and "Colloquy in Black Rock," celebrating the feast of Corpus Christi. In 1947 Lowell was named poetry consultant to the Library of Congress (now poet laureate consultant in poetry), a position he held for one year.

After being divorced in 1948, Lowell married the writer and critic Elizabeth Hardwick the next year (divorced 1972); his third wife was the Irish journalist and novelist Lady Caroline Blackwood (married 1972). In 1951 he published a book of dramatic monologues, *Mills of the Kavanaughs*. After a few years abroad, Lowell settled in Boston in 1954. His *Life Studies* (1959), which won the National Book Award for poetry, contains an autobiographical essay, "91 Revere Street," as well as a series of 15 confessional poems. Chief among these are "Waking in Blue," which tells of his confinement in a mental hospital, and "Skunk Hour," which conveys his mental turmoil with dramatic intensity.

Lowell's activities in the civil-rights and antiwar campaigns of the 1960s lent a more public note to his next three books of poetry: *For the Union Dead* (1964), *Near the Ocean* (1967), and *Notebook 1967–68* (1969). The last-named work is a poetic record of a tumultuous year in the poet's life and exhibits the interrelation between politics, the individual, and his culture. Lowell's trilogy of plays, *The Old Glory*, which views American culture over the span of history, was published in 1965 (rev. ed. 1968). His later poetry volumes include *The Dolphin* (1973), which won him a second Pulitzer Prize, and *Day by Day* (1977). His translations include *Phaedra* (1963) and *Prometheus Bound* (1969); *Imitations* (1961), free renderings of various European poets; and *The Voyage and Other Versions of Poems by Baudelaire* (1968).

In his poetry Lowell expressed the major tensions—both public and private—of his time with technical mastery and haunting authenticity. His earlier poems, dense with clashing images and discordant sounds, convey a view of the world whose bleakness is relieved by a religious mysticism compounded as much of doubt as of faith. Lowell's later poetry is composed in a more relaxed and conversational manner.

# GWENDOLYN BROOKS

(b. June 7, 1917, Topeka, Kansas, U.S.—
d. December 3, 2000, Chicago, Illinois)

Gwendolyn Brooks was an American poet whose works deal with the everyday life of urban blacks. She was the first African American poet to win the

Pulitzer Prize (1950), and in 1968 she was named the poet laureate of Illinois.

Brooks graduated from Wilson Junior College in Chicago in 1936. Her early verses appeared in the *Chicago Defender*, a newspaper written primarily for that city's African American community. Her first published collection, *A Street in Bronzeville* (1945), reveals her talent for making the ordinary life of her neighbours extraordinary. *Annie Allen* (1949), for which she won the Pulitzer Prize, is a loosely connected series of poems related to an African American girl's growing up in Chicago. The same theme was used for Brooks's novel *Maud Martha* (1953).

*The Bean Eaters* (1960) contains some of her best verse. Her *Selected Poems* (1963) was followed in 1968 by *In the Mecca*, half of which is a long narrative poem about people in the Mecca, a vast, fortresslike apartment building erected on the South Side of Chicago in 1891, which had long since deteriorated into a slum. The second half of the book contains individual poems, among which the most noteworthy are "Boy Breaking Glass" and "Malcolm X." Brooks also wrote a book for children, *Bronzeville Boys and Girls* (1956). The autobiographical *Report from Part One* (1972) was an assemblage of personal memoirs, interviews, and letters; it was followed, though much later, by *Report from Part Two* (1996). Her other works include *Primer for Blacks* (1980), *Young Poet's Primer* (1980), *To Disembark* (1981), *The Near-Johannesburg Boy, and Other Poems* (1986), *Blacks* (1987), *Winnie* (1988), and *Children Coming Home* (1991).

In 1985–86 Brooks was Library of Congress consultant in poetry (now poet laureate consultant in poetry), and in 1989 she received a lifetime achievement award from the National Endowment for the Arts. She became a professor of English at Chicago State University in 1990, a position she held until her death.

# AUGUSTO ROA BASTOS

(b. June 13, 1917, Iturbe, Paraguay — d. April 26, 2005, Asunción)

Augusto Roa Bastos was a Latin American novelist, short-story writer, and film scriptwriter of national and international fame.

Born in a country village, Roa Bastos attended military school in Asunción in 1925 and fought in the Chaco War (1932–35) against Bolivia. While a student, he also gained an appreciation of classical Spanish literature by reading in his uncle's library. His first book of poetry, *El ruiseñor de la aurora* (1942; "The Nightingale of the Dawn"), which he later renounced, is an imitation of the Spanish masters. The novel *Fulgencio Miranda* (written 1941) and a number of plays successfully performed during the 1940s were never published. Of a considerable amount of poetry written in the late 1940s, only the pamphlet *El naranjal ardiente* (1960; "The Burning Orange Grove") was published.

In 1947 civil war forced Roa Bastos into exile in Buenos Aires, Argentina, where he lived until 1976, serving as cultural attaché in the embassy and working as a journalist. His first collection of short stories, *El trueno entre las hojas* (1953; "Thunder Among the Leaves"), which he also adapted as a film script, describes the Paraguayan experience with emphasis on violence and social injustice. Roa Bastos began to experiment with magic realism, in which realistic descriptions are enhanced by myths and expressionistic techniques.

Roa Bastos's novel *Hijo de hombre* (1960; *Son of Man*) was an overwhelming critical and popular success. It recreates Paraguay's history from the dictatorship of José Gaspar de Francia early in the 19th century through the

Chaco War. By carefully juxtaposing alternate narrative voices, Roa Bastos creates a tension that signals the moral and political stagnation of Paraguay and indicates that the only solution is for the common man to suffer and sacrifice himself for all humanity. In 1960 he adapted the novel for a film, and during the 1960s he wrote other film scripts.

Stories collected in *El baldío* (1966; "The Untilled") treat tenderly and understandingly the problems of Paraguayan exiles. In some of the stories there is a clear indictment of civil war atrocities. The story collections *Los pies sobre el agua* (1967; "The Feet on the Water") and *Madera quemada* (1967; "Burnt Madeira") rework psychologically and existentially themes used earlier.

Roa Bastos's most ambitious work, the novel *Yo, el supremo* (1974; *I, the Supreme*, in bilingual edition), is based on the life of Francia and covers more than a hundred years of Paraguayan history.

From 1976 to 1985 Roa Bastos taught at the University of Toulouse II in France. After 1989, when General Alfredo Stroessner's dictatorship in Paraguay ended, Roa Bastos moved freely between Paraguay and France. His later novels include *Vigilia del almirante* (1992; "Vigil of the Admiral"), *El fiscal* (1993; "The Prosecutor"), and *Contravida* (1994; "Counterlife"). In 1989 he was awarded the Cervantes Prize.

# SIR ARTHUR C. CLARKE

(b. December 16, 1917, Minehead, Somerset, England—d. March 19, 2008, Colombo, Sri Lanka)

The English writer Sir Arthur Charles Clarke is notable for both his science fiction and his nonfiction.

Clarke was interested in science from childhood, but he lacked the means for higher education. He worked as a government auditor from 1936 to 1941 and joined a small, advanced group that called itself the British Interplanetary Society. From 1941 to 1946 Clarke served in the Royal Air Force, becoming a radar instructor and technician. While in the service he published his first science-fiction stories and in 1945 wrote an article entitled "Extra-Terrestrial Relays" for *Wireless World*. The article envisioned a communications satellite system that would relay radio and television signals throughout the world; this system was in operation two decades later.

In 1948 Clarke secured a bachelor of science degree from King's College in London. He went on to write more than 20 novels and 30 nonfiction books and is especially known for such novels as *Against the Fall of Night* (1953), *Childhood's End* (1953), *The City and the Stars* (1956), *Rendezvous with Rama* (1973; winner of Nebula and Hugo awards), *The Fountains of Paradise* (1979; winner of Nebula and Hugo awards), and *The Songs of Distant Earth* (1986). Collections of Clarke's essays and lectures include *Voices from the Sky* (1965), *The View from Serendip* (1977), *Ascent to Orbit: A Scientific Autobiography* (1984), *Astounding Days: A Science Fictional Autobiography* (1989), and *By Space Possessed* (1993).

In the 1950s Clarke developed an interest in undersea exploration and moved to Sri Lanka, where he embarked on a second career combining skin diving and photography; he produced a succession of books, the first of which was *The Coast of Coral* (1956).

Stanley Kubrick's hugely successful film *2001: A Space Odyssey* (1968) was based on Clarke's short story *The Sentinel* (1951), which Clarke and Kubrick subsequently developed into a novel (1968), published under the same name as the movie. A sequel novel, *2010: Odyssey Two* (1982), by Clarke alone, was released as a film in 1984. In 1997 he published *3001: The Final Odyssey*. Clarke was knighted in 2000.

# HEINRICH BÖLL

(b. December 21, 1917, Cologne, Germany—
d. July 16, 1985, Bornheim-Merten, near Cologne, West Germany)

The German writer Heinrich Böll was the winner of the Nobel Prize for Literature in 1972. Böll's ironic novels on the travails of German life during and after World War II capture the changing psychology of the German nation.

The son of a cabinetmaker, Böll graduated from high school in 1937. He was called into compulsory labour service in 1938 and then served six years as a private and corporal in the German army, fighting on the Russian and other fronts. Böll's wartime experiences—being wounded, deserting, becoming a prisoner of war—were central to the art of a writer who remembered the "frightful fate of being a soldier and having to wish that the war might be lost." After the war he settled in his native Cologne.

Böll's earliest success came with short stories, the first of which were published in 1947; these were later collected in *Wanderer, kommst du nach Spa* (1950; *Traveller, If You Come to Spa*). In his early novels *Der Zug war pünktlich* (1949; *The Train Was on Time*) and *Wo warst du Adam?* (1951; *Adam, Where Art Thou?*), he describes the grimness and despair of soldiers' lives. The uneasiness of reality is explored in the life of a mechanic in *Das Brot der frühen Jahre* (1955; *The Bread of Our Early Years*) and in a family of architects in *Billard um halb zehn* (1959; *Billiards at Half-Past Nine*), which, with its interior monologues and flashbacks, is his most complex novel. In the popular *Ansichten eines Clowns* (1963; *The Clown*), the protagonist deteriorates through drinking from being a well-paid entertainer to a begging street musician.

Böll's other writings include *Und sagte kein einziges Wort* (1953; *Acquainted with the Night*) and *Ende einer Dienstfahrt* (1966; *End of a Mission*), in which the trial of a father and son lays bare the character of the townspeople. In his longest novel, *Gruppenbild mit Dame* (1971; *Group Portrait with Lady*), Böll presented a panorama of German life from the world wars to the 1970s through the accounts of the many people who have figured in the life of his middle-aged "lady," Leni Pfeiffer. *Die verlorene Ehre der Katharina Blum* (1974; *The Lost Honour of Katharina Blum*) attacked modern journalistic ethics as well as the values of contemporary Germany. *Was soll aus dem Jungen bloss werden?; oder, Irgendwas mit Büchern* (1981; *What's to Become of the Boy?; or, Something to Do with Books*) is a memoir of the period 1933–37. The novel *Der Engel schwieg* (*The Silent Angel*) was written in 1950 but first published posthumously in 1992; in it a German soldier struggles to survive in war-ravaged Cologne after World War II. *Der blasse Hund* (1995; *The Mad Dog*) collected previously unpublished short stories, while another early novel, *Kreuz ohne Liebe* ("Cross Without Love"), was first published in 2003.

A Roman Catholic and a pacifist, Böll developed a highly moral but individual vision of the society around him. A frequent theme of his was the individual's acceptance or refusal of personal responsibility. Böll used austere prose and frequently sharp satire to present his antiwar, nonconformist point of view. He was widely regarded as the outstanding humanist interpreter of his nation's experiences in World War II.

# DAME MURIEL SPARK

(b. February 1, 1918, Edinburgh, Scotland—
d. April 13, 2006, Florence, Italy)

The British writer Dame Muriel Spark (née Camberg) is best known for the satire and wit with which the serious themes of her novels are presented.

Spark was educated in Edinburgh and later spent some years in Central Africa; the latter served as the setting for her first volume of short stories, *The Go-Away Bird and Other Stories* (1958). She returned to Great Britain during World War II and worked for the Foreign Office, writing propaganda. She then served as general secretary of the Poetry Society and editor of *The Poetry Review* (1947–49). She later published a series of critical biographies of literary figures and editions of 19th-century letters, including *Child of Light: A Reassessment of Mary Wollstonecraft Shelley* (1951; rev. ed., *Mary Shelley*, 1987), *John Masefield* (1953), and *The Brontë Letters* (1954). Spark converted to Roman Catholicism in 1954.

Until 1957 Spark published only criticism and poetry. With the publication of *The Comforters* (1957), however, her talent as a novelist—an ability to create disturbing, compelling characters and a disquieting sense of moral ambiguity—was immediately evident. Her third novel, *Memento Mori* (1959), was adapted for the stage in 1964 and for television in 1992. Her best-known novel is probably *The Prime of Miss Jean Brodie* (1961), which centres on a domineering teacher at a girls' school. It also became popular in its stage (1966) and film (1969) versions.

Some critics found Spark's earlier novels minor; some of these works—such as *The Comforters, Memento Mori, The Ballad of Peckham Rye* (1960), and *The Girls of Slender Means* (1963)—are characterized by humorous and slightly unsettling fantasy. *The Mandelbaum Gate* (1965) marked a departure toward weightier themes, and the novels that followed—*The Driver's Seat* (1970, film 1974), *Not to Disturb* (1971), and *The Abbess of Crewe* (1974)—have a distinctly sinister tone. Among Spark's later novels are *Territorial Rights* (1979), *A Far Cry from Kensington* (1988), *Reality and Dreams* (1996), and *The Finishing School* (2004). Other works include *Collected Poems I* (1967) and *Collected Stories* (1967). *Curriculum Vitae* (1992) is an autobiography. Spark was made Dame Commander of the British Empire in 1993.

# *Juan José Arreola*

(b. September 21, 1918, Ciudad Guzmán, Mexico—
d. December 3, 2001, Guadalajara)

The Mexican short-fiction writer and humorist Juan José Arreola was a master of brief subgenres, such as the short story, the epigram, and the sketch. He published only one novel, *La feria* (1963; *The Fair*). His collection of stories *Confabulario* (1952) has been reprinted in several expanded editions and was translated into English as *Confabulario and Other Inventions*.

One of 14 children, Arreola had to leave school at age eight. He tried his hand at several professions, including journalism, teaching, and editing. He also studied acting in Mexico and in France, where he worked as an extra in the Comédie Française from 1945 to 1946. When he returned to Mexico City, he took an editorial position with a respected firm.

As a writer, Arreola's trademark was his humour, which fluctuated between the witty and the cosmic. He was obsessively drawn to the absurd and enjoyed satirizing modern technology and its monstrous by-products. One of Arreola's fixations was the absurdity of religious belief and what he denounced as God's unequal relationship to humankind. This is the theme of *El silencio de Dios* (*God's Silence*).

Like the Argentine writer Jorge Luis Borges, Arreola cultivated the hybrid subgenre of the essay-story, a combination that lends authority to quite outlandish propositions. *El guardagujas* (*The Switchman*) is Arreola's most anthologized piece. It is without question his most representative. A stranded railroad traveler waits for months to board a train that never arrives, only to discover that schedules, routes, and even the landscapes seen from the windows of railroad cars are fake. Some literal-minded readers have interpreted the story as a criticism of the Mexican railroad system, others as an allegory of Mexican society as a whole. The story is both, as well as an allegory of modern technological society and a critique of the entire universe, whose functioning seems to be in the hands of a very minor employee, a switchman who is like an incompetent minor god.

# *A*LEKSANDR *S*OLZHENITSYN

(b. December 11, 1918, Kislovodsk, Russia—
d. August 3, 2008, Troitse-Lykovo, near Moscow)

Aleksandr Solzhenitsyn was a Russian novelist and historian who was awarded the Nobel Prize for Literature in 1970.

Solzhenitsyn was born into a family of Cossack intellectuals and was brought up by his mother (his father was killed in an accident before his birth). He attended the University of Rostov-na-Donu, graduating in mathematics, and took correspondence courses in literature at Moscow State University. He fought in World War II, achieving the rank of captain of artillery; in 1945, however, he was arrested for writing a letter in which he criticized Joseph Stalin and spent eight years in prisons and labour camps, after which he spent three more years in enforced exile. Rehabilitated in 1956, he was allowed to settle in Ryazan, in central Russia, where he became a mathematics teacher and began to write.

Encouraged by the loosening of government restraints on cultural life that was a hallmark of the de-Stalinizing policies of the early 1960s, Solzhenitsyn submitted his short novel *Odin den iz zhizni Ivana Denisovicha* (1962; *One Day in the Life of Ivan Denisovich*) to the leading Soviet literary periodical *Novy Mir* ("New World"). The novel quickly appeared in that journal's pages and met with immediate popularity, Solzhenitsyn becoming an instant celebrity. *Ivan Denisovich*, based on Solzhenitsyn's own experiences, described a typical day in the life of an inmate of a forced-labour camp during the Stalin era. The impression made on the public by the book's simple, direct language and by the obvious authority with which it treated the daily struggles and material hardships of camp life was magnified by its being one of the first Soviet literary works of the post-Stalin era to directly describe such a life. The book produced a political sensation both abroad and in the Soviet Union, where it inspired a number of other writers to produce accounts of their imprisonment under Stalin's regime.

Solzhenitsyn's period of official favour proved to be short-lived, however. Ideological strictures on cultural activity in the Soviet Union tightened with Nikita Khrushchev's fall from power in 1964, and Solzhenitsyn met first with increasing criticism and then with overt harassment from the authorities when he emerged as an eloquent opponent of repressive government policies. After the publication of a collection of his short stories in 1963, he was denied further official publication of his work, and he resorted to circulating them in the form of samizdat ("self-published") literature—i.e., as illegal literature circulated clandestinely—as well as publishing them abroad.

The following years were marked by the foreign publication of several ambitious novels that secured Solzhenitsyn's international literary reputation. *V kruge pervom* (1968; *The First Circle*) was indirectly based on his years spent working in a prison research institute as a mathematician. The book traces the varying responses of scientists at work on research for the secret police as they must decide whether to cooperate with the authorities and thus remain within the research prison or to refuse their services and be thrust back into the brutal conditions of the labour camps. *Rakovy korpus* (1968; *Cancer Ward*) was based on Solzhenitsyn's hospitalization and successful treatment for terminally diagnosed cancer during his forced exile in Kazakhstan during the mid-1950s. The main character, like Solzhenitsyn himself, was a recently released inmate of the camps.

In 1970 Solzhenitsyn was awarded the Nobel Prize for Literature, but he declined to go to Stockholm to receive the prize for fear he would not be readmitted to the Soviet Union by the government upon his return. His next novel to be published outside the Soviet Union was *Avgust 1914* (1971; *August 1914*), a historical novel treating Germany's crushing victory over Russia in their initial military engagement of World War I, the Battle of Tannenburg.

The novel centred on several characters in the doomed 1st Army of the Russian general A.V. Samsonov and indirectly explored the weaknesses of the tsarist regime that eventually led to its downfall by revolution in 1917.

In December 1973 the first parts of *Arkhipelag Gulag* (*The Gulag Archipelago*) were published in Paris after a copy of the manuscript had been seized in the Soviet Union by the KGB. (*Gulag* is an acronym formed from the official Soviet designation of its system of prisons and labour camps.) *The Gulag Archipelago* is Solzhenitsyn's attempt to compile a literary-historical record of the vast system of prisons and labour camps that came into being shortly after the Bolsheviks seized power in Russia (1917) and that underwent an enormous expansion during the rule of Stalin (1924–53). Various sections of the work describe the arrest, interrogation, conviction, transportation, and imprisonment of the Gulag's victims as practiced by Soviet authorities over four decades. The work mingles historical exposition and Solzhenitsyn's own autobiographical accounts with the voluminous personal testimony of other inmates that he collected and committed to memory during his imprisonment.

Upon publication of the first volume of *The Gulag Archipelago*, Solzhenitsyn was immediately attacked in the Soviet press. Despite the intense interest in his fate that was shown in the West, he was arrested and charged with treason on February 12, 1974. Solzhenitsyn was exiled from the Soviet Union on the following day, and in December he took possession of his Nobel Prize.

In 1975 a documentary novel, *Lenin v Tsyurikhe: glavy* (*Lenin in Zurich: Chapters*), appeared, as did *Bodalsya telyonok s dubom* (*The Oak and the Calf*), an autobiographical account of literary life in the Soviet Union. The second and third volumes of *The Gulag Archipelago* were published in 1974–75. Solzhenitsyn traveled to the United

States, where he eventually settled on a secluded estate in Cavendish, Vermont. The brief *The Mortal Danger* (1980), translated from an essay Solzhenitsyn wrote for the journal *Foreign Affairs*, analyzes what he perceived to be the perils of American misconceptions about Russia. In 1983 an extensively expanded and revised version of *August 1914* appeared in Russian as the first part of a projected series, *Krasnoe koleso* (*The Red Wheel*); other volumes (or uzly ["knots"]) in the series were *Oktyabr 1916* ("October 1916"), *Mart 1917* ("March 1917"), and *Aprel 1917* ("April 1917").

In presenting alternatives to the Soviet regime, Solzhenitsyn tended to reject Western emphases on democracy and individual freedom and instead favoured the formation of a benevolent authoritarian regime that would draw upon the resources of Russia's traditional Christian values. The introduction of *glasnost* ("openness") in the late 1980s brought renewed access to Solzhenitsyn's work in the Soviet Union. In 1989 the Soviet literary magazine *Novy Mir* published the first officially approved excerpts from *The Gulag Archipelago*. Solzhenitsyn's Soviet citizenship was officially restored in 1990.

Solzhenitsyn ended his exile and returned to Russia in 1994. He subsequently made several public appearances and even met privately with Russian Pres. Boris Yeltsin. In 1997 Solzhenitsyn established an annual prize for writers contributing to the Russian literary tradition. Installments of his autobiography, *Ugodilo zernyshko promezh dvukh zhernovov: ocherki izgnaniia* ("The Little Grain Managed to Land Between Two Millstones: Sketches of Exile"), were published from 1998 to 2003, and his history of Russian Jews, *Dvesti let vmeste, 1795–1995* ("Two Hundred Years Together"), was published in 2001–02. In 2007 Solzhenitsyn was awarded Russia's prestigious State Prize for his contribution to humanitarian causes.

# J·D· SALINGER

(b. January 1, 1919, New York, New York, U.S.—
d. January 27, 2010, Cornish, New Hampshire)

Jerome David Salinger was an American writer whose novel *The Catcher in the Rye* (1951) won critical acclaim and devoted admirers, especially among the post-World War II generation of college students. His corpus of published works also consists of short stories that were printed in magazines, including the *The Saturday Evening Post*, *Esquire*, and *The New Yorker*.

Salinger was the son of a Jewish father and a Christian mother, and, like Holden Caulfield, the hero of *The Catcher in the Rye*, he grew up in New York City, attending public schools and a military academy. After brief periods at New York and Columbia Universities, he devoted himself entirely to writing, and his stories began to appear in periodicals in 1940. After Salinger's return from service in the U.S. Army (1942–46), his name and writing style became increasingly associated with *The New Yorker* magazine, which published almost all of his later stories. Some of the best of these made use of his wartime experiences: "For Esmé—with Love and Squalor" (1950) describes a U.S. soldier's poignant encounter with two British children; "A Perfect Day for Bananafish" (1948) concerns the suicide of the sensitive, despairing veteran Seymour Glass.

Major critical and popular recognition came with the publication of *The Catcher in the Rye*, whose central character, a sensitive, rebellious adolescent, relates in authentic teenage idiom his flight from the "phony" adult world, his search for innocence and truth, and his final collapse on a psychiatrist's couch. The humour and colourful language

*J.D. Salinger.* San Diego Historical Society/Hulton Archive/
Getty Images

of *The Catcher in the Rye* place it in the tradition of Mark Twain's *Adventures of Huckleberry Finn* and the stories of the American satirist Ring Lardner, but its hero, like most of Salinger's child characters, views his life with an added dimension of precocious self-consciousness. *Nine Stories* (1953), a selection of Salinger's short stories, added to his reputation. Several of his published pieces feature the siblings of the fictional Glass family, beginning with Seymour's appearance in "A Perfect Day for Bananafish." In works such as *Franny and Zooey* (1961) and *Raise High the Roof Beam, Carpenters and Seymour: An Introduction* (1963), the introspective Glass children, influenced by their eldest brother and his death, navigate questions about spirituality and enlightenment.

The reclusive habits of Salinger in his later years made his personal life a matter of speculation among devotees, and his small literary output was a subject of controversy among critics. The last work Salinger published during his lifetime was a novella titled *Hapworth 16, 1924,* which appeared in *The New Yorker* in 1965. In 1974 *The Complete Uncollected Short Stories of J.D. Salinger*, an unauthorized two-volume work of his early pieces, was briefly released to the public, but sales were halted when Salinger filed a lawsuit for copyright infringement.

# *LAWRENCE FERLINGHETTI*

(b. March 24, 1919, Yonkers, New York, U.S.)

The American poet Lawrence Ferlinghetti was one of the founders of the Beat movement in San Francisco in the mid-1950s. His City Lights bookshop was an early gathering place of the Beats, and the publishing arm of City Lights was the first to print the Beats' books of poetry.

Ferlinghetti's father died shortly before Lawrence was born, his mother was placed in a mental hospital, and a female relative took him to France, where he spent most of his childhood. Later, they lived on a Long Island, New York, estate on which she was employed as a governess. He was a U.S. naval officer during World War II, and he received a B.A. at the University of North Carolina, an M.A. at Columbia University, and a doctorate at the Sorbonne in 1951.

In 1951 Ferlinghetti settled in San Francisco, and in 1953 he opened the City Lights Pocket Book Shop, which quickly became a gathering place for the city's literary avant garde. In 1955 Ferlinghetti's new City Lights press published his verse collection *Pictures of the Gone World*, which was the first paperback volume of the Pocket Poets series. Allen Ginsberg's *Howl and Other Poems* (1956) was originally published as the fourth volume in the series. City Lights Books printed other works by Ginsberg as well as books by Jack Kerouac, Gregory Corso, Denise Levertov, William Burroughs, William Carlos Williams, and foreign authors.

Ferlinghetti's own lucid, good-natured, witty verse was written in a conversational style and was designed to be read aloud; it was popular in coffee houses and campus auditoriums and struck a responsive chord in disaffected youth. His collection *A Coney Island of the Mind* (1958), with its notable verse "Autobiography," became the largest-selling book by any living American poet in the second half of the 20th century. The long poem *Tentative Description of a Dinner Given to Promote the Impeachment of President Eisenhower* (1958) was also popular. Ferlinghetti's later poems continued to be politically oriented, as such titles as *One Thousand Fearful Words for Fidel Castro* (1961), *Where Is Vietnam?* (1965), *Tyrannus Nix?* (1969), and *Who Are We Now?* (1976) suggest. Retrospective collections of his poems were published as *Endless Life* (1981) and *These Are My Rivers* (1995). In 1988 Ferlinghetti published a short novel, *Love in the Days of Rage*, about a romance during the student revolution in France in 1968.

*A Far Rockaway of the Heart*, a sequel to *A Coney Island of the Mind*, appeared in 1997. In 1998 Ferlinghetti was named poet laureate of San Francisco, the first poet so honoured by the city. Two years later he published *What Is Poetry?*, a book of prose poetry, which was followed by the collection *How to Paint Sunlight* (2001) and *Americus: Part I* (2004), a history of the United States in verse.

# DAME IRIS MURDOCH

(b. July 15, 1919, Dublin, Ireland—
d. February 8, 1999, Oxford, Oxfordshire, England)

Dame Jean Iris Murdoch was a British novelist and philosopher noted for her psychological novels that contain philosophical and comic elements.

After an early childhood spent in London, Murdoch went to Badminton School, Bristol, and from 1938 to 1942 studied at Somerville College, Oxford. Between 1942 and 1944 she worked in the British Treasury and then for two years as an administrative officer with the United Nations Relief and Rehabilitation Administration. In 1948 she was elected a fellow of St. Anne's College, Oxford.

Murdoch's first published work was a critical study, *Sartre, Romantic Rationalist* (1953). This was followed by two novels, *Under the Net* (1954) and *The Flight from the Enchanter* (1956), that were admired for their intelligence, wit, and high seriousness. These qualities, along with a rich comic sense and a gift for analyzing the tensions and complexities in sophisticated sexual relationships, continued to distinguish her work. With what is perhaps her finest book, *The Bell* (1958), Murdoch began to attain wide recognition as a novelist. She went on to a highly prolific career with such novels as *A Severed Head* (1961), *The Red and the Green* (1965), *The Nice and the Good* (1968), *The Black Prince* (1973), *Henry and Cato* (1976), *The Sea, the Sea* (1978, Booker Prize), *The Philosopher's Pupil* (1983), *The Good Apprentice* (1985), *The Book and the Brotherhood* (1987), *The Message to the Planet* (1989), and *The Green Knight* (1993). Murdoch's last novel, *Jackson's Dilemma* (1995), was not well received; some critics attributed the novel's flaws to the Alzheimer's disease with which she had been diagnosed in 1994. Murdoch's husband, the novelist John Bayley, chronicled her struggle with the disease in his memoir, *Elegy for Iris* (1999).

Murdoch's novels typically have convoluted plots in which innumerable characters representing different philosophical positions undergo kaleidoscopic changes in their relations with each other. Realistic observations of 20th-century life among middle-class professionals are interwoven with extraordinary incidents that partake of the macabre, the grotesque, and the wildly comic. The novels illustrate Murdoch's conviction that although human beings think they are free to exercise rational control over their lives and behaviour, they are actually at the mercy of the unconscious mind, the determining effects of society at large, and other, more inhuman, forces. In addition to producing novels, Murdoch wrote plays, verse, and works of philosophy and literary criticism.

# *DORIS LESSING*

(b. October 22, 1919, Kermānshāh, Persia [now Iran])

The British writer Doris Lessing (née Tayler) is known for her novels and short stories, which are largely concerned with people involved in the social and political upheavals of the 20th century. She was awarded the Nobel Prize for Literature in 2007.

Her family was living in Persia at the time of her birth but moved to a farm in Southern Rhodesia (now Zimbabwe), where she lived from age five until she settled in England in 1949. In her early adult years she was an active communist. *In Pursuit of the English* (1960) tells of her initial months in England, and *Going Home* (1957) describes her reaction to Rhodesia on a return visit. In 1994 she published the first volume of an autobiography, *Under My Skin*; a second volume, *Walking in the Shade*, appeared in 1997.

Her first published book, *The Grass Is Singing* (1950), is about a white farmer and his wife and their African servant in Rhodesia. Among her most substantial works is the series *Children of Violence* (1952–69), a five-novel sequence that centres on Martha Quest, who grows up in southern Africa and settles in England. *The Golden Notebook* (1962), in which a woman writer attempts to come to terms with the life of her times through her art, is one of the most complex and the most widely read of her novels. *The Memoirs of a Survivor* (1975) is a prophetic fantasy that explores psychological and social breakdown. A master of the short story, Lessing has published several collections, including *The Story of a Non-Marrying Man* (1972) and *Stories* (1978);

her African stories are collected in *This Was the Old Chief's Country* (1951) and *The Sun Between Their Feet* (1973).

Lessing turned to science fiction in a five-novel sequence titled *Canopus in Argos: Archives* (1979–83). The novels *The Diary of a Good Neighbour* (1983) and *If the Old Could...* (1984) were published pseudonymously under the name Jane Somers to dramatize the problems of unknown writers. Subsequent novels include *The Good Terrorist* (1985), about a group of revolutionaries in London, and *The Fifth Child* (1988), a horror story, to which *Ben, in the World* (2000) is a sequel. *The Sweetest Dream* (2001) is a semiautobiographical novel set primarily in London during the 1960s, while the parable-like novel *The Cleft* (2007) considers the origins of human society. Her collection of essays *Time Bites* (2004) displays her wide-ranging interests, from women's issues and politics to Sufism.

# ISAAC ASIMOV

(b. January 2, 1920, Petrovichi, Russia—
d. April 6, 1992, New York, New York, U.S.)

Isaac Asimov was an American author and biochemist as well as a highly successful and prolific writer of science fiction and of science books for the layperson. He published about 500 volumes.

Asimov was brought to the United States at age three. He grew up in Brooklyn, New York, graduating from Columbia University in 1939 and taking a Ph.D. there in 1948. He then joined the faculty of Boston University, with which he remained associated thereafter.

Asimov began contributing stories to science-fiction magazines in 1939 and in 1950 published his first book, *Pebble in the Sky*. His trilogy of novels, *Foundation*, *Foundation and Empire*, and *Second Foundation* (1951–53), which recounts the collapse and rebirth of a vast interstellar empire in the universe of the future, is his most famous work of science fiction. In the short-story collection *I, Robot* (1950; film 2004), he developed a set of ethics for robots and intelligent machines that greatly influenced other writers' treatment of the subject. His other novels and collections of stories included *The Stars, like Dust* (1951), *The Currents of Space* (1952), *The Caves of Steel* (1954), *The Naked Sun* (1957), *Earth Is Room Enough* (1957), *Foundation's Edge* (1982), and *The Robots of Dawn* (1983). His *Nightfall* (1941) is thought by many to be the finest science-fiction short story ever written. Among Asimov's books on various topics in science, written with lucidity and humour, are *The Chemicals of Life* (1954), *Inside the Atom* (1956), *The World of Nitrogen* (1958), *Life and Energy* (1962), *The Human Brain* (1964), *The Neutrino* (1966), *Science, Numbers, and I* (1968), *Our World in Space* (1974), and *Views of the Universe* (1981). He also published two volumes of autobiography.

# RICHARD ADAMS

(b. May 9, 1920, Wash Common, Berkshire
[now West Berkshire], England)

The English author Richard Adams is known for redefining anthropomorphic fiction, most notably with *Watership Down* (1972; film 1978), a novel that naturalistically depicts the travails of a group of wild European rabbits (*Oryctolagus cuniculus*) seeking a new home.

Adams was raised in a rural community outside Newbury, Berkshire, where he led an isolated childhood mostly occupied by exploring his bucolic surroundings.

He enrolled at Worcester College, Oxford, in 1938, but the advent of World War II the next year necessitated the postponement of his studies. In 1940 he enlisted in the Royal Army Service Corps, joining an airborne company. Following the war, Adams completed a bachelor's degree in modern history at Oxford (1948). He found work with the civil service, eventually advancing to assistant secretary in the precursor to the Department of the Environment in 1968. (He cowrote the version of the Clean Air Act passed that year.)

Largely immersed in work and raising a family (he married in 1949), Adams did not begin writing until 1966. While on a car trip with his daughters, he began telling them a story about a warren of rabbits; the girls urged him to put the story to paper. Adams penned the tale over the next two years, consulting Welsh naturalist R.M. Lockley's natural history study *The Private Life of the Rabbit* (1964) to ensure the accurate depiction of his rabbit protagonists, who leave their oppressive warren after it is threatened by a housing development. What emerged was a sui generis work of fiction: unlike much anthropomorphic literature, the animal characters in *Watership Down*, though able to talk, behave as they would in the wild, fighting, copulating, and defecating.

The profits allowed Adams to begin writing full-time in 1974. *Shardik* (1974) relates the formation of a religion centred on a giant bear; the protagonists are human. *The Plague Dogs* (1977; film 1982) explores issues of animal rights through the tale of two dogs that escape from a research facility—possibly carrying the bubonic plague. The novels *The Girl in a Swing* (1980; film 1988) and *Maia* (1984) drew attention for their graphic depictions of sexuality. Adams took a different approach to anthropomorphism with *Traveller* (1988), told from the perspective of Robert E. Lee's horse. He returned to his intrepid lagomorphs with

*Tales from Watership Down* in 1996. *Daniel* (2006) concerns a former slave who becomes an abolitionist.

Adams cowrote two works of nonfiction with Max Hooper, *Nature Through the Seasons* (1975) and *Nature Day and Night* (1978), and another with Lockley, *Voyage Through the Antarctic* (1982). His autobiography, *The Day Gone By*, was published in 1990.

Adams was president of the Royal Society for the Prevention of Cruelty to Animals (1980–82). He was inducted into the Royal Society of Literature in 1975.

# CHARLES BUKOWSKI

(b. August 16, 1920, Andernach, Germany —
d. March 9, 1994, San Pedro, California, U.S.)

The American author Charles Bukowski is noted for his use of violent images and graphic language in poetry and fiction that depict survival in a corrupt, blighted society.

Bukowski lived most of his life in Los Angeles. He briefly attended Los Angeles City College (1939–41) and worked at menial jobs while writing short stories, the first of which were published in the mid-1940s. After a 10-year period during which he abandoned writing and traveled across the U.S. living the life of a destitute alcoholic drifter, he returned to Los Angeles and began publishing poetry in 1955. Beginning with *Flower, Fist and Bestial Wail* (1959), volumes of his poetry appeared almost annually via small underground publishing houses. By 1963, the year he published *It Catches My Heart in Its Hands*—a collection of poetry about alcoholics, prostitutes, losing gamblers, and down-and-out people—Bukowski had a loyal following. Notable later poetry collections include *Mockingbird Wish Me Luck*

(1972), *Love Is a Dog from Hell* (1977), *War All the Time* (1984), and *You Get So Alone at Times That It Just Makes Sense* (1986). Though he had begun his career as one of the ultimate "cult authors," his work was so popular and influential that by the time of his death he was one of the best-known American authors and an established part of the 20th-century literary canon. Bukowski was such a prolific writer that his production outstripped his own life span; numerous collections of his previously unpublished poetry appeared posthumously, such as *Slouching Toward Nirvana* (2005) and *The People Look Like Flowers At Last* (2007).

Bukowski's short stories and novels are unsparingly realistic and usually comic. They often observe the thoughts and actions of Bukowski's alter ego Henry Chinaski, a hard-drinking unskilled worker, a lover of classical music, and a gambler on the horses. Collections of his stories include *Notes of a Dirty Old Man* (1969), taken from his underground newspaper column of that name, *Erections, Ejaculations, Exhibitions, and General Tales of Ordinary Madness* (1972), and *Hot Water Music* (1983). His later novels include *Post Office* (1971), *Factotum* (1975), and *Ham on Rye* (1982). *Hollywood* (1989), also a novel, took as its subject the filming of the 1987 motion picture *Barfly*, a semiautobiographical comedy about alcoholic lovers on skid row for which Bukowski wrote the screenplay (published 1984). The novel *Pulp* was published posthumously in 1994.

# ZHANG AILING

(b. September 9, 1920, Shanghai, China—
found dead September 8, 1995, Los Angeles, California, U.S.)

Zhang Ailing (Chang Ai-ling, also called Eileen Chang) was a Chinese writer whose sad, bitter love stories gained her a large devoted audience as well as critical acclaim.

A descendant of the famous late Qing statesman Li Hongzhang, Zhang attended a traditional private school in her early childhood. Her mother arranged a Western-style education for her at age nine; she learned English, oil painting, and piano. She became familiar with traditional Chinese novels such as *Hongloumeng* (*Dream of the Red Chamber*) and *Hai shang hua lie zhuan* ("A Biography of Flower from the Sea"), and she tried her hand at writing.

In 1939 Zhang enrolled at the University of Hong Kong. However, when her education there was halted two years later by the Japanese invasion, she returned to Shanghai. She pursued a writing career, beginning with film scripts and romantic works. In 1943 she came to prominence with the publication in journals of the novella *Jinsuoji* ("The Golden Cangue") and the stories *Chenxiangxie—diyilu xiang* ("Scraps of Agalloch Eaglewood [a precious medicinal herb]—The First Charge in the Incense Burner") and *Qingcheng zhi lian* ("Love in a Fallen City"; film, 1984). Using the "trifling matters between the sexes" as the theme of her stories, she accurately described the desires, imaginations, and personalities of urban residents. Her short-story collection *Chuanqi* (1944; "The Legend") and her prose anthology *Liuyan* (1944; "The Gossip") not only sold well but also successfully combined elegance and accessibility. When the Sino-Japanese War ended in 1945, however, Zhang's reputation was damaged because she was the best-known writer in Shanghai during the Japanese occupation and her then-husband, Hu Lanchen, had collaborated with the Japanese.

Zhang moved to Hong Kong in 1952 and to the United States three years later. Two of her best-known novels were published during that period: *Yangge* (1954; *The Rice Sprout Song*; written in English but first published in Chinese), the work that won Zhang an audience in the West, and *Chidi zhi lian* (1954; *Naked Earth*). Both were critical of communist society. Zhang married Ferdinand Reyher, an American writer, in 1956 and became a U.S. citizen in 1960. In 1961 she traveled to Hong Kong via Taiwan. After writing several film scripts, she returned to the United States in 1962. Though Zhang held visiting positions at several American universities over the years, she became increasingly reclusive, revising her works and studying *Dream of the Red Chamber*. She wrote a novel, *Yuannu* (1966; *The Rouge of the North*), based on her earlier novella *Jinsuoji*; it was adapted as a motion picture in 1988. With the reprinting of a large number of her older works, there emerged in Taiwan and Hong Kong a revival of interest in Zhang. Starting in the mid-1980s, her popularity gradually spread to mainland China. Her works were collected in *Zhang Ailing quanji*, 16 vol. (1991–94; "The Complete Works of Zhang Ailing").

# CLARICE LISPECTOR

(b. December 10, 1920, Chechlnik, Ukraine, Russian Empire—
d. December 9, 1977, Rio de Janeiro, Brazil)

The novelist and short-story writer Clarice Lispector was one of Brazil's most important literary figures and is considered to be among the greatest women writers of the 20th century.

Escaping the Jewish pogroms that were part of life in Ukraine and other parts of the Russian Empire in the late

19th and early 20th century, Lispector at age five immigrated with her parents and two older sisters to Brazil. There her mother died some four years later of syphilis, contracted from a group of Russian soldiers who had raped her. Lispector studied law for a time and then took up journalism.

Her first novel, *Perto do coração selvagem* (1944; *Near to the Wild Heart*), published when she was 24 years old, won critical acclaim for its sensitive interpretation of adolescence. In her later works, such as *A maçã no escuro* (1961; *The Apple in the Dark*), *A paixão segundo G.H.* (1964; *The Passion According to G.H.*), and *Água viva* (1973; "Living Water"), her characters, alienated and searching for meaning in life, gradually gain a sense of awareness of themselves and accept their place in an arbitrary, yet eternal, universe.

Lispector's finest prose is found in her short stories. Collections such as *Laços de família* (1960; *Family Ties*) and *A legião estrangeira* (1964; "The Foreign Legion") focus on personal moments of revelation in the everyday lives of the protagonists and the lack of meaningful communication among individuals in a contemporary urban setting.

Lispector achieved international fame with works that depict a highly personal, almost existentialist view of the human dilemma and are written in a prose style characterized by a simple vocabulary and elliptical sentence structure. She is notoriously difficult to translate. In contrast to the regional or national social concerns expressed by many of her Brazilian contemporaries, her artistic vision transcends time and place; her characters, in elemental situations of crisis, are frequently female and only incidentally modern or Brazilian.

# *ALEX HALEY*

(b. August 11, 1921, Ithaca, New York, U.S.—
d. February 10, 1992, Seattle, Washington)

Alex Haley was an American writer whose works of historical fiction and reportage depicted the struggles of African Americans.

Although his parents were teachers, Haley was an indifferent student. He began writing to avoid boredom during voyages while serving in the U.S. Coast Guard (1939–59). His first major work, *The Autobiography of Malcolm X* (1965), was an authoritative and widely read narrative based on Haley's interviews with the Black Muslim spokesman. The work is recognized as a classic of African American literature.

Haley's greatest success was *Roots: The Saga of an American Family* (1976). This saga covers seven American generations, from the enslavement of Haley's African ancestors to his own genealogical quest. The work forcefully shows relationships between generations and between races. *Roots* was adapted as a multi-episode television program, which, when first broadcast in January 1977, became one of the most popular shows in the history of American television and galvanized attention on African American issues and history. That same year Haley won a special Pulitzer Prize. A successful sequel was first broadcast in February 1979 as *Roots: The Next Generations*.

*Roots* spurred much interest in family history, and Haley created the Kinte Foundation (1972) to store records that aid in tracing black genealogy. Haley later admitted that his saga was partly fictional; the book was also the subject of a plagiarism suit, which Haley settled out of court.

In 1978 Haley's boyhood home in Henning, Tennessee, north of Memphis, was restored and opened to the public. On the same grounds, the state later constructed the Alex Haley Interpretive Center (2010), which educated visitors in genealogical methodology.

# JACK KEROUAC

(b. March 12, 1922, Lowell, Massachusetts, U.S.—
d. October 21, 1969, St. Petersburg, Florida)

Jean-Louis Lebris de Kerouac was an American novelist, poet, and leader of the Beat movement whose most famous book, *On the Road* (1957), had broad cultural influence before it was recognized for its literary merits. *On the Road* captured the spirit of its time as no other work of the 20th century had since F. Scott Fitzgerald's *The Great Gatsby* (1925).

## Childhood and Early Influences

Lowell, Massachusetts, a mill town, had a large French Canadian population; while Kerouac's mother worked in a shoe factory and his father worked as a printer, Kerouac attended a French Canadian school in the morning and continued his studies in English in the afternoon. He spoke joual, a Canadian dialect of French, and so, though he was an American, he viewed his country as if he were a foreigner. Kerouac subsequently went to the Horace Mann School, a preparatory school in New York City, on a football scholarship. There, two of his fellow students whom he befriended had a particular impact on his life: Henri Cru helped him find jobs as a merchant seaman, and Seymour Wyse introduced him to jazz.

In 1940 Kerouac enrolled at Columbia University, where he met two writers who would become life-long friends: Allen Ginsberg and William S. Burroughs. Together with Kerouac they are the seminal figures of the literary movement known as Beat, a term introduced to Kerouac by Herbert Huncke, a Times Square junkie, petty thief, hustler, and writer. It meant "down-and-out" as well as "beatific" and therefore signified the bottom of existence (from a financial and an emotional point of view) as well as the highest, most spiritual high.

Kerouac's childhood and early adulthood were marked by loss: his brother Gerard died in 1926, when Gerard was nine. Kerouac's boyhood friend Sebastian Sampas died in 1944 and his father, Leo, in 1946. In a deathbed promise to Leo, Kerouac pledged to care for his mother, Gabrielle, affectionately known as Memere. Kerouac married three times: to Edie Parker (1944, annulled 1946); to Joan Haverty (1951), with whom he had a daughter, Jan Michelle; and to Stella Sampas (1966), the sister of Sebastian, who had died at Anzio, Italy, during World War II.

## On the Road *and Other Early Work*

By the time Kerouac and Burroughs met in 1944, Kerouac had already written a million words. His boyhood ambition had been to write the "great American novel." His first novel, *The Town & the City* (1950), received favourable reviews but was considered derivative of the novels of Thomas Wolfe, whose *Time and the River* (1935) and *You Can't Go Home Again* (1940) were then popular. In his novel Kerouac articulated the "New Vision," that "everything was collapsing," a theme that would dominate his grand design to have all his work taken together as "one vast book"—*The Legend of Duluoz*.

Yet Kerouac was unhappy with the pace of his prose. The music of bebop jazz artists Thelonious Monk and Charlie Parker began to drive Kerouac toward his "spontaneous bop prosody," as Ginsberg later called it, which took shape in the late 1940s through various drafts of his second novel, *On the Road*. The original manuscript, a scroll written in a three-week blast in 1951, is legendary: composed of approximately 120 feet (37 metres) of paper taped together and fed into a manual typewriter, the scroll allowed Kerouac the fast pace he was hoping to achieve. He also hoped to publish the novel as a scroll so that the reader would not be encumbered by having to turn the pages of a book. Rejected for publication at first, it finally was printed in 1957. In the interim, Kerouac wrote several more "true-life" novels, *Doctor Sax* (1959), *Maggie Cassidy* (1959), and *Tristessa* (1960) among them.

Kerouac found himself a national sensation after *On the Road* received a rave review from *The New York Times* critic Gilbert Millstein. While Millstein extolled the literary merits of the book, to the American public the novel represented a departure from tradition. Kerouac, though, was disappointed with having achieved fame for what he considered the wrong reason: little attention went to the excellence of his writing and more to the novel's radically different characters and its characterization of hipsters and their nonconformist celebration of sex, jazz, and endless movement. The character Dean Moriarty (based on Neal Cassady, another important influence on Kerouac's style) was an American archetype, embodying "IT," an intense moment of heightened experience achieved through fast driving, talking, or "blowing" (as a horn player might) or in writing. In *On the Road* Sal Paradise explains his fascination with others who have "IT," such as Dean

*Jack Kerouac, c. 1965.* Hulton Archive/Getty Images

Moriarty and Rollo Greb as well as jazz performers: "The only ones for me are the mad ones, the ones who are mad to live, mad to talk, mad to be saved." These are characters for whom the perpetual now is all.

Readers often confused Kerouac with Sal Paradise, the amoral hipster at the centre of his novel. The critic Norman Podhoretz famously wrote that Beat writing was an assault against the intellect and against decency. This misreading dominated negative reactions to *On the Road*. Kerouac's rebellion, however, is better understood as a quest for the solidity of home and family, what he considered "the hearthside ideal." He wanted to achieve in his writing that which he could find neither in the promise of America nor in the empty spirituality of Roman Catholicism; he strived instead for the serenity that he had discovered in his adopted Buddhism. Kerouac felt that the Beat label marginalized him and prevented him from being treated as he wanted to be treated, as a man of letters in the American tradition of Herman Melville and Walt Whitman.

## Sketching, Poetry, and Buddhism

Despite the success of the "spontaneous prose" technique Kerouac used in *On the Road*, he sought further refinements to his narrative style. Following a suggestion by Ed White, a friend from his Columbia University days, that he sketch "like a painter, but with words," Kerouac sought visual possibilities in language by combining spontaneous prose with sketching. *Visions of Cody* (written in 1951–52 and published posthumously in 1972), an in-depth, more poetic variation of *On the Road* describing a buddy trip and including transcripts of his conversation with Cassady (now fictionalized as Cody), is the most successful realization of the sketching technique.

As he continued to experiment with his prose style, Kerouac also bolstered his standing among the Beat writers as a poet supreme. With his sonnets and odes he ranged across Western poetic traditions. He also experimented with the idioms of blues and jazz in such works as *Mexico City Blues* (1959), a sequential poem comprising 242 choruses. After he met the poet Gary Snyder in 1955, Kerouac's poetry, as well as that of Ginsberg and fellow Beats Philip Whalen and Lew Welch, began to show the influence of the haiku, a genre mostly unknown to Americans at that time. (The haiku of Bashō, Buson, Masaoka Shiki, and Issa had not been translated into English until the pioneering work of R.H. Blyth in the late 1940s.) While Ezra Pound had modeled his poem *In a Station of the Metro* (1913) after Japanese haiku, Kerouac, departing from the 17-syllable, 3-line strictures, redefined the form and created an American haiku tradition. In the posthumously published collection *Scattered Poems* (1971), he proposed that the "Western haiku" simply say a lot in three short lines:

*Above all, a Haiku must be very simple and free of all poetic trickery and make a little picture and yet be as airy and graceful as a Vivaldi Pastorella.*

In his pocket notebooks, Kerouac wrote and rewrote haiku, revising and perfecting them. He also incorporated his haiku into his prose. His mastery of the form is demonstrated in his novel *The Dharma Bums* (1958).

Kerouac turned to Buddhist study and practice from 1953 to 1956, after his "road" period and in the lull between composing *On the Road* in 1951 and its publication in 1957. In the fall of 1953 he finished *The Subterraneans* (it would be published in 1958). Fed up with the world after the failed love affair upon which the book was based, he read Henry David Thoreau and fantasized a life outside civilization.

He immersed himself in the study of Zen, beginning his genre-defying *Some of the Dharma* in 1953 as reader's notes on Dwight Goddard's *A Buddhist Bible* (1932); the work grew into a massive compilation of spiritual material, meditations, prayers, haiku, and musings on the teaching of Buddha. In an attempt to replicate the experience of Han Shan, a reclusive Chinese poet of the Tang dynasty (618–907), Kerouac spent 63 days atop Desolation Peak in Washington state. Kerouac recounted this experience in *Desolation Angels* (1965) using haiku as bridges (connectives in jazz) between sections of spontaneous prose. In 1956 he wrote a sutra, *The Scripture of the Golden Eternity*. He also began to think of his entire oeuvre as a "Divine Comedy of the Buddha," thereby combining Eastern and Western traditions.

## Later Work

By the 1960s Kerouac had finished most of the writing for which he is best known. In 1961 he wrote *Big Sur* in 10 days while living in the cabin of Lawrence Ferlinghetti, a fellow Beat poet, in California's Big Sur region. Two years later Kerouac's account of his brother's death was published as the spiritual *Visions of Gerard*. Another important autobiographical book, *Vanity of Duluoz* (1968), recounts stories of his childhood, his schooling, and the dramatic scandals that defined early Beat legend.

In 1969 Kerouac was broke, and many of his books were out of print. An alcoholic, he was living with his third wife and his mother in St. Petersburg, Florida, where he spent his time in local bars. A week after he had been beaten by fellow drinkers whom he had antagonized, he died of internal hemorrhaging in front of his television while watching *The Galloping Gourmet* — the ultimate ending for a writer who came to be known as the "martyred king of the Beats."

*Jack Kerouac: Collected Poems* (2012) gathered all of his published poetry collections along with poems that appeared in his fiction and elsewhere. The volume also contained six previously unpublished poems.

Kerouac's presence found new life on the screen with the release of three movies: film versions of his novels *On the Road* (2012) and *Big Sur* (2013), and a dramatization of New York's early Beat movement called *Kill Your Darlings* (2013), the latter two films premiering at the prestigious Sundance Film Festival in Park City, Utah.

# Sir Kingsley Amis

(b. April 16, 1922, London, England—d. October 22, 1995, London)

The novelist, poet, critic, and teacher Sir Kingsley Amis created in his first novel, *Lucky Jim*, a comic figure that became a household word in Great Britain in the 1950s.

Amis was educated at the City of London School and at St. John's College, Oxford (B.A., 1949). His education was interrupted during World War II by his service as a lieutenant in the Royal Corps of Signals. From 1949 to 1961 he taught at universities in Wales, England, and the United States.

Amis's first novel, *Lucky Jim* (1954, film 1957), was an immediate success and remains his most popular work. Its disgruntled antihero, a young university instructor named Jim Dixon, epitomized a newly important social group that had risen by dint of scholarships from lower-middle-class and working-class backgrounds only to find the more comfortable perches still occupied by the well-born. *Lucky Jim* prompted critics to group Amis with the Angry Young Men, a group of working-class and lower-middle-class

British writers of the 1950s who expressed similar social discontent. Amis's next novel, *That Uncertain Feeling* (1955), had a similar antihero. A visit to Portugal resulted in the novel *I Like It Here* (1958), while observations garnered from a teaching stint in the United States were expressed in the novel *One Fat Englishman* (1963).

Amis went on to write more than 40 books, including some 20 novels, many volumes of poetry, and several collections of essays. His apparent lack of sympathy with his characters and his sharply satirical rendering of well-turned dialogue were complemented by his own curmudgeonly public persona. Notable among his later novels were *The Green Man* (1969), *Jake's Thing* (1978), and *The Old Devils* (1986). As a poet, Amis was a representative member of a group sometimes called "The Movement," whose poems began appearing in 1956 in the anthology *New Lines*. Poets belonging to this school wrote understated and disciplined verse that avoided experimentation and grandiose themes. In 1990 Amis was knighted, and his *Memoirs* were published in 1991. His son Martin Amis also became a well-known novelist.

# Alain Robbe-Grillet

(b. August 18, 1922, Brest, France—d. February 18, 2008, Caen)

Alain Robbe-Grillet was the leading theoretician of the *nouveau roman* ("new novel"), the French "anti-novel" that emerged in the 1950s. He was also a screenwriter and film director.

Robbe-Grillet was trained as a statistician and agronomist. He claimed to write novels for his time, especially attentive "to the ties that exist between objects, gestures, and situations, avoiding all psychological and ideological 'commentary' on the actions of the characters" (*Pour un nouveau roman*, 1963; *Toward a New Novel; Essays on Fiction*). Robbe-Grillet's world is neither meaningful nor absurd; it merely exists. Omnipresent is the object—hard, polished, with only the measurable characteristics of pounds, inches, and wavelengths of reflected light. It overshadows and eliminates plot and character. The story is composed of recurring images, either actually recorded by an objective eye or drawn from reminiscences and dreams.

If Robbe-Grillet's fiction, with its timetables, careful inventories of things, and reports on arrivals and departures, owes anything to the traditional novel, it is to the detective story. His first work, *Les Gommes* (1953; *The Erasers*), deals with a murder committed by the man who has come to investigate it. *Le Voyeur* (1955; *The Voyeur*) deals with the murder of a young girl by a passing stranger. In *La Jalousie* (1957; *Jealousy*), a jealous husband views the actions of his wife and her suspected lover through a louvre shutter (*jalousie*). Among his later novels are *Dans le labyrinthe* (1959; *In the Labyrinth*), *Instantanés* (1962; *Snapshots*), *La Maison de rendez-vous* (1966; *The House of Assignation*), *Projet pour une révolution à New York* (1970; *Project for a Revolution in New York*), *Topologie d'une cité famtôme* (1976; *Topology of a Phantom City*), *Un Régicide* (1978; "A Regicide"), and *Djinn* (1981). Robbe-Grillet continued to write into the early 21st century; novels from this period include *La Reprise* (2001; *Repetition*) and *Un Roman sentimental* (2007; "A Sentimental Novel"), the latter of which concerns incest and pedophilia. His autobiography, *Le Miroir qui revient* (*Ghosts in the Mirror*), was published in 1984.

Robbe-Grillet's techniques were dramatized in the motion pictures he directed, among them *L'Immortelle* (1963; "The Immortal"), *Trans-Europ-Express* (1966), and *L'Homme qui ment* (1968; *The Man Who Lies*). His best-known work in the medium, however, is the screenplay for

Alain Resnais's film *L'Année dernière à Marienbad* (1961; *Last Year at Marienbad*). Ultimately, Robbe-Grillet's work raises questions about the ambiguous relationship of objectivity and subjectivity.

Robbe-Grillet was the recipient of numerous honours. In 2004 he was elected to the French Academy.

# KURT VONNEGUT

(b. November 11, 1922, Indianapolis, Indiana, U.S.—
d. April 11, 2007, New York, New York)

The American writer Kurt Vonnegut is noted for his wryly satirical novels in which he frequently used postmodern techniques as well as elements of fantasy and science fiction to highlight the horrors and ironies of 20th-century civilization. Much of Vonnegut's work is marked by an essentially fatalistic worldview that none-theless embraces modern humanist beliefs.

Vonnegut grew up in Indianapolis in a well-to-do family, although his father, an architect, was unemployed during much of the Great Depression. As a teenager, Vonnegut wrote for his high school newspaper, and he continued the activity at Cornell University in Ithaca, New York, where he majored in biochemistry before leaving in 1943 to enlist in the U.S. Air Force. Captured by the Germans during World War II, he was one of the survivors of the firebombing of Dresden, Germany, in February 1945. After the war Vonnegut took graduate courses in anthropology at the University of Chicago while working as a reporter. He was later employed as a public relations writer in upstate New York, but his reservations about what he considered the deceitfulness of the profession led him to pursue fiction writing full-time.

In the early 1950s Vonnegut began publishing short stories. Many of them were concerned with technology and the future, which led some critics to classify Vonnegut as a science-fiction writer, though he resisted the label. His first novel, *Player Piano* (1952), elaborates on those themes, visualizing a completely mechanized and automated society whose dehumanizing effects are unsuccessfully resisted by the scientists and workers in a New York factory town. For his second novel, *The Sirens of Titan* (1959), Vonnegut imagined a scenario in which the entire history of the human race is considered an accident attendant on an alien planet's search for a spare part for a spaceship.

Vonnegut abandoned science-fiction tropes altogether in *Mother Night* (1961; film 1996), a novel about an American playwright who serves as a spy in Nazi Germany. In *Cat's Cradle* (1963) some Caribbean islanders, who practice a religion consisting of harmless trivialities, come into contact with a substance discovered by an atomic scientist that eventually destroys all life on Earth. (In 1963 the University of Chicago granted Vonnegut a master's degree in anthropology after he submitted *Cat's Cradle* as a thesis.) The novel was particularly significant in its development of a slyly irreverent voice that constantly called attention to its own artifice; a similar "metafictional" style would characterize much of Vonnegut's subsequent work. *God Bless You, Mr. Rosewater* (1965) centres on the title character, an eccentric philanthropist, but also introduces the writer Kilgore Trout, a fictional alter ego of Vonnegut who appears throughout his oeuvre.

Although Vonnegut's work had already gained a popular audience by the late 1960s, the publication of *Slaughterhouse-Five; or, The Children's Crusade* (1969; film 1972) cemented his reputation. Explicitly drawing on his Dresden experience, Vonnegut crafted an absurdist nonlinear narrative in which the bombing raid serves as a symbol of the cruelty and destructiveness of war through the centuries. Critics lauded *Slaughterhouse-Five* as a modern-day classic. *Breakfast of Champions; or, Goodbye Blue Monday!* (1973; film 1999)—about a Midwestern businessman who becomes obsessed with Trout's books—is a commentary on writing, fame, and American social values, interspersed with drawings by Vonnegut. Though reviews were mixed, it quickly became a best-seller. Vonnegut's next two novels were less successful. *Slapstick; or, Lonesome No More!* (1976; film 1982) focuses on a pair of grotesque siblings who devise a program to end loneliness, and *Jailbird* (1979) is a postmodern pastiche rooted in 20th-century American social history.

While Vonnegut remained prolific throughout the 1980s, he struggled with depression and in 1984 attempted suicide. His later novels include *Deadeye Dick* (1982), which revisits characters and settings from *Breakfast of Champions*; *Galápagos* (1985), a fantasy of human evolution told from a detached future perspective; *Bluebeard* (1987), the fictional autobiography of an aging painter; *Hocus Pocus* (1990), about a college professor turned prison warden; and *Timequake* (1997), a loosely structured meditation on free will.

Vonnegut also wrote several plays, including *Happy Birthday, Wanda June* (1970; film 1971); several works of nonfiction, such as the collection *Wampeters, Foma & Granfalloons* (1974); and several collections of short stories, chief among which was *Welcome to the Monkey House* (1968). In 2005 he published *A Man Without a Country: A Memoir of Life in George W. Bush's America*, a collection of essays and speeches inspired in part by contemporary politics. Vonnegut's posthumously published works include *Armageddon in Retrospect* (2008), a collection of fiction and nonfiction that focuses on war and peace, and a number of previously unpublished short stories, assembled in *Look at the Birdie* (2009) and *While Mortals Sleep* (2011).

Vonnegut was elected a member of the American Academy of Arts and Sciences in 1973. In 2010 the Kurt Vonnegut Memorial Library opened in Indianapolis. In addition to promoting the work of Vonnegut, the non-profit organization serves as a cultural and educational resource centre, including a museum, an art gallery, and a reading room.

# JOSÉ SARAMAGO

(b. November 16, 1922, Azinhaga, Portugal—
d. June 18, 2010, Lanzarote, Canary Islands, Spain)

The Portuguese novelist and man of letters José Saramago was awarded the Nobel Prize for Literature in 1998.

The son of rural labourers, Saramago grew up in great poverty in Lisbon. After holding a series of jobs as mechanic and metalworker, Saramago began working in a Lisbon publishing firm and eventually became a journalist and translator. He joined the Portuguese Communist Party in 1969, published several volumes of poems, and served as editor of a Lisbon newspaper in 1974–75 during the cultural thaw that followed the overthrow of the dictatorship of António Salazar. An anticommunist backlash followed in which Saramago lost his position, and in his 50s he began writing the novels that would eventually establish his international reputation.

One of Saramago's most important novels is *Memorial do convento* (1982; "Memoirs of the Convent"; Eng. trans. *Baltasar and Blimunda*). With 18th-century Portugal (during the Inquisition) as a backdrop, it chronicles the efforts of a handicapped war veteran and his lover to flee their situation by using a flying machine powered by human will. Saramago alternates this allegorical fantasy with grimly realistic descriptions of the construction of the Mafra Convent by thousands of labourers pressed into service by King John V. Another ambitious novel, *O ano da morte de Ricardo Reis* (1984; *The Year of the Death of Ricardo Reis*), juxtaposes the romantic involvements of its narrator, a poet-physician who returns to Portugal at the start of the Salazar dictatorship, with long dialogues that examine human nature as revealed in Portuguese history and culture. Saramago's practice of setting whimsical parables against realistic historical backgrounds in order to comment ironically on human foibles is exemplified in two novels: *A jangada de pedra* (1986; *The Stone Raft*; film 2002), which explores the situation that ensues when the Iberian Peninsula breaks off from Europe and becomes an island, and *O evangelho segundo Jesus Cristo* (1991; *The Gospel According to Jesus Christ*), which posits Christ as an innocent caught in the machinations of God and Satan. The outspoken atheist's ironic comments in *The Gospel According to Jesus Christ* were deemed too cutting by the Roman Catholic Church, which pressured the Portuguese government to block the book's entry for a literary prize in 1992. As a result of what he considered censorship, Saramago went into self-imposed exile on the Canary Islands for the remainder of his life.

Among Saramago's other novels are his first, *Manual de pintura e caligrafia* (1976; *Manual of Painting and Calligraphy*), and such subsequent works as *Historia do cerco de Lisboa* (1989; *The History of the Siege of Lisbon*), *Todos os nomes* (1997; *All the Names*), *O homem duplicado* (2002; *The Double*), *As intermitências da morte* (2005; *Death with Interruptions*), and *A viagem do elefante* (2008; *The Elephant's Journey*). *Ensaio sobre a cegueira* (1995; "Essay on Blindness"; Eng. trans. *Blindness*; film 2008) and *Ensaio sobre a lucidez* (2004; "Essay on Lucidity"; Eng. trans. *Seeing*) are companion novels. In 2012 his novel *Claraboya* ("Skylight"), which had been written in the 1950s but languished in a Portuguese publishing house for decades, was posthumously published.

Saramago also wrote poetry, plays, and several volumes of essays and short stories, as well as autobiographical works. His memoir *As pequenas memórias* (2006; *Small*

*José Saramago at a reading of his work, Guadalajara, Mex., 2006.*
Ivan Garcia/AFP/Getty Images

*Memories*) focuses on his childhood. When he received the Nobel Prize in 1998, his novels were widely read in Europe but less well known in the United States; he subsequently gained popularity worldwide. He was the first Portuguese-language writer to win the Nobel Prize.

# *WILLIAM GADDIS*

(b. December 29, 1922, New York, New York, U.S.—
d. December 16, 1998, East Hampton, New York)

William Gaddis was an American novelist of complex, satiric works who is considered one of the best of the post-World War II Modernist writers.

After incomplete studies at Harvard University (1941–45), Gaddis worked as a fact-checker for *The New Yorker* magazine for two years and then traveled widely in Central America and Europe, holding a variety of jobs. He first gained note as an author with the publication of his controversial novel *The Recognitions* (1955). This book, rich in language and imagery, began as a parody of Faust but developed into a multileveled examination of spiritual bankruptcy that alternately was considered a brilliant masterpiece and incomprehensibly excessive. It became an underground classic, but, discouraged by the harsh critical reception of his book, Gaddis worked as a freelance writer for various corporations and published nothing for 20 years. His second novel, *JR* (1975), uses long stretches of cacophonous dialogue to depict what its author viewed as the greed, hypocrisy, and banality of the world of American business. Gaddis's third novel, *Carpenter's Gothic* (1985), is even more pessimistic in its depiction of moral chaos in modern America. The law, lawyers, and especially the litigiousness rampant in contemporary American society are examined in *A Frolic of His Own* (1994). Gaddis's last work of fiction, *Agapē Agape*, a rambling first-person narrative of a dying man obsessed with the history of the player piano, was published posthumously in 2002, as was the collection *The Rush for Second Place: Essays and Occasional Writings*.

Gaddis's fiction shows the influence of the writings of James Joyce and in turn influenced the work of Thomas Pynchon; it contains long dialogues and monologues connected by a minimal plotline and structured with scant punctuation. His books belong to a style of literature characterized by the absence of distinctive incidents and by the pervasive use of black humour in dealing with a chaotic mass of associations. They create a radical way of viewing the world by which the reader can reassess his own situation.

# OUSMANE SEMBÈNE

(b. January 1, 1923, Ziguinchor-Casamance, Senegal, French West Africa—d. June 9/10, 2007, Dakar, Senegal)

The Senegalese writer and film director Ousmane Sembène is known for his historical and political themes.

Sembène spent his early years as a fisherman on the Casamance coast. He studied at the School of Ceramics at Marsassoum and then moved to Dakar, where he worked as a bricklayer, plumber, and apprentice mechanic until he was drafted into the French army in 1939. In 1942, during World War II, he joined the Free French forces and landed in France for the first time in 1944. After demobilization he remained in France, working as a docker in Marseille, and became a militant trade unionist.

Sembène taught himself to read and write in French and in 1956 published his first novel, *Le Docker noir* (*Black Docker*), based on his experiences in Marseille. After a spinal disorder forced him to give up physical labour, he made literature his livelihood. Among the works that followed were *Ô pays, mon beau peuple!* (1957; "O My Country, My Good People"), *Les Bouts de bois de Dieu* (1960; *God's Bits of Wood*), which depicts an African workers' railroad strike and the attempts to combat colonialism, a volume of short stories titled *Voltaïque* (1962; *Tribal Scars and Other Stories*), *L'Harmattan* (1964; "The Wind"), and *Xala* (1973), which also provided the subject of one of his best films (1974). In 1987 the novella collection *Niiwam; suivi de Taaw* (*Niiwam; and Taaw*) was published.

About 1960 Sembène developed an interest in motion pictures, in an attempt to reach an African popular audience, 80 percent of whom did not know French or have access to books in any language. After studying at the Moscow Film School, Sembène returned to Africa and made three short-subject films, all reflecting a strong social commitment. His 1966 feature film, *La Noire de...* (*Black Girl*), was considered the first major film produced by an African filmmaker. It depicts the virtual enslavement of an illiterate girl from Dakar employed as a servant by a French family. The film won a major prize at the 1967 Cannes international film festival.

With *Mandabi* ("The Money Order"), a comedy of daily life and corruption in Dakar, Sembène in 1968 made the revolutionary decision to film in the Wolof language. His masterpiece, *Ceddo* (1977; "Outsiders"), an ambitious, panoramic account of aspects of African religions, was also in Wolof and was banned in his native Senegal. *Camp de Thiaroye* (1987; "The Camp at Thiaroye") depicts an event in 1944 in which French troops slaughtered a camp of rebellious African war veterans. *Guelwaar* (1993), a commentary on the fractious religious life of Senegal, tells of the confusion that arises when the bodies of a Muslim and a Catholic (Guelwaar) are switched at the morgue. *Moolaadé* (2004; "Protection"), which received the prize for Un Certain Regard at Cannes, mixed comedy and melodrama to explore the practice of female circumcision.

The writer-director's cinematic achievements are examined in *A Call to Action: The Films of Ousmane Sembene*, edited by Sheila Petty (1996).

# NORMAN MAILER

(b. January 31, 1923, Long Branch, New Jersey, U.S. —
d. November 10, 2007, New York, New York)

The American novelist and journalist Norman Mailer is best known for using a form of journalism — called New Journalism — that combines the imaginative subjectivity of literature with the more objective qualities of journalism. Both Mailer's fiction and his nonfiction made a radical critique of the totalitarianism he believed inherent in the centralized power structure of 20th- and 21st-century America.

Mailer grew up in Brooklyn and graduated from Harvard University in 1943 with a degree in aeronautical engineering. Drafted into the army in 1944, he served in the Pacific until 1946. While he was enrolled at the Sorbonne, in Paris, he wrote *The Naked and the Dead* (1948), hailed immediately as one of the finest American novels to come out of World War II. Mailer's success at age 25 aroused the expectation that he would develop from a war novelist into the leading literary figure of the postwar generation. But Mailer's search for themes and forms to give meaningful expression to what he saw as the problems of his time committed him to exploratory works that had little general appeal. His second novel, *Barbary Shore* (1951), and *The Deer Park* (1955) were greeted with critical hostility and mixed reviews, respectively. His next important work was a long essay, *The White Negro* (1957), a sympathetic study of a marginal social type—the "hipster."

In 1959, when Mailer was generally dismissed as a one-book author, he made a bid for attention with the book *Advertisements for Myself,* a collection of unfinished stories, parts of novels, essays, reviews, notebook entries, or ideas for fiction. The miscellany's naked self-revelation won the admiration of a younger generation seeking alternative styles of life and art. Mailer's subsequent novels, though not critical successes, were widely read as guides to life. *An American Dream* (1965) is about a man who murders his wife, and *Why Are We in Vietnam?* (1967) is about a young man on an Alaskan hunting trip.

A controversial figure whose egotism and belligerence often antagonized both critics and readers, Mailer did not command the same respect for his fiction that he received for his journalism, which conveyed actual events with the subjective richness and imaginative complexity of a novel. *The Armies of the Night* (1968), for example, was based on the Washington peace demonstrations of October 1967, during which Mailer was jailed and fined for an act of civil disobedience; it won a Pulitzer Prize and a National Book Award. A similar treatment was given the Republican and Democratic presidential conventions in *Miami and the Siege of Chicago* (1968) and the Moon exploration in *Of a Fire on the Moon* (1970).

In 1969 Mailer ran unsuccessfully for mayor of New York City. Among his other works are his essay collections *The Presidential Papers* (1963) and *Cannibals and Christians* (1966); *The Executioner's Song* (1979), a Pulitzer Prize-winning novel based on the life of convicted murderer

Gary Gilmore; *Ancient Evenings* (1983), a novel set in ancient Egypt, the first volume of an uncompleted trilogy; *Tough Guys Don't Dance* (1984), a contemporary mystery thriller; and the enormous *Harlot's Ghost* (1991), a novel focusing on the Central Intelligence Agency. In 1995 Mailer published *Oswald's Tale*, an exhaustive nonfictional portrayal of U.S. Pres. John F. Kennedy's assassin. Mailer's final two novels intertwined religion and historical figures: *The Gospel According to the Son* (1997) is a first-person "memoir" purportedly written by Jesus Christ, and *The Castle in the Forest* (2007), narrated by a devil, tells the story of Adolf Hitler's boyhood.

In 2003 Mailer published two works of nonfiction: *The Spooky Art*, his reflections on writing, and *Why Are We at War?*, an essay questioning the Iraq War. *On God* (2007) records conversations about religion between Mailer and the scholar Michael Lennon.

# *BRENDAN BEHAN*

(b. February 9, 1923, Dublin, Ireland—d. March 20, 1964, Dublin)

Brendan Behan was an Irish author noted for his earthy satire and powerful political commentary.

Reared in a family active in revolutionary and left-wing causes against the British, Behan at the age of eight began what became a lifelong battle with alcoholism. After leaving school in 1937, he learned the house-painter's trade while concurrently participating in the Irish Republican Army (IRA) as a courier.

Behan was arrested in England while on a sabotage mission and sentenced (February 1940) to three years in a reform school at Hollesley Bay, Suffolk. He wrote an autobiographical account of this detention in *Borstal Boy* (1958).

He was deported to Dublin in 1942 and was soon involved in a shooting incident in which a policeman was wounded. He was convicted of attempted murder and sentenced to 14 years. He served at Mountjoy Prison, Dublin, the setting of his first play, *The Quare Fellow* (1954), and later at the Curragh Military Camp, County Kildare, from which he was released under a general amnesty in 1946. While imprisoned, he perfected his Irish, the language he used for his delicately sensitive poetry and for *An Giall* (1957), the initial version of his second play, *The Hostage* (1958).

Subsequent arrests followed, either for revolutionary activities or for drunkenness, which also forced various hospitalizations. In 1948 Behan went to Paris to write. Returning to Dublin in 1950, he wrote short stories and scripts for Radio Telefís Éireann and sang on a continuing program, *Ballad Maker's Saturday Night*. In 1953 he began in the *Irish Press* a column about Dublin, later collected (1963) in *Hold Your Hour and Have Another*, with illustrations by his wife, Beatrice Salkeld, whom he had married in 1955.

*The Quare Fellow* opened at the small Pike Theatre, Dublin, in 1954 and was an instant success. A tragicomedy concerning the reactions of jailors and prisoners to the hanging of a condemned man (the "quare [unusual] fellow"), it presents an explosive statement on capital punishment. The play was subsequently performed in London (1956) and in New York City (1958). *The Hostage*, however, is considered to be his masterwork, in which ballads, slapstick, and fantasies satirize social conditions and warfare with a personal gaiety that emerges from anguish. The play deals with the tragic situation of an English soldier whom the IRA holds as a hostage in a brothel to prevent the execution of one of their own men. A success in London, the play opened in 1960 off Broadway, New York City, where Behan became a celebrated personality.

Behan's last works, which he dictated on tape, were *Brendan Behan's Island* (1962), a book of Irish anecdotes; *The Scarperer* (1964), a novel about a smuggling adventure, first published serially in the *Irish Press*; *Brendan Behan's New York* (1964); and *Confessions of an Irish Rebel* (1965), further memoirs.

# JOSEPH HELLER

(b. May 1, 1923, Brooklyn, New York, U.S.—
d. December 12, 1999, East Hampton, New York)

Joseph Heller was an American writer whose novel *Catch-22* (1961) was one of the most significant works of protest literature to appear after World War II. The satirical novel was a popular success, and a film version appeared in 1970.

During World War II, Heller flew 60 combat missions as a bombardier with the U.S. Air Force in Europe. After receiving an M.A. at Columbia University in 1949, he studied at the University of Oxford (1949–50) as a Fulbright scholar. He taught English at Pennsylvania State University (1950–52) and worked as an advertising copywriter for the magazines *Time* (1952–56) and *Look* (1956–58) and as promotion manager for *McCall's* (1958–61), meanwhile writing *Catch-22* in his spare time.

Released to mixed reviews, *Catch-22* developed a cult following with its dark surrealism. Centring on the antihero Captain John Yossarian, stationed at an airstrip on a Mediterranean island during World War II, the novel portrays the airman's desperate attempts to stay alive. The "catch" in *Catch-22* involves a mysterious Air Force regulation that asserts that a man is considered insane if he willingly continues to fly dangerous combat missions; but, if he makes the necessary formal request to be relieved of such missions, the very act of making the request proves that he is sane and therefore ineligible to be relieved. The term *catch-22* thereafter entered the English language as a reference to a proviso that trips one up no matter which way one turns.

Heller's later novels, including *Something Happened* (1974), an unrelievedly pessimistic novel, *Good as Gold* (1979), a satire on life in Washington, D.C., and *God Knows* (1984), a wry, contemporary-vernacular monologue in the voice of the biblical King David, were less successful. *Closing Time*, a sequel to *Catch-22*, appeared in 1994. His final novel, *Portrait of an Artist, as an Old Man* (2000), was published posthumously, as was *Catch As Catch Can: The Collected Stories and Other Writings* (2003). Heller also wrote an autobiography, *Now and Then: From Coney Island to Here* (1998), and his dramatic work includes the play *We Bombed in New Haven* (1968).

# *YVES BONNEFOY*

(b. June 24, 1923, Tours, France)

Perhaps the most important French poet of the latter half of the 20th century, Yves Bonnefoy is also a respected critic, scholar, and translator.

Bonnefoy's father was a railroad employee, his mother a teacher. After studying mathematics at the University of Poitiers, the young poet moved to Paris, where he came under the influence of the Surrealists. His first poetry collection, *Du mouvement et de l'immobilité de Douve* (1953; *On the Motion and Immobility of Douve*), explored the relation of poetry to life. In Bonnefoy's thought, poetry might be said to be a closed universe that only lives when it is shattered by an intuition of the "real world." He spoke of poetry as at its best expressing "temps transfiguré par l'instant" ("time transfigured by the moment"), a conceptual, progressive world shattered and enlivened by an instant's intuition brought by a ray of sun or other phenomenon of the natural world. His own poetry illustrated his thought in several volumes, including *Ce qui fut sans lumière* (1987; *In the Shadow's Light*), *Début et fin de la neige* (1991; *The Beginning and End of Snow*), and *Les Planches courbes* (2001; *The Curved Planks*). *New and Selected Poems* (1995) contains poems from across his oeuvre in the original French alongside their English translations. *La Longue Chaîne de l'ancre* (2008; "The Long Chain of the Anchor") includes both poems and short stories.

Bonnefoy translated many of Shakespeare's most significant works, including *Julius Caesar* (1960), *Hamlet* (1962), *King Lear* (1965), and *Romeo and Juliet* (1968), into French. He also translated works by John Donne and William Butler Yeats. Bonnefoy analyzed the complexities of the translation process in *Théâtre et poésie: Shakespeare et Yeats* (1998; "Theatre and Poetry: Shakespeare and Yeats") and *Sous l'horizon du langage* (2002; "Beneath the Horizon of Language"), selections from which were published in English as *Shakespeare and the French Poet* (2004).

Bonnefoy taught at numerous universities in both France and the United States. He held the chair in comparative poetics at the Collège de France between 1981 and 1994. He explored the visual arts as well as literature in *Alberto Giacometti: biographie d'une œuvre* (1991; *Alberto Giacometti: A Biography of His Work*) and *Goya, les peintures noires* (2006; "Goya, the Black Paintings"). Several of his essays were brought together in the English-language volume *The Lure and the Truth of Painting* (1993). Bonnefoy also compiled the *Dictionnaire des mythologies et des religions des sociétés traditionelles et du monde antique* (1981; "Dictionary of Mythologies and Religions of Traditional Societies and the Ancient World"; Eng. trans. *Mythologies*). In 2007 he was awarded the Franz Kafka Prize in recognition of his contributions to literature.

# WISŁAWA SZYMBORSKA

(b. July 2, 1923, Bnin [now part of Kórnik], Poland—
d. February 1, 2012, Kraków)

W isława Szymborska was a Polish poet whose intelligent and empathic explorations of philosophical, moral, and ethical issues won her the Nobel Prize for Literature in 1996.

Szymborska's father was the steward on a count's family estate. When she was eight, the family moved to Kraków, and she attended high school there. Between 1945 and 1948 she studied literature and sociology at Kraków's Jagiellonian University. Her first published poem, "Szukam słowa" ("I Seek the Word"), appeared in a Kraków newspaper in March 1945. *Dlatego żyjemy* (1952; "That's Why We Are Alive"), her first volume of poetry, was an attempt to conform to Socialist Realism, the officially approved literary style of Poland's communist regime. In 1953 she joined the editorial staff of *Życie Literackie* ("Literary Life"), a weekly magazine of intellectual interests, and remained there until 1981. During this period she gained a reputation not only as a poet but also as a book reviewer and translator of French poetry. In the 1980s she wrote for the underground press under the pseudonym Stanczykówna and also wrote for a magazine in Paris.

Between 1952 and 1993 Szymborska published more than a dozen volumes of poetry. She later disowned the first two volumes, which contain poems in the style of Socialist Realism, as not indicative of her true poetic intentions. Her third volume, *Wołanie do Yeti* (1957; "Calling Out to Yeti"), marked a clear shift to a more personal style of poetry and expressed her dissatisfaction with communism (Stalinism in particular). Subsequent volumes, such as *Sól* (1962; "Salt"), *Sto pociech* (1967; "No End of Fun"), and *Wszelki wypadek* (1972; "Could Have"), contain poems noteworthy for their precise, concrete language and ironic detachment. Selections of her poems were translated into English and published in such collections as *Sounds, Feelings, Thoughts: Seventy Poems* (1981), *People on a Bridge: Poems* (1990), *View with a Grain of Sand* (1995), *Monologue of a Dog* (2005), and *Here* (2010).

# ITALO CALVINO

(b. October 15, 1923, Santiago de las Vegas, Cuba—
d. September 19, 1985, Siena, Italy)

Italo Calvino was an Italian journalist, short-story writer, and novelist whose whimsical and imaginative fables made him one of the most important Italian fiction writers in the 20th century.

Calvino left Cuba for Italy in his youth. He joined the Italian Resistance during World War II and after the war settled in Turin, obtaining his degree in literature while working for the Communist periodical *L'Unità* and for the publishing house of Einaudi. From 1959 to 1966 he edited, with Elio Vittorini, the left-wing magazine *Il Menabò di letteratura*.

Two of Calvino's first fictional works were inspired by his participation in the Italian Resistance: the Neorealistic novel *Il sentiero dei nidi di ragno* (1947; *The Path to the Nest of Spiders*), which views the Resistance through the experiences of an adolescent as helpless in the midst of events as the adults around him; and the collection of stories entitled *Ultimo viene il corvo* (1949; *Adam, One Afternoon, and Other Stories*).

Calvino turned decisively to fantasy and allegory in the 1950s, producing the three fantastic tales that brought him international acclaim. The first of these fantasies, *Il visconte dimezzato* (1952; "The Cloven Viscount," in *The Nonexistent Knight & the Cloven Viscount*), is an allegorical story of a man split in two—a good half and an evil half—by a cannon shot; he becomes whole through his love for a peasant girl. The second and most highly praised fantasy, *Il barone rampante* (1957; *The Baron in the Trees*), is a whimsical tale of a 19th-century nobleman who one day decides to climb into the trees and who never sets foot on the ground again. From the trees he does, however, participate fully in the affairs of his fellow men below. The tale wittily explores the interaction and tension between reality and imagination. The third fantasy, *Il cavaliere inesistente* (1959; "The Nonexistent Knight," in *The Nonexistent Knight & the Cloven Viscount*), is a mock epic chivalric tale. Among Calvino's later works of fantasy is *Le cosmicomiche* (1965; *Cosmicomics*), a stream-of-consciousness narrative that treats the creation and evolution of the universe. In the later novels *Le città invisibili* (1972; *Invisible Cities*), *Il castello dei destini incrociate* (1973; *The Castle of Crossed Destinies*), and *Se una notte d'inverno un viaggiatore* (1979; *If on a Winter's Night a Traveler*), Calvino uses playfully innovative structures and shifting viewpoints in order to examine the nature of chance, coincidence, and change. *Una pietra sopra: Discorsi di letteratura e società* (1980; *The Uses of Literature*) is a collection of essays he wrote for *Il Menabò*.

# *Nadine Gordimer*

(b. November 20, 1923, Springs, Transvaal, South Africa)

Nadine Gordimer is a South African novelist and short-story writer whose major theme was exile and alienation. She received the Nobel Prize for Literature in 1991.

Gordimer was born into a privileged white middle-class family and began reading at an early age. By the age of 9 she was writing, and she published her first story in a magazine when she was 15. Her wide reading informed her about the world on the other side of apartheid—the official South African policy of racial segregation—and that discovery in time developed into strong political opposition to apartheid. Never an outstanding scholar, she attended the University of Witwatersrand for one year. In addition to writing, she lectured and taught at various schools in the United States during the 1960s and '70s.

Gordimer's first book was *The Soft Voice of the Serpent* (1952), a collection of short stories. In 1953 a novel, *The Lying Days*, was published. Both exhibit the clear, controlled, and unsentimental technique that became her hallmark. Her stories concern the devastating effects of apartheid on the lives of South Africans—the constant tension between personal isolation and the commitment to social justice, the numbness caused by the unwillingness to accept apartheid, the inability to change it, and the refusal of exile.

In 1974 Gordimer won the Booker Prize for *The Conservationist* (1974). Later novels include *Burger's Daughter* (1979), *July's People* (1981), *A Sport of Nature* (1987), and *My Son's Story* (1990). Gordimer addressed environmental issues in *Get a Life* (2005), the story of a South African ecologist who, after receiving thyroid treatment, becomes radioactive to others. *No Time Like the Present* (2012) follows veterans of the battle against apartheid as they deal with the issues facing modern South Africa. She also wrote a number of short-story collections, including *A Soldier's Embrace* (1980), *Crimes of Conscience* (1991), and *Loot and Other Stories* (2003). *Living in Hope and History: Notes from Our Century* (1999) is a collection of essays, correspondence, and reminiscences. In 2007 Gordimer was awarded the French Legion of Honour.

# *Abe Kōbō*

(b. March 7, 1924, Tokyo, Japan — d. January 22, 1993, Tokyo)

The Japanese novelist and playwright Abe Kōbō (a pseudonym of Abe Kimifusa) was noted for his use of bizarre and allegorical situations to underline the isolation of the individual.

He grew up in Mukden (now Shenyang), in Manchuria, where his father, a physician, taught at the medical college. In middle school his strongest subject was mathematics, but he was also interested in collecting insects and had begun to immerse himself in the writings of Fyodor Dostoyevsky, Franz Kafka, Rainer Maria Rilke, Edgar Allan Poe, and Lewis Carroll. Abe went to Japan in 1941 to attend high school. In 1943 he began studying medicine at the Tokyo Imperial University (now the University of Tokyo), but he returned to Manchuria in 1945 without obtaining a degree. Repatriated to Japan in 1946, he was graduated in medicine in 1948 on condition that he never practice. By this time, however, he was deeply involved in literary activity. He published in 1947 at his own expense *Mumei shishū* ("Poems of an Unknown"), and in the following year his novel *Owarishi michi no shirube ni* ("The Road Sign at the End of the Street"), published commercially, was well received. In 1951 his short novel *Kabe* ("The Wall") was awarded the Akutagawa Prize, establishing his reputation. In 1955 Abe wrote his first plays, beginning a long association with the theatre.

Since the early 1950s, Abe had been a member of the Japanese Communist Party, but his visit to eastern Europe in 1956 proved disillusioning. He attempted to leave the party in 1958 when the Soviet army invaded Hungary, but he was refused, only to be expelled in 1962. In that same year *Suna no onna* (*The Woman in the Dunes*), Abe's most popular (and probably his best) novel, was published to general acclaim. It was made into an internationally successful film in 1964.

From the mid-1960s his works were regularly translated on both sides of the Iron Curtain. They include *Daiyon kampyōki* (1959; *Inter Ice Age 4*), *Tanin no kao* (1964; *The Face of Another*), *Moetsukita chizu* (1967; *The Ruined Map*), *Hako otoko* (1973; *The Box Man*), *Mikkai* (1977; *Secret Rendezvous*), *Hakobune Sakura-maru* (1984; *The Ark Sakura*), and *Kangarū nōto* (1991; *Kangaroo Notebook*). *Beyond the Curve*, a translation into English of short stories drawn from various periods of his career, was published in 1991.

Abe formed the Abe Kōbō Studio, a theatrical company, in 1973. He regularly wrote one or two plays a year for the company and served as its director. The best-known of his plays, *Tomodachi* (1967; *Friends*), was performed in the United States and France. In theatre, as well as in the novel, he stood for the avant-garde and experimental. Several of his most successful plays appear in *Three Plays by Kōbō Abe* (1993), translated into English by Donald Keene.

# JAMES BALDWIN

(b. August 2, 1924, New York, New York—
d. December 1, 1987, Saint-Paul, France)

James Baldwin was an American essayist, novelist, and playwright whose eloquence and passion on the subject of race in America made him an important voice, particularly in the late 1950s and early 1960s, in the United States and, later, through much of western Europe.

The eldest of nine children, he grew up in poverty in the black ghetto of Harlem in New York City. From age 14 to 16 he was active during out-of-school hours as a preacher in a small revivalist church, a period he wrote about in his semiautobiographical first and finest novel, *Go Tell It on the Mountain* (1953), and in his play about a woman evangelist, *The Amen Corner* (performed in New York City, 1965).

After graduation from high school, he began a restless period of ill-paid jobs, self-study, and literary apprenticeship in Greenwich Village, the then-bohemian quarter of New York City. He left in 1948 for Paris, where he lived for the next eight years. (In later years, from 1969, he became a self-styled "transatlantic commuter," living alternatively in the south of France and in New York and New England.) His second novel, *Giovanni's Room* (1956), deals with the white world and concerns an American in Paris torn between his love for a man and his love for a woman. Between the two novels came a collection of essays, *Notes of a Native Son* (1955).

In 1957 he returned to the United States and became an active participant in the civil rights struggle that swept the nation. His book of essays, *Nobody Knows My Name*

(1961), explores black-white relations in the United States. This theme also was central to his novel *Another Country* (1962), which examines sexual as well as racial issues.

*The New Yorker* magazine gave over almost all of its November 17, 1962, issue to a long article by Baldwin on the Black Muslim separatist movement and other aspects of the civil rights struggle. The article became a best-seller in book form as *The Fire Next Time* (1963). His bitter play about racist oppression, *Blues for Mister Charlie* ("Mister Charlie" being a black term for a white man), played on Broadway to mixed reviews in 1964.

Though Baldwin continued to write until his death—publishing works including *Going to Meet the Man* (1965), a collection of short stories; the novels *Tell Me How Long the Train's Been Gone* (1968), *If Beale Street Could Talk* (1974), and *Just Above My Head* (1979); and *The Price of the Ticket* (1985), a collection of autobiographical writings—none of his later works achieved the popular and critical success of his early work.

# TRUMAN CAPOTE

(b. September 30, 1924, New Orleans, Louisiana, U.S.—
d. August 25, 1984, Los Angeles, California)

Truman Capote was an American novelist, short-story writer, and playwright. His early writing extended the Southern Gothic tradition, but he later developed a more journalistic approach in the novel *In Cold Blood* (1965), which remains his best-known work.

Born Truman Persons, he was young when his parents divorced, and he spent his childhood with various elderly relatives in small towns in Louisiana and Alabama. (He owed his surname to his mother's remarriage, to Joseph Garcia Capote.) He attended private schools and eventually joined his mother and stepfather at Millbrook, Connecticut, where he completed his secondary education at Greenwich High School.

Capote drew on his childhood experiences for many of his early works of fiction. Having abandoned further schooling, he achieved early literary recognition in 1945 when his haunting short story "Miriam" was published in *Mademoiselle* magazine; it won the O. Henry Memorial Award the following year, the first of four such awards Capote was to receive. His first novel, *Other Voices, Other Rooms* (1948), was acclaimed as the work of a young writer of great promise. The book is a sensitive portrayal of a homosexually inclined boy's search for his father and his own identity through a nightmarishly decadent Southern world. The short story "Shut a Final Door" (O. Henry Award, 1946) and other tales of loveless and isolated persons were collected in *A Tree of Night* (1949). The quasi-autobiographical novel *The Grass Harp* (1951) is a story of nonconforming innocents who retire temporarily from life to a tree house, returning renewed to the real world. One of Capote's most popular works, *Breakfast at Tiffany's* (1958; film 1961), is a novella about a young, fey Manhattan playgirl.

Capote's increasing preoccupation with journalism was reflected in the "nonfiction novel" *In Cold Blood,* a chilling account of a multiple murder committed by two young psychopaths in Kansas. Capote spent six years interviewing the principals in the case, and the critical and popular success of his novel about them was the high point of his dual careers as a writer and a celebrity socialite. For though a serious writer, Capote was also a party-loving sybarite who became a darling of the rich and famous of high society. Endowed with a quirky but attractive character, he entertained television audiences with outrageous tales recounted in his distinctively high-pitched Southern drawl.

Capote's later writings never approached the success of his earlier ones. In the late 1960s he adapted two short stories about his childhood, "A Christmas Memory" and "The Thanksgiving Visitor," for television. *The Dogs Bark* (1973) consists of collected essays and profiles over a 30-year span, while the collection *Music for Chameleons* (1980) includes both fiction and nonfiction. In later years Capote's growing dependence on drugs and alcohol stifled his productivity. Moreover, selections from a projected work that he considered to be his masterpiece, a social satire entitled *Answered Prayers,* appeared in *Esquire* magazine in 1975 and raised a storm among friends and foes who were harshly depicted in the work (under the thinnest of disguises). He was thereafter ostracized by his former celebrity friends. *Answered Prayers* remained unfinished at his death.

# DENNIS BRUTUS

(b. November 28, 1924, Salisbury, Southern Rhodesia [now Harare, Zimbabwe]—d. December 26, 2009, Cape Town, South Africa)

Dennis Brutus was a poet whose works centre on his sufferings and those of his fellow blacks in South Africa.

For 14 years Brutus taught English and Afrikaans in South Africa. As the white minority government increased restrictions on the black population, he became involved in a series of antiapartheid-related activities, including efforts to end discrimination in sports. The government subsequently banned him from teaching, writing, publishing, attending social or political meetings, and pursuing his studies in law at the University of the Witwatersrand. In 1963 his refusal to abide by the ban resulted in an 18-month prison term. His campaigns eventually led to South Africa's suspension from the 1964 Olympic Games. Due in part to Brutus's continued pressure on the International Olympic Committee, South Africa was later officially expelled from the Olympics and did not compete again until 1992.

After leaving South Africa in 1966 with a Rhodesian passport, Brutus made his home in England and then taught at the University of Denver (Colorado, U.S.). In 1971 he became professor of African literature at Northwestern University, Evanston, Illinois. In 1983, after engaging in a protracted legal struggle, he won the right to stay in the United States as a political refugee. Brutus accepted a position teaching African literature at the University of Pittsburgh in 1986. After his retirement from that position in 1999, he continued to lecture and write prolifically, often lending his talents to the various social causes championed by the Centre for Civil Society at the University of KwaZulu-Natal in South Africa.

Brutus's first collection of poetry, *Sirens, Knuckles and Boots* (1963), was published in Nigeria while he was in prison. His verse, while political in nature, is highly developed and restrained: "...all our land is scarred with terror / rendered unlovely and unlovable; / sundered are we and all our passionate surrender / but somehow tenderness survives" (from "Somehow We Survive"). Even in *Letters to Martha and Other Poems from a South African Prison* (1968), which records his experiences of misery and loneliness as a political prisoner, Brutus exhibits a restrained artistic control and combines lovingness with anger.

*China Poems*, written when Brutus visited China as vice president of the South African Table Tennis Board in 1973 but published in 1975, contains a series of short poems paying homage to *chüeh-chü*, a Chinese verse form. The poems in *Salutes and Censures* (1982) constitute Brutus's most explicit and forceful work; the collection juxtaposes drawings and newspaper clippings with verse indicting the brutality of apartheid. Later works such as *Airs and Tributes* (1989), *Still the Sirens* (1993), and *Leafdrift* (2005) continue in the protest vein, punctuated by acknowledgment of the achievements in the struggle against racism.

# *M*ISHIMA *Y*UKIO

(b. January 14, 1925, Tokyo—d. November 25, 1970, Tokyo)

The prolific writer Mishima Yukio (a pseudonym of Hiraoka Kimitake) is regarded by many critics as the most important Japanese novelist of the 20th century.

Mishima was the son of a high civil servant and attended the aristocratic Peers School in Tokyo. During World War II, having failed to qualify physically for military service, he worked in a Tokyo factory and after the war studied law at the University of Tokyo. In 1948–49 he worked in the banking division of the Japanese Ministry of Finance. His first novel, *Kamen no kokubaku* (1949; *Confessions of a Mask*), is a partly autobiographical work that describes with exceptional stylistic brilliance a homosexual who must mask his abnormal sexual preferences from the society around him. The novel gained Mishima immediate acclaim, and he began to devote his full energies to writing.

He followed up his initial success with several novels whose main characters are tormented by various physical or psychological problems or who are obsessed by unattainable ideals that make everyday happiness impossible

As 1970 drew to a close, Mishima Yukio's final impassioned speech found no purchase among his audience, and so he committed seppuku (also known as hari-kari), the ritualized method of Japanese suicide. **AFP/Getty Images**

for them. Among these works are *Ai no kawaki* (1950; *Thirst for Love*), *Kinjiki* (1954; *Forbidden Colours*), and *Shiosai* (1954; *The Sound of Waves*). *Kinkaku-ji* (1956; *The Temple of the Golden Pavilion*) is the story of a troubled young acolyte at a Buddhist temple who burns down the famous building because he himself cannot attain to its beauty. *Utage no ato* (1960; *After the Banquet*) explores the twin themes of middle-aged love and corruption in Japanese politics. In addition to novels, short stories, and essays, Mishima also wrote plays in the form of the Japanese Nō drama, producing reworked and modernized versions of the traditional stories. His plays include *Sado kōshaku fujin* (1965; *Madame de Sade*) and *Kindai nōgaku shu* (1956; *Five Modern Nōh Plays*).

Mishima's last work, *Hōjō no umi* (1965–70; *The Sea of Fertility*), is a four-volume epic that is regarded by many as his most lasting achievement. Its four separate novels, *Haru no yuki* (*Spring Snow*), *Homma* (*Runaway Horses*), *Akatsuki no tera* (*The Temple of Dawn*), and *Tennin gosui* (*The Decay of the Angel*), are set in Japan and cover the period from about 1912 to the 1960s. Each of them depicts a different reincarnation of the same being: as a young aristocrat in 1912, as a political fanatic in the 1930s, as a Thai princess before and after World War II, and as an evil young orphan in the 1960s. These books effectively communicate Mishima's own increasing obsession with blood, death, and suicide, his interest in self-destructive personalities, and his rejection of the sterility of modern life.

Mishima's novels are typically Japanese in their sensuous and imaginative appreciation of natural detail, but their solid and competent plots, their probing psychological analysis, and a certain understated humour helped make them widely read in other countries.

The short story "Yukoku" ("Patriotism") from the collection *Death in Midsummer, and Other Stories* (1966) revealed Mishima's own political views and proved prophetic of his own end. The story describes, with obvious admiration, a young army officer who commits seppuku, or ritual disembowelment, to demonstrate his loyalty to the Japanese emperor. Mishima was deeply attracted to the austere patriotism and martial spirit of Japan's past, which he contrasted unfavourably with the materialistic, Westernized people and the prosperous society of Japan in the postwar era. Mishima himself was torn between these differing values. Although he maintained an essentially Western life-style in his private life and had a vast knowledge of Western culture, he raged against Japan's imitation of the West. He diligently developed the age-old Japanese arts of karate and kendo and formed a controversial private army of about 80 students, the Tate no Kai (Shield Society), with the idea of preserving the Japanese martial spirit and helping protect the emperor (the symbol of Japanese culture) in case of an uprising by the left or a Communist attack.

On November 25, 1970, after having that day delivered the final installment of *The Sea of Fertility* to his publisher, Mishima and four Shield Society followers seized control of the commanding general's office at a military headquarters near downtown Tokyo. He gave a 10-minute speech from a balcony to a thousand assembled servicemen in which he urged them to overthrow Japan's post-World War II constitution, which forbids war and Japanese rearmament. The soldiers' response was unsympathetic, and Mishima then committed seppuku in the traditional manner, disemboweling himself with his sword, followed by decapitation at the hands of a follower. This shocking event aroused much speculation as to Mishima's motives, and regret that his death had robbed the world of such a gifted writer.

# RUSSELL HOBAN

(b. February 4, 1925, Lansdale, Pennsylvania, U.S.—
d. December 13, 2011, London, England)

The American novelist and children's writer Russell Hoban combined myth, fantasy, humour, and philosophy to explore issues of self-identity.

Hoban attended the Philadelphia Museum School of Industrial Art and served in the U.S. Army (1943–45) before beginning his career as an advertising artist and copywriter. He moved to London in 1969. His first book, *What Does It Do and How Does It Work?* (1959), developed from his drawings of construction machinery. He then started writing fiction for children. One of his most enduring creations is the anthropomorphic badger Frances, who is featured with her family and friends in a series of books beginning with *Bedtime for Frances* (1960). Fear and mortality intrude on the fantasy story *The Mouse and His Child* (1967; film 1977), one of Hoban's best-known books. His other notable works for children include *The Sorely Trying Day* (1964), *Charlie the Tramp* (1967), *Emmet Otter's Jug-Band Christmas* (1971), *How Tom Beat Captain Najork and His Hired Sportsmen* (1974), *Dinner at Alberta's* (1975), *Jim Hedgehog and the Lonesome Tower* (1992), *M.O.L.E.: Much Overworked Little Earthmover* (1993), *Trouble on Thunder Mountain* (1999), and *Jim's Lion* (2001). Before 1971 most of Hoban's books for children were illustrated by his first wife, Lillian Hoban.

Among Hoban's novels for adults are *The Lion of Boaz-Jachin and Jachin-Boaz* (1973), *Kleinzeit* (1974), and *Turtle Diary* (1975; film 1985). *Riddley Walker* (1980), probably Hoban's best-known novel, is set in the future in an

England devastated by nuclear war. Events are narrated in a futuristic form of English. Hoban's later writings include the novels *Pilgermann* (1983); *The Medusa Frequency* (1987), the story of an author who deals with his writer's block by electrifying his brain, which produces a series of imagined interlocutors, including the disembodied head of Orpheus; *The Moment Under the Moment* (1992); *Fremder* (1996); *Amaryllis Night and Day* (2001); *Linger Awhile* (2006), about a dead B-movie actress from the 1950s who is reanimated at the behest of a love-struck 83-year-old widower; and *My Tango with Barbara Strozzi* (2007).

# *PRAMOEDYA ANANTA TOER*

(b. February 20, 1925, Blora, Java, Dutch East Indies [now in Indonesia] — d. April 30, 2006, Jakarta, Indonesia)

The Javanese novelist and short-story writer Pramoedya Ananta Toer was the preeminent prose writer of postindependence Indonesia.

Pramoedya, the son of a schoolteacher, went to Jakarta while a teenager and worked as a typist there under the Japanese occupation during World War II. When the Indonesian revolt against renewed Dutch colonial rule broke out in 1945, he joined the nationalists, working in radio and producing an Indonesian-language magazine before he was arrested by the Dutch authorities in 1947. He wrote his first published novel, *Perburuan* (1950; *The Fugitive*), during a two-year term in a Dutch prison camp (1947–49). This work describes the flight of an anti-Japanese rebel back to his home in Java.

After Indonesia gained independence in 1949, Pramoedya produced a stream of novels and short stories that established his reputation. The novel *Keluarga gerilja* (1950; "Guerrilla Family") chronicles the tragic consequences of divided political sympathies in a Javanese family during the Indonesian Revolution against Dutch rule, while *Mereka jang dilumpuhkan* (1951; "The Paralyzed") depicts the odd assortment of inmates Pramoedya became acquainted with in the Dutch prison camp. The short stories collected in *Subuh* (1950; "Dawn") and *Pertjikan revolusi* (1950; "Sparks of Revolution") are set during the Indonesian Revolution, while those in *Tjerita dari Blora* (1952; "Tales of Bora") depict Javanese provincial life in the period of Dutch rule. The sketches in *Tjerita dari Djakarta* (1957; "Tales of Jakarta") examine the strains and injustices Pramoedya perceived within Indonesian society after independence had been achieved. In these early works Pramoedya evolved a rich prose style that incorporates Javanese everyday speech and images from classical Javanese culture.

By the late 1950s Pramoedya had become sympathetic toward the Indonesian Communist Party, and after 1958 he abandoned fiction for essays and cultural criticism that reflect a left-wing viewpoint. By 1962 he had become closely aligned with communist-sponsored cultural groups. As a result, he was jailed by the army in the course of its bloody suppression of a communist coup in 1965. During his imprisonment he wrote a series of four historical novels that further enhanced his reputation. Two of these, *Bumi manusia* (1980; *This Earth of Mankind*) and *Anak semua bangsa* (1980; *Child of All Nations*), met with great critical and popular acclaim in Indonesia after their publication, but the government subsequently banned them from circulation, and the last two volumes of the tetralogy, *Jejak langkah* (1985; *Footsteps*) and *Rumah kaca* (1988; *House of Glass*), had to be published abroad. These late works comprehensively depict Javanese society under

Dutch colonial rule in the early 20th century. In contrast to Pramoedya's earlier works, they are written in a plain, fast-paced narrative style.

Following his release from prison in 1979, Pramoedya was kept under house arrest in Jakarta until 1992. The autobiography *Nyanyi sunyi seorang bisu* (*The Mute's Soliloquy*) was published in 1995.

# *FLANNERY O'CONNOR*

(b. March 25, 1925, Savannah, Georgia, U.S.—
d. August 3, 1964, Milledgeville, Georgia)

Mary Flannery O'Connor was an American novelist and short-story writer whose works, usually set in the rural American South and often focusing on alienation, are concerned with the relationship between the individual and God.

O'Connor grew up in a prominent Roman Catholic family in her native Georgia. She lived in Savannah until her adolescence, but the worsening of her father's lupus erythematosus forced the family to relocate in 1938 to the home in rural Milledgeville where her mother had been raised. After graduating from Georgia State College for Women (now Georgia College & State University) in 1945, she studied creative writing at the University of Iowa Writers' Workshop.

Her first published work, a short story, appeared in the magazine *Accent* in 1946. Her first novel, *Wise Blood* (1952; film 1979), explored, in O'Connor's own words, the "religious consciousness without a religion." *Wise Blood* consists of a series of near-independent chapters—many of which originated in previously published short stories—that tell the tale of Hazel Motes, a man who returns home from military service and founds the Church Without Christ, which leads to a series of interactions with the grotesque inhabitants of his hometown. The work combines the keen ear for common speech, caustic religious imagination, and flair for the absurd that were to characterize her subsequent work. With the publication of further short stories, first collected in *A Good Man Is Hard to Find, and Other Stories* (1955), she came to be regarded as a master of the form. The collection's eponymous story has become possibly her best-known work. In it O'Connor creates an unexpected agent of salvation in the character of an escaped convict called The Misfit, who kills a quarreling family on vacation in the Deep South.

Her other works of fiction are a novel, *The Violent Bear It Away* (1960), and the short-story collection *Everything That Rises Must Converge* (1965). A collection of occasional prose pieces, *Mystery and Manners*, appeared in 1969. *The Complete Stories*, published posthumously in 1971, contained several stories that had not previously

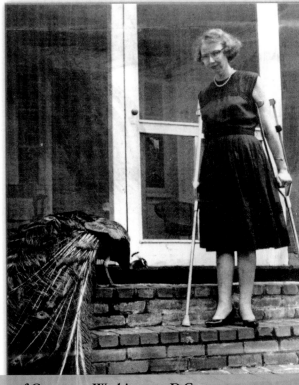

*Flannery O'Connor.* Library of Congress, Washington, D.C.; neg. no. LC USZ 62 108013

appeared in book form; it won a National Book Award in 1972.

Disabled for more than a decade by the lupus erythematosus she inherited from her father, which eventually proved fatal, O'Connor lived modestly, writing and raising peafowl on her mother's farm at Milledgeville. The posthumous publication of her letters, under the title *The Habit of Being* (1979), and her book reviews and correspondence with local diocesan newspapers, published as *The Presence of Grace, and Other Book Reviews* (1983), provided valuable insight into the life and mind of a writer whose works defy conventional categorization. O'Connor's corpus is notable for the seeming incongruity of a devout Catholic whose darkly comic works commonly feature startling acts of violence and unsympathetic, often depraved, characters. She explained the prevalence of brutality in her stories by noting that violence "is strangely capable of returning my characters to reality and preparing them to accept their moment of grace." It is this divine stripping of man's comforts and hubris, along with the attendant degradation of the corporeal, that stands as the most salient feature of O'Connor's work.

# ROSARIO CASTELLANOS

(b. May 25, 1925, Mexico City, Mexico—
d. August 7, 1974, Tel Aviv, Israel)

The novelist, short-story writer, poet, essayist, and diplomat Rosario Castellanos was probably the most important female Mexican writer of the 20th century. Her 1950 master's thesis, *Sobre cultura femenina* ("On Feminine Culture"), became a turning point for modern

Mexican women writers, who found in it a profound call to self-awareness.

Castellanos was the daughter of landowners from Chiapas and spent her formative years on a ranch near the Guatemalan border. She received an excellent education in Mexico and Europe. From 1960 to 1966 she was press director for the National Autonomous University of Mexico. Afterward, she held several visiting professorships in the United States and then returned to Mexico to accept the chair in comparative literature at the National Autonomous University. In 1971 Castellanos became Mexico's ambassador to Israel, and she died there three years later, accidentally electrocuted in her Tel Aviv home.

Castellanos was passionately interested in the works of two women writers: Saint Teresa of Ávila, the Spanish 16th-century religious activist and author, and Sor Juana Inés de la Cruz, the Mexican nun-poet of the 17th century. Profoundly Catholic, her own verse also recalls the poetry of Saint John of the Cross. It expresses at once indignation at social injustice and ecstasy before the beauty of creation. Castellanos's poetry is as powerful and original as that of her contemporary Octavio Paz, although she is best known for her prose works. Her most famous novel, *Oficio de tinieblas* (1962; *The Book of Lamentations*), recreates an Indian rebellion that occurred in the city of San Cristóbal de las Casas in the 19th century, but Castellanos sets it in the 1930s, when her own family suffered from the reforms brought about by Lázaro Cárdenas del Rio in the wake of the Mexican Revolution. Castellanos donated the land she inherited to the destitute Indians of Chiapas.

In 1972 Castellanos published her collected poetry in a volume entitled *Poesía no eres tú* ("Poetry Is Not You"; Eng. trans., *The Selected Poems*, by Magda Bogin), a polemical allusion to a well-known verse by Spanish Romantic poet

Gustavo Adolfo Bécquer, in which he tells his beloved that she is poetry.

# JOHN HAWKES

(b. August 17, 1925, Stamford, Connecticut, U.S.—
d. May 15, 1998, Providence, Rhode Island)

John Hawkes was an American author whose novels achieve a dreamlike (often nightmarish) intensity through the suspension of traditional narrative constraints. He considered a story's structure his main concern; in one interview he stated that plot, character, and theme are "the true enemies of the novel."

The son of a businessman, Hawkes was an only child. Between the ages of 10 and 15 he lived in Alaska with his family, who then moved to New York City. Hawkes attended Harvard University, taking time out during World War II to serve as an ambulance driver in Italy and Germany but returning to achieve a B.A. in 1949. He worked at Harvard University Press from 1949 to 1955 and then taught at Harvard until 1958; for the next 30 years he taught at Brown University.

Hawkes's first novel, *The Cannibal* (1949), depicts harbingers of a future apocalypse amid the rubble of postwar Germany. *The Beetle Leg* (1951) is a surreal parody of the pulp western. In 1954 he published two novellas, *The Goose on the Grave* and *The Owl*, both set in Italy.

With *The Lime Twig* (1961), a dark thriller set in postwar London, Hawkes attracted the critical attention that would place him in the front rank of avant-garde, postmodern American writers. His next novel, *Second Skin* (1964), is the first-person confessional of a retired naval officer. *The Blood Oranges* (1971; film 1997), *Death, Sleep, & the Traveler*

(1974), and *Travesty* (1976) explore the concepts of marriage and freedom to unsettling effect. *The Passion Artist* (1979) and *Virginie: Her Two Lives* (1982) are tales of sexual obsession. Hawkes's later works include *Adventures in the Alaskan Skin Trade* (1985), whose narrator is a middle-aged woman; *Whistlejacket* (1988); *Sweet William: A Memoir of Old Horse* (1993), written in the voice of a horse; *The Frog* (1996); and *An Irish Eye* (1997), whose narrator is a 13-year-old female orphan. He also published *The Innocent Party* (1966), a collection of short plays, and *Lunar Landscapes* (1969), a volume of short stories and novellas. *Humors of Blood & Skin: A John Hawkes Reader* was published in 1984.

Hawkes's prose is poetic, irrational, and often comic. He himself said, "The imagination should always uncover new worlds for us. I want to try to create a world, not represent it."

# GORE VIDAL

(b. October 3, 1925, West Point, New York, U.S.—
d. July 31, 2012, Los Angeles, California)

Eugene Luther Gore Vidal, Jr., was a prolific American novelist, playwright, and essayist who was noted for his irreverent and intellectually adroit novels.

Vidal graduated from Phillips Exeter Academy in New Hampshire in 1943 and served in the U.S. Army in World War II. Thereafter he resided in many parts of the world—the east and west coasts of the United States, Europe, North Africa, and Central America. His first novel, *Williwaw* (1946), which was based on his wartime experiences, was praised by the critics, and his third novel, *The City and the Pillar* (1948), shocked the public with its direct and unadorned examination of a homosexual main character. Vidal's next five novels, including *Messiah* (1954), were received coolly by critics and were commercial failures. Abandoning novels, he turned to writing plays for the stage, television, and motion pictures and was successful in all three media. His best-known dramatic works from the next decade were *Visit to a Small Planet* (produced for television 1955; on Broadway 1957; for film 1960) and *The Best Man* (play 1960; film 1964).

Vidal returned to writing novels with *Julian* (1964), a sympathetic fictional portrait of Julian the Apostate, the 4th-century pagan Roman emperor who opposed Christianity. *Washington, D.C.* (1967), an ironic examination of political morality in the U.S. capital, was the first of a series of several popular novels known as the Narratives of Empire, which vividly re-created prominent figures and events in American history—*Burr* (1973), *1876* (1976), *Lincoln* (1984), *Empire* (1987), *Hollywood* (1990), and *The Golden Age* (2000). *Lincoln*, a compelling portrait of President Abraham Lincoln's complex personality as viewed through the eyes of some of his closest associates during the American Civil War, is particularly notable. Another success was the comedy *Myra Breckinridge* (1968; film 1970), in which Vidal lampooned both transsexuality and contemporary American culture.

In *Rocking the Boat* (1962), *Reflections upon a Sinking Ship* (1969), *The Second American Revolution and Other Essays (1976–82)* (1982), *United States: Essays, 1952–1992* (1993; National Book Award), *Imperial America: Reflections on the United States of Amnesia* (2004), and other essay collections, Vidal incisively analyzed contemporary American politics and government. He also wrote the autobiographies *Palimpsest: A Memoir* (1995), *Point to Point Navigation: A Memoir, 1964 to 2006* (2006), and *Snapshots in History's Glare* (2009). Vidal was noted for his outspoken political opinions and for the witty and satirical observations he

*Gore Vidal*, c. *1955.* Hulton Archive/Getty Images

was wont to make as a guest on talk shows. He also occasionally worked as an actor, notably in the films *Bob Roberts* (1992) and *Gattaca* (1997).

---

# DARIO FO

---

(b. March 24, 1926, Leggiuno-Sangiano, Italy)

The Italian avant-garde playwright, manager-director, and actor-mime Dario Fo was awarded the Nobel Prize for Literature in 1997. A theatrical caricaturist with a flair for social agitation, he often faced government censure.

Fo's first theatrical experience was collaborating on satirical revues for small cabarets and theatres. He and his wife, the actress Franca Rame, founded the Campagnia Dario Fo–Franca Rame in 1959, and their humorous sketches on the television show "Canzonissima" soon made them popular public personalities. They gradually developed an agitprop theatre of politics, often blasphemous and scatological, but rooted in the tradition of commedia dell'arte and blended with what Fo called "unofficial leftism."

In 1968 Fo and Rame founded another acting group, Nuova Scena, with ties to the Italian Communist Party, and in 1970 they started the Collettivo Teatrale La Comune and began to tour factories, parks, and gymnasiums. Fo wrote about 70 plays, coauthoring some of them with Rame. Among his most popular plays are *Morte accidentale di un anarchico* (1974; *Accidental Death of an Anarchist*) and *Non si paga, non si paga!* (1974; *We Can't Pay? We Won't Pay!*). As a performer, Fo is best known for his solo tour de force *Mistero Buffo* (1973; "Comic Mystery"), based on medieval mystery plays but so topical that the shows changed with each audience.

His later works, some of which were written with Rame, include *Tutta casa, letto e chiesa* (1978; "All House, Bed, and Church"; Eng. trans. *Adult Orgasm Escapes from the Zoo*), *Clacson, trombette, e pernacchi* (1981; *Trumpets and Raspberries*), *Female Parts* (1981), *Coppia aperta* (1983; *The Open Couple—Wide Open Even*), *L'uomo nudo e l'uomo in frak* (1985; *One Was Nude and One Wore Tails*), and *Il papa e la strega* (1989; *The Pope and the Witch*).

# *Harper Lee*

(b. April 28, 1926, Monroeville, Alabama, U.S.)

The American writer Nelle Harper Lee is nationally acclaimed for her one novel, *To Kill a Mockingbird* (1960).

Harper Lee was the daughter of Amasa Coleman Lee, a lawyer who was by all accounts apparently rather like the hero-father of her novel in his sound citizenship and warmheartedness. The plot of *To Kill a Mockingbird* was based in part on his unsuccessful youthful defense of two African American men convicted of murder.

Lee attended the University of Alabama (spending a year as an exchange student at Oxford) but left for New York City before obtaining her own law degree. In New York she worked as an airline reservationist but soon received financial aid from friends that allowed her to write full-time. With the help of an editor, she transformed a series of short stories into *To Kill a Mockingbird*.

The narrator of the novel is lawyer Atticus Finch's six-year-old daughter, "Scout." Scout and her brother,

Jem, learn the principles of racial justice and social tolerance from their father, whose just and compassionate acts include an unpopular defense of a black man falsely accused of raping a white girl. They also develop tolerance and the strength to follow their convictions in their acquaintance and eventual friendship with a recluse who has been demonized by the community. *To Kill a Mockingbird* received a Pulitzer Prize in 1961. Criticism of its tendency to sermonize has been matched by praise of its insight and stylistic effectiveness. It became a memorable film in 1962 and was filmed again in 1997.

After a few years in New York, Lee divided her time between that city and her hometown of Monroeville, Alabama. In addition to her novel, she wrote a few short essays, including the 1983 "Romance and High Adventure," devoted to Alabama history. In 2007 Lee was awarded the Presidential Medal of Freedom.

# ALLEN GINSBERG

(b. June 3, 1926, Newark, New Jersey, U.S.—
d. April 5, 1997, New York, New York)

Allen Ginsberg was an American poet whose epic poem *Howl* (1956) is considered to be one of the most significant products of the Beat movement.

Ginsberg grew up in Paterson, New Jersey, where his father, Louis Ginsberg, himself a poet, taught English. Allen Ginsberg's mother, whom he mourned in his long poem *Kaddish* (1961), was confined for years in a mental hospital. Ginsberg was influenced in his work by the poet William Carlos Williams, particularly toward the use of natural speech rhythms and direct observations of unadorned actuality.

While at Columbia University, where his anarchical proclivities pained the authorities, Ginsberg became close friends with Jack Kerouac and William Burroughs, who were later to be numbered among the Beats. After leaving Columbia in 1948, Ginsberg traveled widely and worked at a number of jobs from cafeteria floor mopper to market researcher.

*Howl*, Ginsberg's first published book, laments what he believed to have been the destruction by insanity of the "best minds of [his] generation." Dithyrambic and prophetic, owing something to the romantic bohemianism of Walt Whitman, it also dwells on homosexuality, drug addiction, Buddhism, and Ginsberg's revulsion from what he saw as the materialism and insensitivity of post-World War II America.

*Empty Mirror*, a collection of earlier poems, appeared along with *Kaddish and Other Poems* in 1961, followed by *Reality Sandwiches* in 1963. *Kaddish*, one of Ginsberg's most important works, is a long confessional poem in which the poet laments his mother's insanity and tries to come to terms with both his relationship to her and with her death. In the early 1960s Ginsberg began a life of ceaseless travel, reading his poetry at campuses and coffee bars, traveling abroad, and engaging in left-wing political activities. He became an influential guru of the American youth counterculture in the late 1960s. He acquired a deeper knowledge of Buddhism, and increasingly a religious element of love for all sentient beings entered his work.

His later volumes of poetry included *Planet News* (1968); *The Fall of America: Poems of These States, 1965–1971* (1972), which won the National Book Award; *Mind Breaths: Poems 1972–1977* (1978); and *White Shroud: Poems 1980–1985* (1986). His *Collected Poems 1947–1980* appeared in 1984. *Collected Poems, 1947–1997* (2006) is the first comprehensive one-volume collection of Ginsberg's published poetry.

*The Letters of Allen Ginsberg* was published in 2008, and a collection edited by Bill Morgan and David Stanford that focuses on Ginsberg's correspondence with Kerouac was published as *Jack Kerouac and Allen Ginsberg: The Letters* in 2010.

# FRANK O'HARA

(b. June 27, 1926, Baltimore, Maryland, U.S.—
d. July 25, 1966, Fire Island, New York)

The American poet Frank O'Hara gathered images from an urban environment to represent personal experience.

O'Hara was drawn to both poetry and the visual arts for much of his life. He studied at Harvard University (B.A., 1950) and the University of Michigan (M.A., 1951). During the 1960s, as an assistant curator at the Museum of Modern Art in New York City, O'Hara sent his fine criticism of current painting and sculpture to such periodicals as *Art News*, and he wrote catalogs for exhibits that he arranged. Meanwhile, local theatres were producing many of his experimental one-act plays, including *Try! Try!* (1960), about a soldier's return to his wife and her new lover.

O'Hara, however, considered himself primarily a poet. His pieces, which mark him as a member of the New York school of poets, are a mixture of quotations, gossip, phone numbers, commercials—any mote of experience that he found appealing. O'Hara also drew inspiration from non-literary sources, including free-form jazz and the abstract paintings of acquaintances such as Jackson Pollock and Larry Rivers, whose work he championed in art criticism. (His interest in both poetry and visual art came together with a series of "poem-paintings" he produced in collaboration with the artist Norman Bluhm in 1960.) The results vary from the merely idiosyncratic to the dynamic and humorous. His reputation grew in the 1960s to the point that he was considered one of the most important and influential postwar American poets at the time of his death, at age 40, after being hit by a car while on vacation.

O'Hara's first volume of poetry was *A City Winter and Other Poems* (1952). His most celebrated collections are *Meditations in an Emergency* (1957) and *Lunch Poems* (1964). *The Collected Poems of Frank O'Hara* (1971) and its successor, *Selected Poems* (2008), were published posthumously.

# Ana María Matute

(b. July 26, 1926, Barcelona, Spain)

The Spanish novelist Ana María Matute is known for her sympathetic treatment of the lives of children and adolescents, their feelings of betrayal and isolation, and their rites of passage. She often interjected such elements as myth, fairy tale, the supernatural, and fantasy into her works.

Matute's education suffered because of childhood illnesses, the family's frequent moves between Barcelona and Madrid, and the disruptions of the Spanish Civil War (1936–39), which left her family largely housebound in Barcelona. She broke the monotony of the war years by editing a magazine for her siblings. While in her teens, she published short stories.

Matute frequently used biblical allusion in her works and often used the story of Cain and Abel to symbolize the familial division caused by the Spanish Civil War; her first novel was titled *Los Abel* (1948; "The Abel Family").

She followed up with *Fiesta al noroeste* (1953; *Celebration in the Northwest*), *Pequeño teatro* (1954; "Little Theatre"), and *Los hijos muertos* (1958; *The Lost Children*). Matute then wrote a trilogy consisting of *Primera memoria* (1959; U.K. title, *Awakening*; U.S. title, *School of the Sun*), about children thrust into an adult world by the Spanish Civil War; a war novel, *Los soldados lloran de noche* (1964; *Soldiers Cry by Night*); and *La trampa* (1969; "The Trap"), in which the children of *Primera memoria* are presented as adults. Matute set *La torre vigía* (1971; "The Watchtower") in 10th-century Europe to examine the themes of chivalry, idealism, poverty, and prejudice. Her novel *Olvidado Rey Gudú* ("Forgotten King Gudú"), a massive allegorical folk epic that spans four generations in the story of rulers, gnomes, witches, and other creatures in the mythical medieval kingdom of Olar, was published in 1996. Among her later works are *Aranmanoth* (2000) and *Paraíso inhabitado* (2008; "Uninhabited Paradise").

In addition to the novels for which she is best known, Matute wrote several collections of short stories, including *Los niños tontos* (1956; "The Foolish Children"), *Algunos muchachos* (1968; *The Heliotrope Wall*), and *La puerta de la luna: cuentos completos* (2010; "The Door of the Moon: Complete Stories"). She also wrote several works for children. In 2010 she was named the recipient of the Cervantes Prize, the most prestigious literary award in the Spanish-speaking world.

# ROBERT BLY

(b. December 23, 1926, Madison, Minnesota, U.S.)

The American poet, translator, editor, and author Robert Bly is perhaps best known to the public at large as the author of *Iron John: A Book About Men* (1990, reprinted 2001 as *Iron John: Men and Masculinity*). Drawing upon Jungian psychology, myth, legend, folklore, and fairy tales (the title is taken from a story by the Brothers Grimm), the book demonstrates Bly's masculinist convictions. Though it had many detractors, it proved an important, creative, and best-selling work on the subject of manhood and masculinity for a budding men's movement in the United States.

After serving in the U.S. Navy, Bly studied at St. Olaf College in Northfield, Minnesota (1946–47), Harvard University (B.A., 1950), and the University of Iowa (M.A., 1956). In 1958 he cofounded the magazine *The Fifties* (its name changed with the decades), which published translations and poetry by Bly and other important young poets. Bly's first collection of poems, *Silence in the Snowy Fields* (1962), reveals his sense of man in nature. It was followed by *The Light Around the Body* (1968), which won a National Book Award.

Further volumes of poems and prose poems include *Sleepers Joining Hands* (1973), *This Body Is Made of Camphor and Gopherwood* (1977), *This Tree Will Be Here for a Thousand Years* (1979), *Morning Poems* (1997), and *Eating the Honey of Words* (1999). His poems of *The Man in the Black Coat Turns* (1981) explore themes of male grief and the father-son connection that he developed further in *Iron John* and also *The Maiden King: The Reunion of Masculine and Feminine* (1999), written with Marion Woodman.

A collection of Bly's prose poems appeared in 1992 under the title *What Have I Ever Lost by Dying?*. Such later collections as *Meditations on the Insatiable Soul* (1994) and *The Urge to Travel Long Distances* (2005) are preoccupied with the pastoral landscape of Minnesota. Bly employed the Arabic ghazal form in the poems comprising *The Night Abraham Called to the Stars* (2001) and *My Sentence Was a*

*Thousand Years of Joy* (2005). He also released a volume of poems protesting the Iraq War, *The Insanity of Empire* (2004). Bly dubbed the poems in *Turkish Pears in August* (2007) "ramages," referencing *rameau*, the French word for branch; they each contain 85 syllables and focus on a certain vowel sound. His collection *Talking into the Ear of a Donkey* (2011) consists of poems in a vast range of forms, including haiku and a return to the ghazal.

Bly translated the work of many poets, ranging from Rainer Maria Rilke (German) and Tomas Tranströmer (Swedish) to Pablo Neruda and Antonio Machado (Spanish). Additionally, he translated several works from Norwegian, including Knut Hamsun's novel *Hunger* (1890; translated 1967) and Henrik Ibsen's play *Peer Gynt* (1867; translated 2008). He also reworked English translations of poetry by the Indian mystic Kabir (translated from Bengali by Rabindranath Tagore) and the Indian poet Mīrzā Asadullāh Khān Ghālib (translated from Urdu by Sunil Datta).

Bly was named the first poet laureate of Minnesota in 2008.

# GÜNTER GRASS

(b. October 16, 1927, Danzig [now Gdańsk, Poland])

The German poet, novelist, playwright, sculptor, and printmaker Günter Grass became the literary spokesman for the German generation that grew up in the Nazi era and survived the war with his extraordinary first novel *Die Blechtrommel* (1959; *The Tin Drum*). In 1999 he was awarded the Nobel Prize for Literature.

In his native Danzig, Grass passed through the Hitler Youth movement and was drafted during World

War II. As he revealed in 2006, he was called up to the Waffen-SS (the elite military wing of the Nazi Party) at age 17, two years after he had been refused as a volunteer for submarine duty. He was wounded in battle and became a prisoner of war in 1945. Later, while an art student in Düsseldorf, he supported himself as a dealer in the black market, a tombstone cutter, and a drummer in a jazz band. Encouraged by the writers' association Gruppe 47 (an association of writers that aimed to return German literature to its pre-Nazi traditions), he produced poems and plays, at first with little success. In 1956 he went to Paris and wrote *Die Blechtrommel* (film 1979). This exuberant picaresque novel, written in a variety of styles, imaginatively distorts and exaggerates his personal experiences—the Polish-German dualism of Danzig, the creeping Nazification of average families, the attrition of the war years, the coming of the Russians, and the complacent atmosphere of West Germany's postwar "economic miracle." Underlying the anarchic fantasy is the moral earnestness that earned Grass the role of "conscience of his generation." It was followed by *Katz und Maus* (1961; *Cat and Mouse*) and an epic novel, *Hundejahre* (1963; *Dog Years*); the three together came to be known as the "Danzig trilogy."

His other novels—always politically topical—include *Örtlich Betäubt* (1969; *Local Anaesthetic*), a protest against the Vietnam War; *Der Butt* (1977; *The Flounder*), a ribald fable of the war between the sexes from the Stone Age to the present; *Das Treffen in Telgte* (1979; *The Meeting at Telgte*), a hypothetical "Gruppe 1647" meeting of authors at the close of the Thirty Years' War; *Kopfgeburten; oder, die Deutschen sterben aus* (1980; *Headbirths; or, The Germans Are Dying Out*), which describes a young couple's agonizing over whether to have a child in the face of a population explosion and the threat of nuclear war; *Die*

*Rättin* (1986; *The Rat*), a vision of the end of the human race that expressed Grass's fear of nuclear holocaust and environmental disaster; and *Unkenrufe* (1992; *The Call of the Toad*), which concerned the uneasy relationship between Poland and Germany. In 1995 Grass published *Ein weites Feld* ("A Broad Field"), an ambitious novel treating Germany's reunification in 1990. The work was vehemently attacked by German critics, who denounced Grass's portrayal of reunification as "misconstrued" and "unreadable." Grass, whose leftist political views were often not well received, was outspoken in his belief that Germany lacked "the politically organized power to renew itself." *Mein Jahrhundert* (1999; *My Century*), a collection of 100 related stories, was less overtly political than many of his earlier works. In it Grass relates the events of the 20th century using a story for each year, each with a different narrator.

Grass was a long-time participant in Social Democratic Party politics in West Berlin, fighting for social and literary causes. When he was awarded the Nobel Prize for Literature in 1999, there were many who believed that his strong, and sometimes unpopular, political beliefs had prevented him from receiving the prize far earlier. Grass's disclosure of his membership in the Waffen-SS, which came just before publication of his memoir *Beim Häuten der Zwiebel* (2006; *Peeling the Onion*), caused widespread controversy, with some arguing that it undercut his moral authority. He had previously claimed that he had been drafted into an air defense unit in 1944. Grass later wrote two more volumes of autobiography, *Die Box* (2008; *The Box*) and *Grimms Wörter: eine Liebeserklärung* (2010; *Grimms' Words: A Declaration of Love*), the latter of which explores Grass's political past through a loving analysis of the Brothers Grimm.

# GABRIEL GARCÍA MÁRQUEZ

(b. March 6, 1928, Aracataca, Colombia)

A Colombian novelist and one of the greatest writers of the 20th century, Gabriel García Márquez was awarded the Nobel Prize for Literature in 1982, mostly for his masterpiece *Cien años de soledad* (1967; *One Hundred Years of Solitude*). He was the fourth Latin American to be so honoured, having been preceded by Chilean poets Gabriela Mistral in 1945 and Pablo Neruda in 1971 and by Guatemalan novelist Miguel Ángel Asturias in 1967. With Jorge Luis Borges, García Márquez is possibly the best-known Latin American writer in history. In addition to his masterly approach to the novel, he is a superb crafter of short stories and an accomplished journalist. In both his shorter and longer fictions, García Márquez achieves the rare feat of being accessible to the common reader while satisfying the most demanding of sophisticated critics.

## Life

Born in the sleepy provincial town of Aracataca, Colombia, García Márquez and his parents spent the first eight years of his life with his maternal grandparents, Colonel Nicolás Márquez and Tranquilina Iguarán de Márquez. After the Colonel's death, they moved to Sucre, a river port. He received a better than average education, but claimed as an adult that his most important literary sources were the stories about Aracataca and his family that his grandfather Nicolás told him. Although he studied law, García

*Gabriel García Márquez, 1990.* Ulf Andersen/Getty Images

Márquez became a journalist, the trade at which he earned his living before attaining literary fame. As a correspondent in Paris during the 1950s he expanded his education, reading a great deal of American literature, some of it in French translation. In the late 1950s he worked in Caracas and then in New York for Prensa Latina, the news service created by the Castro regime. Later he moved to Mexico City, where he wrote the novel that brought him fame and wealth. From 1967 to 1975, he lived in Spain. Subsequently he kept a house in Mexico City and an apartment in Paris, but he also spent much time in Havana, where Fidel Castro (whom García Márquez supported) provided him with a mansion.

## Works

Before 1967 García Márquez had published two novels, *La hojarasca* (1955; *The Leaf Storm*) and *La mala hora* (1962; *In Evil Hour*); a novella, *El coronel no tiene quien le escriba* (1961; *No One Writes to the Colonel*); and a few short stories. Then came *One Hundred Years of Solitude*, in which García Márquez tells the story of Macondo, an isolated town whose history is like the history of Latin America on a reduced scale. While the setting is realistic, there are fantastic episodes, a combination that has come to be known as magic realism, wrongly thought to be the peculiar feature of all Latin American literature. Mixing historical facts and stories with instances of the fantastic is a practice that García Márquez derived from Cuban master Alejo Carpentier, considered to be one of the founders of magic realism. The inhabitants of Macondo are driven by elemental passions—lust, greed, thirst for power—which are thwarted by crude societal, political, or natural forces, as in Greek tragedy and myth.

Continuing his magisterial output, García Márquez issued *El otoño del patriarca* (1975; *The Autumn of the Patriarch*), *Crónica de una muerte anunciada* (1981; *Chronicle of a Death Foretold*), *El amor en los tiempos del cólera* (1985; *Love in the Time of Cholera*; film 2007), *El general en su laberinto* (1989; *The General in His Labyrinth*), and *Del amor y otros demonios* (1994; *Of Love and Other Demons*). The best among these books are *El amor en los tiempos del cólera*, a touching love affair that takes decades to be consummated, and *The General in His Labyrinth*, a chronicle of the South American statesman Simón Bolívar's last days.

In 1996 García Márquez published a journalistic chronicle of drug-related kidnappings in his native Colombia, *Noticia de un secuestro* (*News of a Kidnapping*).

After being diagnosed with cancer in 1999, García Márquez wrote the memoir *Vivir para contarla* (2002; *Living to Tell the Tale*), which focuses on his first 30 years. He returned to fiction with *Memoria de mis putas tristes* (2004; *Memories of My Melancholy Whores*), a novel about a lonely man who finally discovers the meaning of love when he hires a virginal prostitute to celebrate his 90th birthday.

# EDWARD ALBEE

(b. March 12, 1928, Washington, D.C., U.S.)

The American dramatist and theatrical producer Edward Albee is best known for his play *Who's Afraid of Virginia Woolf?* (1962), which displays slashing insight and witty dialogue in its gruesome portrayal of married life.

Albee was the adopted child of a father who had for a time been the assistant general manager of a chain of vaudeville theatres then partially owned by the Albee family. At the time of Albee's adoption, though, both his parents were involved with owning and showing saddle horses. He had a difficult relationship with his parents, particularly with his mother, whom he saw as distant and unloving. Albee grew up in New York City and nearby Westchester county. He was educated at Choate School (graduated 1946) and at Trinity College in Hartford, Connecticut (1946–47). He wrote poetry and an unpublished novel but turned to plays in the late 1950s.

Among Albee's early one-act plays, *The Zoo Story* (1959), *The Sandbox* (1959), and *The American Dream* (1961) were the most successful and established him as an astute critic of American values. But it is his first full-length play, *Who's Afraid of Virginia Woolf?* (film 1966), that remains his most important work. In this play a middle-aged professor, his wife, and a younger couple engage one night in an unrestrained drinking bout that is filled with malicious games, insults, humiliations, betrayals, savage witticisms, and painful, self-revealing confrontations. *Virginia Woolf* won immediate acclaim and established Albee as a major American playwright.

It was followed by a number of full-length works—including *A Delicate Balance* (1966; winner of a Pulitzer Prize), which was based in part on his mother's witty alcoholic sister, and *Three Tall Women* (1994; Pulitzer Prize). The latter play deals with Albee's perceptions and feelings about his mother and is a remarkable portrait achieved by presenting the interaction of three women, who resemble each other, at different stages of life. Among his other plays are *Tiny Alice* (1965), which begins as a philosophical discussion between a lawyer and a cardinal; *Seascape* (1975; also winner of a Pulitzer Prize), a poetic exploration of evolution; and *The Play About the Baby* (1998), on the mysteries of birth and parenthood.

Albee continued to dissect American morality in plays such as *The Goat; or, Who Is Sylvia?* (2002), which depicts the disintegration of a marriage in the wake of the revelation that the husband has engaged in bestiality. In *Occupant* (2001), Albee imagines the sculptor Louise Nevelson being interviewed after her death. Albee also expanded *The Zoo Story* into a two-act play, called *Peter and Jerry* (2004). (The play was retitled *At Home at the Zoo* in 2009.) The absurdist *Me, Myself, & I* (2007) trenchantly analyzes the relationship between a mother and her twin sons.

In addition to writing, Albee produced a number of plays and lectured at schools throughout the country. He was awarded the National Medal of Arts in 1996. A compilation of his essays and personal anecdotes, *Stretching My Mind*, was published in 2005. That year Albee also received a Tony Award for lifetime achievement.

# *Maya Angelou*

(b. April 4, 1928, St. Louis, Missouri, U.S.)

Maya Angelou is an American poet whose several volumes of autobiography explore the themes of economic, racial, and sexual oppression.

Although born in St. Louis, Angelou (who was born Marguerite Johnson) spent much of her childhood in the care of her paternal grandmother in rural Stamps, Arkansas. Raped at the age of eight by her mother's boyfriend, she went through an extended period of muteness. This early life is the focus of Angelou's first autobiographical work, *I Know Why the Caged Bird Sings* (1970). Subsequent volumes of autobiography include *Gather Together in My Name* (1974), *Singin' and Swingin' and Gettin'*

*Merry Like Christmas* (1976), *The Heart of a Woman* (1981), *All God's Children Need Traveling Shoes* (1986), and *A Song Flung Up to Heaven* (2002).

In 1940 Angelou moved with her mother to San Francisco and worked intermittently as a cocktail waitress, a prostitute and madam, a cook, and a dancer. It was as a dancer that she assumed her professional name. Moving to New York City in the late 1950s, Angelou found encouragement for her literary talents at the Harlem Writers' Guild. About the same time, Angelou landed a featured role in a State Department–sponsored production of George Gershwin's opera *Porgy and Bess*; with this troupe she toured 22 countries in Europe and Africa. She also studied dance with Martha Graham and Pearl Primus. In 1961 she performed in Jean Genet's *The Blacks*. That same year, she was persuaded by a South African dissident to whom she was briefly married to move to Cairo, Egypt, where she worked for the *Arab Observer*. She later moved to Ghana and worked on *The African Review*.

Angelou returned to California in 1966 and wrote *Black, Blues, Black* (aired 1968), a 10-part television series about the role of African culture in American life. When her screenplay *Georgia, Georgia* was produced in 1972, Angelou became the first African American woman to have a feature film adapted from one of her own stories. She also acted in such movies as *Poetic Justice* (1993) and *How to Make an American Quilt* (1995) and appeared in several television productions, including the miniseries *Roots* (1977). In 1998 she made her directorial debut with *Down in the Delta* (1998).

Angelou's poetry, collected in such volumes as *Just Give Me a Cool Drink of Water 'fore I Diiie* (1971), *And Still I Rise* (1978), *Now Sheba Sings the Song* (1987), and *I Shall Not Be Moved* (1990), draws heavily on her personal history but employs the points of view of various personae. She also wrote a book of meditations, *Wouldn't Take Nothing for My Journey Now* (1993), and children's books that include *My Painted House, My Friendly Chicken and Me* (1994), *Life Doesn't Frighten Me* (1998), and the *Maya's World* series, which was published in 2004–05 and featured stories of children from various parts of the world.

In 1981 Angelou became a professor of American studies at Wake Forest University, Winston-Salem, North Carolina. Among numerous honours was her invitation to compose and deliver a poem for the inauguration of Pres. Bill Clinton in 1993. In 2011 Angelou was awarded the Presidential Medal of Freedom.

# *WILLIAM TREVOR*

(b. May 24, 1928, Mitchelstown, County Cork, Ireland)

The Irish writer William Trevor Cox is noted for his wry and often macabre short stories and novels.

Trevor was educated at Trinity College, Dublin, and began his career as a teacher and sculptor. He taught both history and art at various schools in Northern Ireland and England, and then in 1960 he moved to London and worked as an advertising copywriter. It was at this time (1960–65) that Trevor began to publish his novels and short stories. Eventually he decided to move to Devon, England, and write full time.

His novels include *The Old Boys* (1964), *The Boarding-House* (1965), *Mrs. Eckdorf in O'Neill's Hotel* (1969), *Elizabeth Alone* (1973), *The Children of Dynmouth* (1976), *Other People's Worlds* (1980), *Fools of Fortune* (1983), *The Silence in the Garden* (1988), *Death in Summer* (1998), *The Story of Lucy Gault* (2002), and *Love and Summer* (2009). He also wrote a number of highly acclaimed collections of short stories, including *Angels at the Ritz and Other Stories* (1975), *The Hill Bachelors* (2000), and *Cheating at Canasta* (2007). These are typically bleak tales featuring moments of reckoning in which characters can no longer seek refuge in the fantasies and illusions that had previously made their lives bearable.

Trevor's story *The Ballroom of Romance* (1972) became a modern classic and was made into an award-winning television play in 1982. Other works by Trevor have been adapted for the screen, most notably the novel *Felicia's Journey* (1994), the film version of which was directed by Atom Egoyan and released in 1999. Influenced by the writings of James Joyce and Charles Dickens, Trevor possessed a keen skill for characterization and irony. His works for the most part focus on the psychology of eccentrics and outcasts.

# MAURICE SENDAK

(b. June 10, 1928, Brooklyn, New York, U.S.—
d. May 8, 2012, Danbury, Connecticut)

Maurice Sendak was an American artist best known for his illustrated children's books.

Sendak was the son of Polish immigrants and received his formal art training at the Art Students League of New York. While attending school, he drew backgrounds for All-American Comics and did window displays for a toy store. The first children's books he illustrated were Marcel Ayme's *The Wonderful Farm* (1951) and Ruth Krauss's *A Hole Is to Dig* (1952). Both were successful, and Sendak went on to illustrate more than 80 children's books by a number of writers including Meindert De Jong, Else Holmelund Minarik, and Randall Jarrell.

With *Kenny's Window* (1956), he began writing some of the stories that he illustrated. These include the tiny

*Maurice Sendak in 2002 standing with an enlarged cardboard cutout of the character Max from his* Where the Wild Things Are *(1963).* James Keyser/Time & Life Pictures/Getty Images

four-volume *Nutshell Library* (1962) and his innovative trilogy composed of *Where the Wild Things Are* (1963; winner of the 1964 Caldecott Medal), *In the Night Kitchen* (1970), and *Outside over There* (1981); a film adaptation of *Where the Wild Things Are*, directed by Spike Jonze, was released in 2009. Among Sendak's other works are *Higglety Pigglety Pop!; or, There Must Be More to Life* (1967), *Seven Little Monsters* (1977), and *Bumble-Ardy* (2011). He also illustrated the pop-up book *Mommy?* (2006).

In addition to his children's books, Sendak was involved in numerous other projects. In 1975 he wrote and directed *Really Rosie*, an animated television special based on some of the children in his stories. It was expanded into a musical play in 1978. In addition to creating opera versions of some of his own stories—including *Where the Wild Things Are*—Sendak designed a number of other works for the stage, notably the city of Houston's production of Mozart's *The Magic Flute* in 1980. In 1983 he designed a production of Tchaikovsky's ballet *The Nutcracker* for Pacific Northwest Ballet in Seattle.

Sendak published *Caldecott & Co.: Notes on Books and Pictures*, a collection of essays and reviews on writers and illustrators, in 1988. He was awarded the National Medal of Arts in 1996. *The Art of Maurice Sendak* by Selma G. Lanes was published in 1980.

# CARLOS FUENTES

(b. November 11, 1928, Panama City, Panama—
d. May 15, 2012, Mexico City, Mexico)

Carlos Fuentes was a Mexican novelist, short-story writer, playwright, critic, and diplomat whose experimental novels won him an international literary reputation.

The son of a Mexican career diplomat, Fuentes was born in Panama and traveled extensively with his family in North and South America and in Europe. He learned English at age four in Washington, D.C. As a young man, he studied law at the University of Mexico in Mexico City and later attended the Institute of Advanced International Studies in Geneva. Fuentes was a member of the Mexican delegation to the International Labour Organization (ILO) in Geneva (1950–52), was in charge of cultural dissemination for the University of Mexico (1955–56), was cultural officer of the ministry (1957–59), and was ambassador to France (1975–77). He also cofounded and edited several periodicals, including *Revista Mexicana de literatura* (1954–58; "Mexican Review of Literature").

Rebelling against his family's middle-class values early in the 1950s, Fuentes became a communist, but he left the party in 1962 on intellectual grounds while remaining an avowed Marxist. His first collection of stories, *Los días enmascarados* (1954, 2nd ed. 1966; "The Masked Days"), re-creates the past realistically and fantastically. His first novel, *La región más transparente* (1958; *Where the Air Is Clear*), which treats the theme of national identity and bitterly indicted Mexican society, won him national prestige. The work is marked by cinematographic techniques, flashbacks, interior monologues, and language from all levels of society, showing influences from many non-Spanish literatures. After this, Fuentes spent most of his time writing but continued to travel widely as he had in his youth.

The novel *Las buenas conciencias* (1959; *The Good Conscience*) emphasizes the moral compromises that mark the transition from a rural economy to a complex middle-class urban one. *Aura* (1962) is a novella that successfully fuses reality and fantasy. *La muerte de Artemio Cruz* (1962; *The Death of Artemio Cruz*), which presents the agony of the last hours of a wealthy survivor of the Mexican Revolution, was translated into several languages and established Fuentes as a major international novelist.

After *Artemio Cruz* came a succession of novels. *Cambio de piel* (1967; *A Change of Skin*) defines existentially a collective Mexican consciousness by exploring and reinterpreting the country's myths. *Terra nostra* (1975; "Our Land," Eng. trans. *Terra nostra*) explores the cultural substrata of New and Old Worlds as the author seeks to understand his cultural heritage. *Diana; o, la cazadora solitaria* (1994; *Diana the Goddess Who Hunts Alone*) is a fictional version of Fuentes's affair with the American actress Jean Seberg. In 1995 he published *La frontera de cristal: una novela en nueve cuentos* (*The Crystal Frontier: A Novel in Nine Stories*), a tale of nine lives as they are affected by a powerful and unscrupulous man. Among Fuentes's other works of fiction are *La cabeza de la hidra* (1978; *The Hydra Head*), *Una familia lejana* (1980; *Distant Relations*), *Gringo viejo* (1985; *The Old Gringo*; film 1989), *Cristóbal nonato* (1987; *Christopher Unborn*), *Los años con Laura Díaz* (1999; *The Years with Laura Díaz*), *Instinto de Inez* (2001; *Inez*), and *La voluntad y la fortuna* (2008; "Will and Fortune").

Fuentes also published collections of stories, including *Constancia, y otras novelas para vírgenes* (1989; *Constancia and Other Stories for Virgins*), *El naranjo; o, los círculos del tiempo* (1993; "The Orange Tree; or, The Circles of Time," Eng. trans. *The Orange Tree*), *Inquieta compañía* (2004; "Disturbing Company"), and *Todas las familias felices* (2006; *Happy Families: Stories*).

Fuentes wrote several plays, including the important *Todos los gatos son pardos* (1970; "All Cats Are Gray"), a drama about the Spanish conquest of Mexico with the pivotal character La Malinche, the quasi-legendary woman agent of Hernán Cortés who is said to have served as a mediator between the Spanish and Mexican civilizations. A revised version of *Todos los gatos* was released in 1991 as *Ceremonias del alba* ("Ceremonies of the Dawn").

Among Fuentes's works of nonfiction are *La nueva novela hispanoamericana* (1969; "The New Hispano-American Novel"), which is his chief work of literary criticism; *Cervantes; o, la crítica de la lectura* (1976; "Cervantes; or, The Critique of Reading," Eng. trans. *Don Quixote; or, The Critique of Reading*), an homage to the great Spanish writer; and his book-length essay on Hispanic cultures, *El espejo enterrado* (1992; *Buried Mirror*), which was published simultaneously in Spanish and English.

Fuentes was undoubtedly one of the foremost Mexican writers of the 20th century. His broad range of literary accomplishments and his articulate humanism made him highly influential in the world's literary communities, particularly in that of Latin America. Several of his novels effect a cosmopolitan dialogue between Mexican culture and that of other countries and study the effect of foreign cultures, especially the Spanish and the North American, on Mexican identity. He pronounced his most ambitious work, *Terra nostra*, an attempt to synthesize the voices of James Joyce in *Ulysses* and Alexandre Dumas in *The Count of Monte Cristo*. Fuentes exhibits a postmodern sensibility in his use of plural voices to explore a subject. In 1987 he was awarded the Cervantes Prize, the most prestigious Spanish-language literary award.

# CHINGIZ AYTMATOV

(b. December 12, 1928, Sheker, Kirgiziya, U.S.S.R. [now in Kyrgyzstan]—d. June 10, 2008, Nürnberg, Germany)

The author, translator, journalist, and diplomat Chingiz Aytmatov is best known as a major figure in Kyrgyz and Russian literature.

Aytmatov's father was a Communist Party official executed during the great purges directed by Soviet leader Joseph Stalin in the late 1930s. Aytmatov's literary career started in 1952, and in 1959 he began writing for *Pravda* as the newspaper's correspondent in Kirgiziya. He achieved major recognition with the collection of short stories *Povesti gor i stepey* (1963; *Tales of the Mountains and Steppes*), for which he was awarded the Lenin Prize in 1963. Although Aytmatov composed in both Russian and Kyrgyz, many of his works, which are predominantly long short stories and novellas, were originally written in the latter language. Major themes in these works are love and friendship, the trials and heroism of wartime, and the emancipation of Kyrgyz youth from restrictive custom and tradition.

Among Aytmatov's most important works are *Trudnaya pereprava* (1956; "A Difficult Passage"), *Litsom k litsu* (1957; "Face to Face"), *Jamila* (1958; Eng. trans. *Jamilia*), *Pervy uchitel* (1967; "The First Teacher"), *Proshchay, Gulsary!* (1967; *Farewell, Gulsary!*), and *Bely parokhod* (1970; *The White Ship*, also published as *The White Steamship*). Subsequent novels, written originally in Russian, include *I dolshe veka dlitsya den* (1981; *The Day Lasts More Than a Hundred Years*), which blends Central Asian folklore traditions with science fiction, as well as *Plakha* (1986; *The Place of the Skull*) and *Tavro Kassandry* (1995; "The Mark of Cassandra"). He also cowrote, with Kaltai Mukhamedzhanov, *Voskhozhdenie na Fudziyamu* (first performed 1973; *The Ascent of Mount Fuji*), a play considered provocative during the Soviet era for its examination of the themes of authority and dissent. Many of Aytmatov's stories appear in English translation in *Piebald Dog Running Along the Shore, and Other Stories* (1989) and *Mother Earth, and Other Stories* (1989).

Aytmatov was made a member of the Supreme Soviet of the U.S.S.R. in 1966. In 1967 he became a member of the Executive Board of the Writers' Union of the U.S.S.R., and he was awarded the Soviet State Prize for literature in 1968, 1977, and 1983. He served as an adviser to Soviet President Mikhail Gorbachev and as the Soviet ambassador to Luxembourg. From the 1990s Aytmatov was the Kyrgyz ambassador to the European Union and several European countries. He also served as a member of parliament in Kyrgyzstan.

# *Philip K. Dick*

(b. December 16, 1928, Chicago, Illinois, U.S.—
d. March 2, 1982, Santa Ana, California)

Philip Kindred Dick was an American science-fiction writer whose novels and short stories often depict the psychological struggles of characters trapped in illusory environments.

Dick worked briefly in radio before studying at the University of California, Berkeley, for one year. The publication of his first story, *Beyond Lies the Wub*, in 1952 launched his full-time writing career, which was marked by extraordinary productivity, as he often-times completed a new work—usually a short story or a novella—every two weeks for printing in pulp paperback collections. He published his first novel, *Solar Lottery*, in 1955. Early in Dick's work the theme emerged that would remain his central preoccupation—that of a reality at variance with what it appeared or was intended to be. In such novels as *Time out of Joint* (1959), *The Man in the High Castle* (1962; Hugo Award winner), and *The Three Stigmata of Palmer Eldritch* (1965), the protagonists must determine their own orientation in an "alternate world." Beginning with *The Simulacra* (1964) and culminating in *Do Androids Dream of Electric Sheep?* (1968; adapted for film as *Blade Runner* [1982]), the illusion centres on artificial creatures at large and grappling with what is authentic in a real world of the future.

After years of drug abuse and mental illness, Dick died impoverished and with little literary reputation outside of science-fiction circles. By the 21st century, however, he was widely regarded as a master of imaginative, paranoid fiction in the vein of Franz Kafka and Thomas Pynchon. While his works can definitively be categorized as science fiction, Dick was notable for focusing not on the trappings of futuristic technology, as many writers in the genre do, but on the discomfiting effects that these radically different—and often dystopian—surroundings have on the characters.

Among Dick's numerous story collections are *A Handful of Darkness* (1955), *The Variable Man and Other Stories* (1957), *The Preserving Machine* (1969), and the posthumously published *I Hope I Shall Arrive Soon* (1985). Several of his short stories and novels have been adapted for film, including *We Can Remember It for You Wholesale* (filmed as *Total Recall* [1990 and 2012]), *Second Variety* (filmed as *Screamers* [1995]), *The Minority Report* (filmed as *Minority Report* [2002]), and *A Scanner Darkly* (1977; film 2006).

# Milan Kundera

(b. April 1, 1929, Brno, Czechoslovakia [now in the Czech Republic])

The Czech novelist, short-story writer, playwright, essayist, and poet Milan Kundera produced works that combine erotic comedy with political criticism and philosophical speculation.

The son of a noted concert pianist and musicologist, Ludvik Kundera, the young Kundera studied music but gradually turned to writing, and he began teaching literature at the Academy of Music and Dramatic Arts in Prague in 1952. He published several collections of poetry in the 1950s, including *Poslední máj* (1955; "The Last May"), an homage to the Communist resistance leader Julius Fučík, and *Monology* (1957; "Monologues"), a volume of love poems that, because of their ironic tone and eroticism, were later condemned by the Czech political authorities. During his early career he moved in and out of the Communist Party: he joined in 1948, was expelled in 1950, and was readmitted in 1956, remaining a member until 1970. According to an article published in 2008 in a Czech magazine, Kundera in 1950, after his expulsion from the party, informed police in Prague of the presence of a Western intelligence agent, who was then arrested and imprisoned for 14 years. Kundera denied the article's claims, which were based on a researcher's discovery of a police report on the arrest.

Several volumes of short stories and a highly successful one-act play, *Majitelé klíčů* (1962; "The Owners of the Keys"), were followed by his first novel and one of his greatest works, *Žert* (1967; *The Joke*), a comic, ironic view of the private lives and destinies of various Czechs during the years of Stalinism; translated into several languages, it achieved great international acclaim. His second novel, *Život je jinde* (1969; *Life Is Elsewhere*), about a hapless, romantic-minded hero who thoroughly embraces the Communist takeover of 1948, was forbidden Czech publication. Kundera had participated in the brief but heady liberalization of Czechoslovakia in 1967–68, and after the Soviet occupation of the country he refused to admit his political errors and consequently was attacked by the authorities, who banned all his works, fired him from his teaching positions, and ousted him from the Communist Party.

In 1975 Kundera was allowed to emigrate (with his wife, Věra Hrabánková) from Czechoslovakia to teach at the University of Rennes (1975–78) in France; in 1979 the Czech government stripped him of his citizenship. In the 1970s and '80s his novels, including *Valčík na rozloučenou* (1976; "Farewell Waltz"; Eng. trans. *The Farewell Party*), *Kniha smíchu a zapomnění* (1979; *The Book of Laughter and Forgetting*), and *Nesnesitelná lehkost bytí* (1984; *The Unbearable Lightness of Being*), were published in France and elsewhere abroad but until 1989 were banned in his homeland. *The Book of Laughter and Forgetting*, one of his most successful works, is a series of wittily ironic meditations on the modern state's tendency to deny and obliterate human memory and historical truth. *Nesmrtelnost* (1990; *Immortality*) explores the nature of artistic creation. *La Lenteur* (1994; *Slowness*) was the first novel Kundera wrote in French, *L'Identité* (1997; *Identity*) his second. Czech émigrés are the central characters of Kundera's *La ignorancia* (2000; *Ignorance*), written in French but first published in Spanish.

Kundera's wide-ranging reflections appear in *L'Art du roman* (1986; *The Art of the Novel*), *Les Testaments trahis* (1993; *Testaments Betrayed*), *Le Rideau* (2005; *The Curtain*), and *Une Rencontre* (2009; *Encounter*).

# eADRIENNE RICH

(b. May 16, 1929, Baltimore, Maryland, U.S.—
d. March 27, 2012, Santa Cruz, California)

A drienne Rich was an American poet, scholar, teacher, and critic whose many volumes of poetry trace a stylistic transformation from formal, well-crafted but imitative poetry to a more personal and powerful style.

Rich attended Radcliffe College (B.A., 1951), and before her graduation her poetry was chosen by W.H. Auden for publication in the Yale Younger Poets series. The resulting volume, *A Change of World* (1951), reflected her mastery of the formal elements of poetry and her considerable restraint. *The Diamond Cutters and Other Poems* (1955) was followed by *Snapshots of a Daughter-in-Law: Poems 1954–1962* (1963), published long after her earlier volumes. This third collection exhibited a change in style, a movement away from the restrained and formal to a looser, more personal form. In the mid-1950s Rich began to date her poems to give them a historical context. Her fourth volume, *Necessities of Life: Poems 1962–1965* (1966), was written almost entirely in free verse.

Throughout the 1960s and '70s Rich's increasing commitment to the women's movement and to a feminist and, after openly acknowledging her homosexuality, lesbian aesthetic politicized much of her poetry. *Leaflets: Poems 1965–1968* (1969) includes a number of translations of poetry from other languages as well as a series of poems echoing the Middle Eastern ghazal genre. Such collections as *Diving into the Wreck: Poems 1971–1972* (1973; National Book Award) and *The Dream of a Common Language: Poems 1974–1977* (1978) express anger at the societal conception of womanhood and further articulate Rich's lesbian identity. Her later volumes *A Wild Patience Has Taken Me This Far: Poems 1978–1981* (1981), *An Atlas of the Difficult World: Poems 1988–1991* (1991), and *Dark Fields of the Republic: Poems 1991–1995* (1995) pay tribute to early feminists and admonish the reader to recall the lessons of history, often through the use of different voices.

In such later collections as *Midnight Salvage: Poems 1995–1998* (1999), *Fox: Poems 1998–2000* (2001), and *The School Among the Ruins: Poems 2000–2004* (2004), Rich turned her gaze to social problems as diverse as cell phone usage and the Iraq War, using forms more elliptical and fragmented than those present in her earlier work. The poems in *Telephone Ringing in the Labyrinth* (2007) and in *Tonight No Poetry Will Serve* (2011) continue to experiment with form and include more reflective passages on Rich's sharp observations on the cultural climate of the day.

Rich also wrote several books of criticism. *Of Woman Born: Motherhood as Experience and Institution* (1976) combines scholarly research with personal reflections on being a mother, while *On Lies, Secrets, and Silence* (1979) traces history through musings on Rich's own various incarnations. In *Blood, Bread, and Poetry* (1986), *What Is Found There: Notebooks on Poetry and Politics* (1993), *Arts of the Possible: Essays and Conversations* (2001), and *A Human Eye: Essays on Art in Society, 1997–2008* (2009), Rich addressed many of the problems plaguing humanity, as well as the role of her art form in addressing them.

Rich turned down the National Medal of the Arts in 1997, publicly claiming that the politics of the Bill Clinton administration conflicted with her ideas about art. She was awarded the Bollingen Prize in 2003. Rich taught at numerous universities across the United States, including Stanford and Cornell.

# URSULA K. LE GUIN

(b. October 21, 1929, Berkeley, California, U.S.)

The American writer Ursula K. Le Guin is best known for tales of science fiction and fantasy imbued with concern for character development and language.

Born Ursula Kroeber, she was the daughter of the distinguished anthropologist A.L. Kroeber and the writer Theodora Kroeber, and she attended Radcliffe College (B.A., 1951) and Columbia University (M.A., 1952). The methods of anthropology influenced her science-fiction stories, which often feature highly detailed descriptions of alien societies. Her first three novels, *Rocannon's World* (1966), *Planet of Exile* (1966), and *City of Illusions* (1967), introduce beings from the planet Hain, who established human life on habitable planets, including Earth. Although her Earthsea series—*A Wizard of Earthsea* (1968), *The Tombs of Atuan* (1971), *The Farthest Shore* (1972), *Tehanu* (1990), *Tales from Earthsea* (2001), and *The Other Wind* (2001)—was written for children, Le Guin's skillful writing and acute perceptions attracted a large adult readership. She tapped the young adult market again with her Annals of the Western Shore series, which includes *Gifts* (2004), *Voices* (2006), and *Powers* (2007). Le Guin also wrote a series of books about cats with wings; the series includes *Catwings Return* and *Jane on Her Own*, both published in 1999.

Le Guin's most philosophically significant novels exhibit the same attention to detail that characterizes her science fiction and high fantasy works. *The Left Hand of Darkness* (1969) is about a race of androgynous people who may become either male or female. In *The Dispossessed* (1974), she examined two neighbouring worlds that are home to antithetical societies, one capitalist, the other anarchic, both of which stifle freedom in particular ways. The destruction of indigenous peoples on a planet colonized by Earth is the focus of *The Word for World Is Forest* (1972). *Always Coming Home* (1985) concerns the Kesh, survivors of nuclear war in California—this includes poetry, prose, legends, autobiography, and a tape recording of Kesh music. In 2008 Le Guin made literary news with *Lavinia*, a metatextual examination of a minor character from Virgil's *Aeneid* and her role in the historical development of early Rome.

Le Guin also wrote many essays on fantasy fiction, feminist issues, writing, and other topics, some of them collected in *The Language of the Night* (1979), *Dancing at the Edge of the World* (1989), *Steering the Craft* (1998), and *The Wave in the Mind* (2004). In 2000 she was awarded the Living Legend medal by the Library of Congress.

# IMRE KERTÉSZ

(b. November 9, 1929, Budapest, Hungary)

The Hungarian author Imre Kertész is best known for his semiautobiographical accounts of the Holocaust. In 2002 he received the Nobel Prize for Literature.

At age 14, Kertész was deported with other Hungarian Jews during World War II to the Auschwitz concentration camp in Nazi-occupied Poland. He was later sent to the Buchenwald camp in Germany, from which he was liberated in May 1945. Returning to Hungary, he worked as a journalist for the newspaper *Világosság* but was dismissed in 1951 following the communist takeover. He refused to submit to the cultural policies imposed by the new regime and turned to translation as a means of supporting himself. Kertész was highly praised as a translator specializing in the works of German-language authors, notably Friedrich Nietzsche, Hugo von Hofmannsthal, Sigmund Freud, Arthur Schnitzler, and Ludwig Wittgenstein.

Kertész was best known for his first and most acclaimed novel, *Sorstalanság* (*Fateless*), which he completed in the mid-1960s but was unable to publish for nearly a decade. When the novel finally appeared in 1975, it received little critical attention but established Kertész as a unique and provocative voice in the dissident subculture within contemporary Hungarian literature. *Sorstalanság* features an adolescent narrator who is arrested and deported to a concentration camp, where he confronts the inexplicable horror of human degradation not with outrage or resistance but with seemingly incomprehensible complacency and detachment. For the narrator the brutal reality of atrocity and evil is reconciled by his inherent and inexorable will to survive—without remorse or a need for retribution. With the fall of communism in Hungary following what was deemed the "quiet revolution" in 1989, Kertész resumed an active literary role. With the publication in 1990 of the first German-language edition of the novel, his literary reputation began to expand in Europe, and the novel was later published in more than 10 languages.

*Sorstalanság* was the first installment in Kertész's semi-autobiographical trilogy reflecting on the Holocaust, and the two other novels—*A kudarc* (1988; "Fiasco") and *Kaddis a meg nem született gyermekért* (1990; *Kaddish for a Child Not Born*)—reintroduced the protagonist of *Sorstalanság*. In 1991 Kertész published *Az angol lobogó* ("The English Flag"), a collection of short stories and other short prose pieces, and he followed that in 1992 with *Gályanapló* ("Galley Diary"), a fictional diary covering the period from 1961 to 1991. Another installment of the diary, from 1991 to 1995, appeared in 1997 as *Valaki más: a változás krónikája* ("I—Another: Chronicle of a Metamorphosis"). His essays and lectures were collected in *A holocaust mint kultúra* (1993; "The Holocaust as Culture"), *A gondolatnyi csend, amig kivégzőoztag újratölt* (1998; "Moments of Silence While the Execution Squad Reloads"), and *A száműzött nyelv* (2001; "The Exiled Language").

# JOHN OSBORNE

(b. December 12, 1929, London, England—
d. December 24, 1994, Shropshire)

John Osborne was a British playwright and film producer whose *Look Back in Anger* (performed 1956) ushered in a new movement in British drama and made him known as the first of the "Angry Young Men."

The son of a commercial artist and a barmaid, Osborne used insurance money from his father's death in 1941 for a boarding-school education at Belmont College, Devon. He hated it and left after striking the headmaster. He went home to his mother in London and briefly tried trade journalism until a job tutoring a touring company of juvenile actors introduced him to the theatre. He was soon acting himself, later becoming an actor-manager for various repertory companies in provincial towns and also trying his hand at playwriting. His first play, *The Devil Inside Him*, was written in 1950 with his friend and mentor Stella Linden, an actress and one of Osborne's first passions.

Osborne made his first appearance as a London actor in 1956, the same year that *Look Back in Anger* was produced by the English Stage Company. Although the form of the play was not revolutionary, its content was unexpected. On stage for the first time were the 20- to 30-year-olds of Great Britain who had not participated in World War

II and found its aftermath shabby and lacking in promise. The hero, Jimmy Porter, although the son of a worker, has, through the state educational system, reached an uncomfortably marginal position on the border of the middle class from which he can see the traditional possessors of privilege holding the better jobs and threatening his upward climb. Jimmy Porter continues to work in a street-market and vents his rage on his middle-class wife and her middle-class friend. No solution is proposed for Porter's frustrations, but Osborne makes the audience feel them acutely.

Osborne's next play, *The Entertainer* (1957), projects a vision of a contemporary Britain diminished from its days of self-confidence. Its hero is a failing comedian, and Osborne uses the decline of the music-hall tradition as a metaphor for the decline of a nation's vitality. In 1958 Osborne and director Tony Richardson founded Woodfall Film Productions, which produced motion pictures of *Look Back in Anger* (1959), *The Entertainer* (1959), and, from a filmscript by Osborne that won an Academy Award, *Tom Jones* (1963), based on the novel by Henry Fielding.

*Luther* (1961), an epic play about the Reformation leader, again showed Osborne's ability to create an actably rebellious central figure. His two *Plays for England* (1962) include *The Blood of the Bambergs*, a satire on royalty, and *Under Plain Cover*, a study of an incestuous couple playing games of dominance and submission.

The tirade of Jimmy Porter is resumed in a different key by a frustrated solicitor in Osborne's *Inadmissible Evidence* (1964). *A Patriot for Me* (1965) portrays a homosexual Austrian officer in the period before World War I, based on the story of Alfred Redl, and shows Osborne's interests in the decline of empire and the perils of the nonconformist. *West of Suez* (1971) revealed a measure of sympathy for a type of British colonizer whose day has waned and antipathy for his ideological opponents, who are made to appear confused and neurotic. Osborne's last play, *Déjàvu* (1992), a sequel to *Look Back in Anger,* revisits Jimmy Porter after a 35-year interval.

As revealed in the first installment of Osborne's autobiography, *A Better Class of Person* (1981), much of the fire in *Look Back in Anger* was drawn from Osborne's own early experience. In it he attacks the mediocrity of lower-middle-class English life personified by his mother, whom he hated, and discusses his volatile temperament. The second part of his autobiography appeared in 1991 under the title *Almost a Gentleman*. Osborne was married five times.

Having come to the stage initially as an actor, Osborne achieved note for his skill in providing actable roles. He is also significant for restoring the tirade—or passionately scathing speech—to a high place among dramatic elements. Most significantly, however, he reoriented British drama from well-made plays depicting upper-class life to vigorously realistic drama of contemporary life.

# *A*DONIS

(b. 1930, Qaṣṣābīn, near Latakia, Syria)

The Syrian-born Lebanese poet and literary critic Adonis (Adūnīs, a pseudonym of ʿAlī Aḥmad Saʿīd) is a leader of the modernist movement in contemporary Arabic poetry.

Adonis was born into a family of farmers and had no formal education until he was in his teens, though his father taught him much about classical Arabic literature. At age 14 he was enrolled in a French-run high school. He published his first volume of poems, *Dalīlah*, in 1950 and received a degree in philosophy at the University of Damascus in 1954. The following year he was imprisoned for six months because of his political views and activities. Adonis then moved to Beirut, where in 1957 he helped Yūsuf al-Khāl found the avant-garde poetry review *Shiʿr* ("Poetry"), and later became a citizen of Lebanon. Among his early volumes of poetry are *Qasāʾid ūlā* (1956; "First Poems") and *Awrāq fī al-rīḥ*(1958; "Leaves in the Wind").

In the 1960s Adonis helped create a new form of Arabic poetry—one characterized by elevated diction and a form of complex Surrealism influenced by the work of Sufi poets—with the publication of such works as *Aghānī Mihyār al-Dimashqī* (1961; *Mihyar of Damascus: His Songs*), *Kitāb al-taḥawwulāt wa al-hijrah fī aqālīm al-nahār wa al-layl* (1965; "The Book of Metamorphosis and Migration in the Regions of Day and Night") and *Al-Masraḥ wa al-marāyā* (1968; "The Stage and the Mirrors"). His later book *Al-Ṣūfiyyah wa al-Suriyāliyyah* (1995; *Sufism and Surrealism*) is an examination of the similarities between the two movements that inspired him. In 1968 he launched the radical journal *Mawāqif* ("Positions"), which expanded its scope beyond literature to include political and cultural commentary. He also wrote innovative prose poems such as the influential *Qabr min ajl New York* (1971; "A Tomb for New York").

In 1973 Adonis received a Ph.D. from St. Joseph University in Beirut, after which he held faculty positions at various universities before settling in Paris in the mid-1980s. Adonis's *Al-Kitāb* (1995; "The Book"), which echoes the name of the Qurʾān, is a structurally complex work exploring Arab history from multiple perspectives. His critical essays were collected in *Zaman al-Shiʿr* (1972; "The Time for Poetry") and *Al-Thābit wa al-mutaḥawwil* (1974; "Stability and Change"). He also wrote *Muqaddimah li al-shiʿr al-ʿArabī* (1979; *An Introduction to Arab Poetics*).

English translations of selected poems appear in *The Blood of Adonis* (1971), *The Transformation of the Lover* (1983), *The Pages of Day and Night* (1994), and *A Time Between Ashes and Roses* (2004).

# *DEREK WALCOTT*

(b. January 23, 1930, Castries, Saint Lucia)

The West Indian poet and playwright Derek Walcott is noted for works that explore the Caribbean cultural experience. He received the Nobel Prize for Literature in 1992.

Walcott was educated at St. Mary's College in Saint Lucia and at the University of the West Indies in Jamaica. He began writing poetry at an early age, taught at schools in Saint Lucia and Grenada, and contributed articles and reviews to periodicals in Trinidad and Jamaica. Productions of his plays began in Saint Lucia in 1950, and he studied theatre in New York City in 1958–59. He lived thereafter in Trinidad and the United States, teaching for part of the year at Boston University.

Walcott is best known for his poetry, beginning with *In a Green Night: Poems 1948–1960* (1962). This book is typical of his early poetry in its celebration of the Caribbean landscape's natural beauty. The verse in *Selected Poems* (1964), *The Castaway* (1965), and *The Gulf* (1969) is similarly lush in style and incantatory in mood as Walcott expresses his feelings of personal isolation, caught between his European cultural orientation and the black folk cultures of his native Caribbean. *Another Life* (1973) is a book-length autobiographical poem. In *Sea Grapes* (1976) and *The Star-Apple Kingdom* (1979), Walcott uses a tenser, more economical style to examine the deep cultural divisions of

*Derek Walcott, 1992.* Horst Tappe/Archive Photos/Getty Images

language and race in the Caribbean. *The Fortunate Traveller* (1981) and *Midsummer* (1984) explore his own situation as a black writer in America who has become increasingly estranged from his Caribbean homeland.

Walcott's *Collected Poems, 1948–1984,* was published in 1986. In his book-length poem *Omeros* (1990), he retells the dramas of Homer's *Iliad* and *Odyssey* in a 20th-century Caribbean setting. The poems in *The Bounty*

(1997) are mostly devoted to Walcott's Caribbean home and the death of his mother. In 2000 Walcott published *Tiepolo's Hound*, a poetic biography of West Indian-born French painter Camille Pissarro with autobiographical references and reproductions of Walcott's paintings. (The latter are mostly watercolours of island scenes. Walcott's father had been a visual artist, and the poet began painting early on.) The book-length poem *The Prodigal* (2004), its setting shifting between Europe and North America, explores the nature of identity and exile. *Selected Poems*, a collection of poetry from across Walcott's career, appeared in 2007. Aging is a central theme in *White Egrets* (2010), a volume of new poems.

Of Walcott's approximately 30 plays, the best-known are *Dream on Monkey Mountain* (produced 1967), a West Indian's quest to claim his identity and his heritage; *Ti-Jean and His Brothers* (1958), based on a West Indian folktale about brothers who seek to overpower the Devil; and *Pantomime* (1978), an exploration of colonial relationships through the Robinson Crusoe story. *The Odyssey: A Stage Version* appeared in 1993. Many of Walcott's plays make use of themes from black folk culture in the Caribbean. The essays in *What the Twilight Says* (1998) are literary criticism. They examine such subjects as the intersection of literature and politics and the art of translation.

# JOHN BARTH

(b. May 27, 1930, Cambridge, Maryland, U.S.)

An American writer, John Barth is best known for novels that combine philosophical depth and complexity with biting satire and boisterous, frequently bawdy humour. Much of Barth's writing is concerned with the seeming impossibility of choosing the right action in a world that has no absolute values.

Barth grew up on the eastern shore of Maryland, the locale of most of his writing, and studied at Johns Hopkins University in Baltimore, where he graduated with an M.A. in 1952. The next year, he began teaching at Pennsylvania State University; he moved in 1965 to the State University of New York at Buffalo as professor of English and writer in residence. He was a professor of English and creative writing at Johns Hopkins University from 1973 to 1995.

Barth's first two novels, *The Floating Opera* (1956) and *The End of the Road* (1958), describe characters burdened by a sense of the futility of all action and the effects of these characters upon the less self-conscious, more active people around them. Barth forsook realism and modern settings in *The Sot-Weed Factor* (1960), a picaresque tale that burlesques the early history of Maryland and parodies the 18th-century English novel. All three novels appeared in revised editions in 1967.

*Giles Goat-Boy* (1966) is a bizarre tale of the career of a mythical hero and religious prophet, set in a satirical microcosm of vast, computer-run universities. His work *Lost in the Funhouse* (1968) consists of short, experimental pieces, some designed for performance, interspersed with short stories based on his own childhood. It was followed by *Chimera* (1972), a volume of three novellas, and *Letters* (1979), an experimental novel. The novels *Sabbatical* (1982) and *The Tidewater Tales* (1987) are more traditional narratives. *Once Upon a Time: A Floating Opera* (1994) combined the genres of novel and memoir in the form of a three-act opera. The novel *Coming Soon!!!* (2001) revisits *The Floating Opera* and is arguably Barth's most conspicuously self-conscious work. *The Book of Ten Nights and a Night* (2004) and *The Development* (2008) are collections of interconnected short stories. *Every Third Thought: A Novel in Five Seasons* (2011) features a character from *The Development* who injures his head and then, with each change of the seasons, experiences moments from his past as if they are taking place in the present.

# JUAN GELMAN

(b. May 30, 1930, Buenos Aires, Argentina)

Juan Gelman is an Argentinian poet and leftist political activist who was exiled from his home country in the 1970s.

Gelman was jailed in the early 1960s during the Peronists' struggle for control of the federal government in Argentina. From the late 1960s to the mid-1970s, he wrote for the magazines *Panorama* and *Crisis* in Buenos Aires. His political activism and his involvement with the Montoneros, a left-wing Peronist group that used violence in its efforts to overthrow the military government, resulted in his being forced into exile in Italy in 1975. He returned to Argentina briefly in 1988 before moving to Mexico.

Gelman released his first collection of poetry, *Violín y otras cuestiones* ("Violin and Other Issues"), in 1956. He published prolifically for the next five decades, with his poetry registering the waxing and waning of his prominence as a political activist during the second half of the 20th century. The poems in *Anunciaciones* (1988; "Annunciations"), for instance, show Gelman withdrawing from the public sphere; through them he reflects on his political life and returns to some of his early interests in language and creativity. Among the most notable themes in Gelman's wide-ranging poetry are his experiences in Argentina during the 1960s and '70s, his exile, and his Jewish heritage, as well as the nature of poetry itself. A selection of his poems appear in English translation in *Unthinkable Tenderness* (1997).

In the late 1990s Gelman returned to public prominence as he tried to locate the child of his son and daughter-in-law, who were among those "disappeared" by the military government during Argentina's Dirty War of the late 1970s and early 1980s. In 2000 the president of Uruguay, Jorge Batlle, acknowledged that Gelman's daughter-in-law had been transported to Uruguay, where she gave birth to a daughter; Gelman and his granddaughter were subsequently reunited.

Beginning in 2000, Gelman received a number of major literary awards, both for new collections of poetry and for his lifetime's work. The most prominent was the Cervantes Prize, the highest literary honour in the Spanish-speaking world. His win confirmed his place as Argentina's most prominent poet at the turn of the 21st century. At the 2008 ceremony in Spain in which Gelman received the prize, King Juan Carlos praised Gelman's poetry for its "strength, sincerity, and spontaneity."

# TED HUGHES

(b. August 17, 1930, Mytholmroyd, Yorkshire, England—
d. October 28, 1998, London)

Ted Hughes was an English poet whose most characteristic verse is without sentimentality, emphasizing the cunning and savagery of animal life in harsh, sometimes disjunctive lines.

At Pembroke College, Cambridge, he found folklore and anthropology of particular interest, a concern that was reflected in a number of his poems. In 1956 he married the American poet Sylvia Plath. The couple moved to the United States in 1957, the year that his first volume of verse, *The Hawk in the Rain,* was published. Other works soon followed, including the highly praised *Lupercal* (1960) and *Selected Poems* (1962, with Thom Gunn, a poet whose work is frequently associated with Hughes's as marking a new turn in English verse).

Hughes stopped writing poetry almost completely for nearly three years following Plath's suicide in 1963 (the couple had separated the previous year), but thereafter he published prolifically, with volumes of poetry such as *Wodwo* (1967), *Crow* (1970), *Wolfwatching* (1989), and *New Selected Poems, 1957–1994* (1995). In his *Birthday Letters* (1998), he addressed his relationship with Plath after decades of silence. As the executor of her estate, Hughes also edited and published several volumes of her work in the period 1965–98, but he was accused of censoring her writings after he revealed that he had destroyed several journals that she had written before her suicide.

Hughes wrote many books for children, notably *The Iron Man* (1968; also published as *The Iron Giant*; film 1999). *Remains of Elmet* (1979), in which he recalled the world of his childhood, is one of many publications he created in collaboration with photographers and artists. He translated Georges Schehadé's play *The Story of Vasco* from the original French and shaped it into a libretto. The resulting opera, from which significant portions of his text were cut, premiered in 1974. A play based on Hughes's original libretto was staged in 2009. His works also include an adaptation of Seneca's *Oedipus* (1968), nonfiction (*Winter Pollen*, 1994), and translations. He edited many collections of poetry, such as *The Rattle Bag* (1982, with Seamus Heaney). A collection of his correspondence, edited by Christopher Reid, was released in 2007 as *Letters of Ted Hughes.* In 1984 Hughes was appointed Britain's poet laureate.

# HAROLD PINTER

(b. October 10, 1930, London, England—
d. December 24, 2008, London)

Harold Pinter was an English playwright who achieved international renown as one of the most complex and challenging post-World War II dramatists. His plays are noted for their use of understatement, small talk, reticence—and even silence—to convey the substance of a character's thought, which often lies several layers beneath, and contradicts, his speech. In 2005 Pinter won the Nobel Prize for Literature.

The son of a Jewish tailor, Pinter grew up in London's East End in a working-class area. He studied acting at the Royal Academy of Dramatic Art in 1948 but left after two terms to join a repertory company as a professional actor. Pinter toured Ireland and England with various acting companies, appearing under the name David Baron in provincial repertory theatres until 1959. After 1956 he began to write for the stage. *The Room* (first produced 1957) and *The Dumb Waiter* (first produced 1959), his first two plays, are one-act dramas that established the mood of comic menace that was to figure largely in his later works. His first full-length play, *The Birthday Party* (first produced 1958; film 1968), puzzled the London audiences and lasted only a week, but later it was televised and revived successfully on the stage.

After Pinter's radio play *A Slight Ache* (first produced 1959) was adapted for the stage (1961), his reputation was secured by his second full-length play, *The Caretaker* (first produced 1960; film 1963), which established him as more than just another practitioner of the then-popular Theatre of the Absurd. His next major play, *The Homecoming* (first produced 1965), helped establish him as the originator of a unique dramatic idiom. Such plays as *Landscape* (first produced 1969), *Silence* (first produced 1969), *Night* (first produced 1969), and *Old Times* (first produced 1971) virtually did away with physical activity on the stage. Pinter's later successes included *No Man's Land* (first produced 1975), *Betrayal* (first produced 1978), *Moonlight* (first produced 1993), and *Celebration* (first produced 2000). From the 1970s on, Pinter did much directing of both his own and others' works.

Pinter's plays are ambivalent in their plots, presentation of characters, and endings, but they are works of undeniable power and originality. They typically begin with a pair of characters whose stereotyped relations and role-playing are disrupted by the entrance of a stranger; the audience sees the psychic stability of the couple break down as their fears, jealousies, hatreds, sexual preoccupations, and loneliness emerge from beneath a screen of bizarre yet commonplace conversation. In *The Caretaker*, for instance, a wheedling, garrulous old tramp comes to live with two neurotic brothers, one of whom underwent electroshock therapy as a mental patient. The tramp's attempts to establish himself in the household upset the precarious balance of the brothers' lives, and they end up evicting him. *The Homecoming* focuses on the return to his London home of a university professor who brings his wife to meet his brothers and father. The woman's presence exposes a tangle of rage and confused sexuality in this all-male household, but in the end she decides to stay with the father and his two sons after having accepted their sexual overtures without protest from her overly detached husband.

Dialogue is of central importance in Pinter's plays and is perhaps the key to his originality. His characters' colloquial ("Pinteresque") speech consists of disjointed and oddly ambivalent conversation that is punctuated by resonant silences. The characters' speech, hesitations, and pauses reveal not only their own alienation and the difficulties they have in communicating but also the many layers of meaning that can be contained in even the most innocuous statements.

In addition to works for the stage, Pinter wrote radio and television dramas and a number of successful motion-picture screenplays. Among the latter are those for three films directed by Joseph Losey, *The Servant* (1963), *Accident* (1967), and *The Go-Between* (1970). He also wrote the screenplays for *The Last Tycoon* (1976), *The French Lieutenant's Woman* (1981), the screen version of his own play *Betrayal* (1983), *The Handmaid's Tale* (1990), and *Sleuth* (2007). Pinter was also a noted poet, and his verse—such as that collected in *War* (2003)—often reflected his political views and involvement in numerous causes. In 2007 Pinter was named a chevalier of the French Legion of Honour.

# CHINUA ACHEBE

(b. November 16, 1930, Ogidi, Nigeria—
d. March 21, 2013, Boston, Massachusetts, U.S.)

The prominent Igbo (Ibo) novelist Albert Chinualumogu Achebe is acclaimed for his unsentimental depictions of the social and psychological disorientation accompanying the imposition of Western customs and values upon traditional African society. His particular concern was with emergent Africa at its moments of crisis; his novels range in subject matter from the first contact of an African village with the white man to the educated African's attempt to create a firm moral order out of the changing values in a large city.

Educated in English at the University of Ibadan, Achebe taught for a short time before joining the staff of the Nigerian Broadcasting Corporation in Lagos, where he served as director of external broadcasting during 1961–66. In 1967 he cofounded a publishing company at Enugu with the poet Christopher Okigbo, who died shortly thereafter in the Nigerian civil war. In 1969 Achebe toured the United States with his fellow writers Gabriel Okara and Cyprian Ekwensi, lecturing at universities. Upon his return to Nigeria he was appointed research fellow at the University of Nigeria and became professor of English, a position he held from 1976 until 1981 (professor emeritus from 1985). He was director (from 1970) of two Nigerian publishers, Heinemann Educational Books Ltd. and Nwankwo-Ifejika Ltd. After an automobile accident in Nigeria in 1990 that left him partially paralyzed, he moved to the United States, where he taught at Bard College in New York. In 2009 Achebe left Bard to join the faculty of Brown University in Providence, Rhode Island.

*Things Fall Apart* (1958), Achebe's first novel, concerns traditional Igbo life at the time of the advent of missionaries and colonial government in his homeland. His principal character cannot accept the new order, even though the old has already collapsed. In *No Longer at Ease* (1960) he portrayed a newly appointed civil servant, recently returned from university study in England, who is unable to sustain the moral values he believes to be correct in the face of the obligations and temptations of his new position.

In *Arrow of God* (1964), set in the 1920s in a village under British administration, the principal character, the chief priest of the village, whose son becomes a zealous Christian, turns his resentment at the position he is placed in by the white man against his own people. *A Man of the People* (1966) and *Anthills of the Savannah* (1987) deal with corruption and other aspects of postcolonial African life.

Achebe also published several collections of short stories and a children's book, *How the Leopard Got His Claws* (1973; with John Iroaganachi). *Beware, Soul-Brother* (1971) and *Christmas in Biafra* (1973) are collections of poetry. *Another Africa* (1998) combines an essay and poems by Achebe with photographs by Robert Lyons. Achebe's books of essays include *Morning Yet on Creation Day* (1975), *Hopes and Impediments* (1988), *Home and Exile* (2000), *The Education of a British-Protected Child* (2009), and *There Was a Country: A Personal History of Biafra* (2012). In 2007 he won the Man Booker International Prize.

# JUAN GOYTISOLO

(b. January 5, 1931, Barcelona, Spain)

Juan Goytisolo is a Spanish novelist, short-story writer, and essayist whose early Neorealist work evolved into avant-garde fiction using structuralist and formalist techniques.

A young child when his mother was killed during the Spanish Civil War, Goytisolo grew up hating the fascist dictatorship and the country's conservative religious values. From 1948 to 1952 he attended the universities of Barcelona and Madrid. From the late 1950s he lived in self-imposed exile in Paris and later in Marrakech, Morocco.

His highly praised first novel, *Juegos de manos* (1954; *The Young Assassins*), concerns a group of students who are intent on murdering a politician and who kill the student they have chosen as the assassin. *Duelo en el paraíso* (1955; *Children of Chaos*), set just after the Spanish Civil War, is about the violence that ensues when children gain power over a small town. After the publication of the short-story collection *Fin de fiesta* (1962; *The Party's Over*), his style grew more experimental, as in the novel *Señas de identidad* (1966; *Marks of Identity*), the first of a trilogy that presents a fictionalized account of Goytisolo's life and celebrates the Moorish roots of contemporary Spain. *Reivindicación del Conde don Julián* (1970; *Count Julian*), which is considered his masterwork, experiments with transforming the Spanish language, seen as a tool of political power. The novel excoriates Spain for its hypocrisy and cruelty. The trilogy concludes with *Juan sin tierra* (1975; *Juan the Landless*).

Later novels by Goytisolo include *Makbara* (1980); *En los reinos de taifa* (1986; *Realms of Strife*); *La saga de los Marx* (1993; *The Marx Family Saga*); *El sitio de los sitios* (1995; *State of Siege*), a postmodern exploration of Sarajevo, Bosnia, and Herzegovina, in the early 1990s; *Carajicomedia* (2000; *A Cock-Eyed Comedy*), a vicious (and humorous) attack on the Roman Catholic Church in Spain and Opus Dei; *Telón de boca* (2003; *The Blind Rider*); and *El exiliado de aquí y allá* (2008; *Exiled from Almost Everywhere*), in which a recently deceased man is introduced to a hereafter of limitless access to cyberspace and then uses it to explore the grisly aspects of the modern world. Goytisolo also wrote travel narratives, critical essays, and a personal memoir, *Coto vedado* (1985; *Forbidden Territory*).

# *E.L. Doctorow*

(b. January 6, 1931, New York, New York, U.S.)

The American novelist Edgar Lawrence Doctorow is known for his skillful manipulation of traditional genres.

Doctorow graduated from Kenyon College (B.A., 1952) and then studied drama and directing for a year at Columbia University. He worked for a time as a script reader for Columbia Pictures in New York City. In 1959 he joined the editorial staff of the New American Library, leaving that post five years later to become editor in chief at Dial Press. He subsequently taught at several colleges and universities, including Sarah Lawrence College from 1971 to 1978. He was a visiting senior fellow at Princeton University in 1980–81 and the following year became Glucksman Professor of English and American Letters at New York University.

Doctorow was noted for the facility with which he appropriated genre conceits to illuminate the historical periods in which he set his novels. His first novel, *Welcome to Hard Times* (1960; film 1967), is a philosophical turn on the western genre. In his next book, *Big As Life* (1966), he used science fiction to explore the human response to crisis. Doctorow's proclivity for harvesting characters from history first became apparent in *The Book of Daniel* (1971; film 1983), a fictionalized treatment of the execution of Julius and Ethel Rosenberg for espionage in 1953. In *Ragtime* (1975; film 1981), historical figures share the spotlight with characters emblematic of the shifting social dynamics of early 20th-century America.

Doctorow then turned to the milieu of the Great Depression and its aftermath in the novels *Loon Lake* (1980), *World's Fair* (1985), and *Billy Bathgate* (1989; film 1991). *The Waterworks* (1994) concerns life in 19th-century New York. *City of God* (2000), consisting of what are ostensibly the journal entries of a writer, splinters into several different narratives, including a detective story and a Holocaust narrative. *The March* (2005) follows a fictionalized version of the Union general William

Tecumseh Sherman on his infamously destructive trek through Georgia, aimed at weakening the Confederate economy, during the American Civil War. Doctorow trained his sights on historical figures of less eminence in *Homer and Langley* (2009), a mythologization of the lives of the Collyer brothers, a pair of reclusive eccentrics whose death in 1947 revealed a nightmarish repository of curiosities and garbage in their Harlem, New York City, brownstone.

Doctorow's essays were collected in several volumes, including *Reporting the Universe* (2003) and *Creationists: Selected Essays, 1993–2006* (2006), which contrasts the creative process as it manifests in literature and in science. Additionally, Doctorow wrote the play *Drinks Before Dinner* (1979) and published the short-story collections *Lives of the Poets* (1984) and *Sweet Land Stories* (2004).

# TONI MORRISON

(b. February 18, 1931, Lorain, Ohio, U.S.)

The American writer Toni Morrison is noted for her examination of black experience (particularly black female experience) within the black community. She received the Nobel Prize for Literature in 1993.

Born Chloe Anthony Wofford, she grew up in the American Midwest in a family that possessed an intense love of and appreciation for black culture. Storytelling, songs, and folktales were a deeply formative part of her childhood. She attended Howard University (B.A., 1953) and Cornell University (M.A., 1955). After teaching at Texas Southern University for two years, she taught at Howard from 1957 to 1964. In 1965 she became a fiction editor. From 1984 she taught writing at the State University of New York at Albany, leaving in 1989 to join the faculty of Princeton University.

Morrison's first book, *The Bluest Eye* (1970), is a novel of initiation concerning a victimized adolescent black girl who is obsessed by white standards of beauty and longs to have blue eyes. In 1973 a second novel, *Sula*, was published; it examines (among other issues) the dynamics of friendship and the expectations for conformity within the community. *Song of Solomon* (1977) is told by a male narrator in search of his identity; its publication brought Morrison to national attention. *Tar Baby* (1981), set on a Caribbean island, explores conflicts of race, class, and sex. The critically acclaimed *Beloved* (1987), which won a Pulitzer Prize for fiction, is based on the true story of a runaway slave who, at the point of recapture, kills her infant daughter in order to spare her a life of slavery. *Jazz* (1992) is a story of violence and passion set in New York City's Harlem during the 1920s. Subsequent novels are *Paradise* (1998), a richly detailed portrait of a black utopian community in Oklahoma, and *Love* (2003), an intricate family story that reveals the myriad facets of love and its ostensible opposite. *A Mercy* (2008) deals with slavery in 17th-century America. In the redemptive *Home* (2012), a traumatized Korean War veteran encounters racism after returning home and later overcomes apathy to rescue his sister.

A work of criticism, *Playing in the Dark: Whiteness and the Literary Imagination*, was published in 1992. Many of her essays and speeches were collected in *What Moves at the Margin: Selected Nonfiction* (edited by Carolyn C. Denard), published in 2008. Additionally, Morrison released several children's books, including *Who's Got Game?: The Ant or the Grasshopper?* and *Who's Got Game?: The Lion or the Mouse?*, both written with her son and published in 2003. *Remember* (2004) chronicles the hardships of black students during the integration of the American public school system; aimed at children, it uses archival photographs juxtaposed with captions speculating on the thoughts of their subjects. She also wrote the libretto for *Margaret Garner* (2005), an opera about the same story that inspired *Beloved*.

The central theme of Morrison's novels is the black American experience; in an unjust society her characters struggle to find themselves and their cultural identity. Her use of fantasy, her sinuous poetic style, and her rich interweaving of the mythic gave her stories great strength and texture.

In 2010 Morrison was made an officer of the French Legion of Honour. Two years later she was awarded the U.S. Presidential Medal of Freedom.

# TOMAS TRANSTRÖMER

(b. April 15, 1931, Stockholm, Sweden)

The Swedish lyrical poet Tomas Tranströmer is noted for his spare but resonant language, particularly his unusual metaphors—more transformative than substitutive—which have been associated with a literary surrealism. His verse is at once revelatory and mysterious. Tranströmer was awarded the Nobel Prize for Literature in 2011.

Tranströmer was brought up by his divorced mother, who was a teacher, and her extended family. As a young man, he performed the then-obligatory service in the Swedish military. His first collection of poetry, *17 dikter* (1954; "Seventeen Poems"), showed the influence of modernism in its spare language and startling imagery, and it met with critical acclaim. Tranströmer earned a degree from the University of Stockholm in 1956 and thereafter made his living as a psychologist and social worker.

His next volumes of poetry, *Hemligheter på vägen* (1958; "Secrets Along the Way"), *Den halvfärdiga himlen* (1962; "The Half-Finished Heaven"), and *Klanger och spår* (1966; "Resonances and Tracks"), are composed in a more personal style, with plainer diction and personal perspective more in evidence. In these and later books, Tranströmer's poetic observations of nature combine richness of meaning with the utmost simplicity of style. As one critic put it: "Tranströmer's poems are acoustically perfect chambers in which all of these contradictory vibrations can be heard without straining." During the mid-1960s, however, Tranströmer began to fall out of favour with a new generation of poets and some critics who accused him of a lack of political commitment. Also in the 1960s he established a correspondence and friendship with the American poet Robert Bly, who translated many of Tranströmer's poems into English.

Bly's first translation of an entire book by Tranströmer was *Mörkerseende* (1970; "Seeing in the Dark"; Eng. trans. *Night Vision*), written during a difficult time for the Swedish poet. Tranströmer's next volume, *Stigar* (1973; "Paths"), included translations into Swedish of some of Bly's work. The Baltic coast, which captured Tranströmer's imagination as a boy, is the setting for *Östersjöar* (1974; *Baltics*). His later works include *Sanningsbarriären* (1978; *The Truth Barrier*), *Det vilda torget* (1983; *The Wild Marketplace*), and *För levande och döda* (1989; *For the Living and the Dead*).

In 1990 Tranströmer was awarded the Neustadt Prize, a biennial international award for lifetime achievement in literature. That same year he had a stroke that robbed him of the ability to speak. Nevertheless, he published a memoir, *Minnena ser mig* (1993; "Memories Look at Me"), and two more books of verse: *Sorgegondolen* (1996; *Sorrow Gondola*), inspired by Franz Liszt's *La lugubre gondola*, and *Den stora gåtan* (2004; *The Great Enigma: New Collected Poems*). A volume of Tranströmer's collected work, *Dikter och prosa 1954–2004* ("Poetry and Prose 1954–2004"), was issued in 2011.

Tranströmer's direct language and powerful images made him the most widely translated Scandinavian poet in the English-speaking world in the later 20th century. Bly's collections of Tranströmer include *Friends, You Drank Some Darkness: Three Swedish Poets, Harry Martinson, Gunnar Ekelöf, and Tomas Tranströmer* (1975), *Tomas Tranströmer: Selected Poems 1954–1986* (1987; with other translators), and *The Half-Finished Heaven: The Best Poems of Tomas Tranströmer* (2001). Tranströmer's poetry has been translated into many other languages as well.

# ALICE MUNRO

(b. July 10, 1931, Wingham, Ontario, Canada)

The Canadian short-story writer Alice Munro (née Laidlaw) gained international recognition with her exquisitely drawn stories, usually set in southwestern Ontario, peopled by characters of Scotch-Irish stock. Munro's work is noted for its precise imagery and narrative style, which is at once lyrical, compelling, economical, and intense, revealing the depth and complexities in the emotional lives of ordinary individuals.

Munro attended the University of Western Ontario and, after two years, left school and moved to Vancouver, British Columbia. Her first collection of stories was published as *Dance of the Happy Shades* (1968). It is one of three

*Alice Munro, 2002.* © **AP Images**

of her collections—the other two being *Who Do You Think You Are?* (1978; also published as *The Beggar Maid: Stories of Flo and Rose*) and *The Progress of Love* (1986)—awarded the annual Governor General's Literary Award for fiction. Her second collection—*The Lives of Girls and Women* (1971), a group of coming-of-age stories—was followed by *Something I've Been Meaning to Tell You* (1974), *The Moons of Jupiter* (1982), *Friend of My Youth* (1986), *A Wilderness Station* (1994), and *The Love of a Good Woman* (1998). Her book *Open Secrets* (1994) contains stories that range in setting from the semicivilized hills of southern Ontario to the mountains of Albania. In *Runaway* (2004) Munro explores the depths of ordinary lives, and *The View from Castle Rock*

(2007) combines history, family memoir, and fiction into narratives of questionable inquiries and obscure replies. In 2009 Munro won the Man Booker International Prize; that same year she published the short-story collection *Too Much Happiness*. Her following collection, *Dear Life* (2012), focuses on moments when a character's life suddenly changes.

Munro's short story about the domestic erosions of Alzheimer's disease, *The Bear Came over the Mountain*, which was originally published in *Hateship, Friendship, Courtship, Loveship, Marriage* (2001), was made into the critically acclaimed film *Away from Her* (2006).

# JOHN LE CARRÉ

(b. October 19, 1931, Poole, Dorset, England)

John le Carré (a pseudonym of David John Moore Cornwell) is an English writer of suspenseful, realistic spy novels based on a wide knowledge of international espionage.

Educated abroad and at the University of Oxford, le Carré taught French and Latin at Eton College from 1956 to 1958. In 1959 he became a member of the British foreign service in West Germany and continued with the agency until 1964. During this time he began writing novels, and in 1961 his first book, *Call for the Dead* (filmed as *The Deadly Affair*, 1966), was published. More a detective story than a spy story, it introduced the shrewd but self-effacing intelligence agent George Smiley, who became le Carré's best-known character and was featured in several later works. Le Carré's breakthrough came with his third novel, *The Spy Who Came In from the Cold* (1963), which centred on Alec Leamas, an aging British intelligence agent ordered to discredit an East German official. Unlike the usual glamorous spies of fiction, Leamas is a lonely and alienated man, without a respectable career or a place in society. Immensely popular, the book was adapted into a highly successful film (1965), as were many of le Carré's later works.

After a string of moderately received novels, le Carré returned to his original protagonist with *Tinker, Tailor, Soldier, Spy* (1974; television miniseries 1979; film 2011), the first in a trilogy centred on Smiley and his nemesis, the Soviet master spy Karla. Their struggle was continued in *The Honourable Schoolboy* (1977) and culminated in *Smiley's People* (1979; miniseries 1982) with a successful attempt by Smiley to force Karla's defection to the West. In *The Little Drummer Girl* (1983; film 1984), a young actress is persuaded by the Israeli secret service to infiltrate a Palestinian terrorist group. Le Carré's later novels include *A Perfect Spy* (1986; miniseries 1987), the story of a double agent; *The Russia House* (1989; film 1990); *The Secret Pilgrim* (1991); *The Night Manager* (1993); and *Our Game* (1995), set after the collapse of the Soviet Union. In *The Constant Gardener* (2001; film 2005), a British diplomat investigates his wife's death and uncovers a corrupt pharmaceutical company. Subsequent works include *Absolute Friends* (2003), in which two Cold War-era intelligence agents reconnect in Europe after the September 11 attacks; *A Most Wanted Man* (2008), which follows the efforts of a terrorist, the son of a KGB colonel, to conceal himself in Hamburg; and *Our Kind of Traitor* (2010), the story of an English couple who, while on a tennis holiday, unwittingly find themselves embroiled in a complicated plot involving the Russian mob, politicians, and international bankers.

# UMBERTO ECO

(b. January 5, 1932, Alessandria, Italy)

The Italian literary critic, novelist, and semiotician (student of signs and symbols) Umberto Eco is best known for his novel *Il nome della rosa* (1980; *The Name of the Rose*).

After receiving a Ph.D. from the University of Turin (1954), Eco worked as a cultural editor for Italian Radio-Television and also lectured at the University of Turin (1956–64). He then taught in Florence and Milan and finally, in 1971, assumed a professorial post at the University of Bologna. His initial studies and researches were in aesthetics, his principal work in this area being *Opera aperta* (1962; rev. ed. 1972, 1976; *The Open Work*), which suggests that in much modern music, Symbolist verse, and literature of controlled disorder (Franz Kafka, James Joyce) the messages are fundamentally ambiguous and invite the audience to participate more actively in the interpretive and creative process. From this work he went on to explore other areas of communication and semiotics in such volumes as *A Theory of Semiotics* (1976) and *Semiotics and the Philosophy of Language* (1984), both written in English. Many of his prolific writings in criticism, history, and communication have been translated into various foreign languages, including *La ricerca della lingua perfetta nella cultura europea* (1993; *The Search for the Perfect Language*) and *Kant e l'ornitorinco* (1997; *Kant and the Platypus*). He edited the illustrated companion volumes *Storia della bellezza* (2004; *History of Beauty*) and *Storia della bruttezza* (2007; *On Ugliness*), and he wrote another pictorial book, *Vertigine della lista* (2009; *The Vertigo of Lists*), produced in conjunction with an exhibition he organized at the Louvre Museum, in which he investigated the Western passion for list making and accumulation. *Costruire il nemico e altri scritti occasionali* (2011; *Inventing the Enemy, and Other Occasional Writings*) collected pieces—some initially presented as lectures—on a wide range of subjects, from fascist reactions to James Joyce's *Ulysses* (1922) to the implications of Wikileaks.

The *Name of the Rose*—in story, a murder mystery set in a 14th-century Italian monastery but, in essence, a questioning of "truth" from theological, philosophical, scholarly, and historical perspectives—became an international best-seller. A film version, directed by Jean-Jacques Annaud, appeared in 1986. Eco continued to explore the connections between fantasy and reality in another best-selling novel, *Il pendolo di Foucault* (1988; *Foucault's Pendulum*).

*L'isola del giorno prima* (1995; *The Island of the Day Before*) uses fictional epistolary fragments—pieced together with narration by Eco himself—to trace the peregrinations of a 17th-century Italian nobleman who is drawn into the search for a means of measuring longitude. The illustrated novel *La misteriosa fiamma della regina Loana* (2004; *The Mysterious Flame of Queen Loana*) traces the efforts of a book dealer to reconstruct his life—having suffered amnesia following a coma—through reviewing literature and periodicals from his youth. *Il cimitero di Praga* (2010; *The Cemetery of Prague*) fictionalizes the creation of the *Protocols of the Learned Elders of Zion* (a fraudulent early-20th-century document that was purported to be a plan for Jewish world domination); Eco's book was used to countenance the anti-Semitism that the *Protocols* had sought to foment.

# ROBERT COOVER

(b. February 4, 1932, Charles City, Iowa, U.S.)

R obert Coover is an American writer of avant-garde fiction, plays, poetry, and essays whose experimental forms and techniques mix reality and illusion, frequently creating otherworldly and surreal situations and effects.

Coover attended Southern Illinois University, Indiana University (B.A., 1953), and the University of Chicago (M.A., 1965). He taught at several universities, notably Brown University in Providence, Rhode Island, where he was a professor of creative writing from 1979 to 2012.

His first, and most conventional, novel, *The Origin of the Brunists* (1966), tells of the rise and eventual disintegration of a religious cult. The protagonist of *The Universal Baseball Association, Inc.* (1968) creates an imaginary baseball league, in which fictitious players take charge of their own lives. Written in the voice of Richard Nixon and satirizing the national mood of the early 1950s, *The Public Burning* (1976) is what Coover called a "factional account" of the trial and execution of Julius and Ethel Rosenberg. Among his other works are *Whatever Happened to Gloomy Gus of the Chicago Bears?* (1987), which casts Nixon as a simpleminded and lascivious football player during the 1930s in a work that skewers the superficial 20th-century notions of the "American Dream"; *Pinocchio in Venice* (1991); *John's Wife* (1996); *Ghost Town* (1998); *The Adventures of Lucky Pierre: Director's Cut* (2002), the tale of an idolized pornographic-film actor who lives in a society of limitless sexual extravagance, and *Noir* (2010), Coover's metafictional take on the hardboiled detective story.

*Robert Coover, 2009.* Dave Pape

Coover's short-story collection *Pricksongs & Descants* (1969) established him as a major figure in postwar American writing, and several of his stories were adapted for theatrical performance, including "The Babysitter" (film 1995), his most-anthologized work, and "Spanking the Maid." In 2002 he published *The Grand Hotels (of Joseph Cornell)*, a collection of 10 poetic vignettes derived from Joseph Cornell's assemblages. Coover explored children's literature through *Stepmother* (2004), an illustrated modern fairy tale for adults, and *A Child Again* (2005), a collection of grotesque retellings of childhood tales.

Coover's often avant-garde work was far from commercially successful, but he had a vast influence on a generation of postmodern writers, including David Foster Wallace, Dave Eggers, and Rick Moody.

# JOHN UPDIKE

(b. March 18, 1932, Reading, Pennsylvania, U.S.—
d. January 27, 2009, Danvers, Massachusetts)

John Updike was an American writer of novels, short stories, and poetry who was known for his careful craftsmanship and realistic but subtle depiction of "American, Protestant, small-town, middle-class" life.

Updike grew up in Shillington, Pennsylvania, and many of his early stories draw on his youthful experiences there. He graduated from Harvard University in 1954. In 1955 he began an association with *The New Yorker* magazine, to which he contributed editorials, poetry, stories, and criticism throughout his prolific career. His poetry—intellectual, witty pieces on the absurdities of modern life—was gathered in his first book, *The Carpentered Hen and Other Tame Creatures* (1958), which was followed by his first novel, *The Poorhouse Fair* (1958). About this time, Updike devoted himself to writing fiction full-time, and several works followed. *Rabbit, Run* (1960), which is considered to be one of his best novels, concerns a former star athlete who is unable to recapture success when bound by marriage and small-town life and flees responsibility. Three subsequent novels, *Rabbit Redux* (1971), *Rabbit Is Rich* (1981), and *Rabbit at Rest* (1990)—the latter two winning Pulitzer Prizes—follow the same character during later periods of his life. *Rabbit Remembered* (2001) returns to characters from those books in the wake of Rabbit's death. *The Centaur* (1963) and *Of the Farm* (1965) are notable among Updike's novels set in Pennsylvania.

Much of Updike's later fiction is set in New England (in Ipswich, Massachusetts), where he lived from the 1960s. Updike continued to explore the issues that confront middle-class America, such as fidelity, religion, and responsibility. The novels *Couples* (1968) and *Marry Me* (1976) expose the evolving sexual politics of the time in East Coast suburbia. Updike set *Memories of the Ford Administration: A Novel* (1992) in the 1970s, infusing the tale of a professor's research on President James Buchanan with observations on sexuality. *In the Beauty of the Lilies* (1996) draws parallels between religion and popular obsession with cinema, while *Gertrude and Claudius* (2000) offers conjectures on the early relationship between Hamlet's mother and her brother-in-law. In response to the cultural shifts that occurred in the United States after the September 11 attacks, Updike released *Terrorist* in 2006.

Updike often expounded upon characters from earlier novels, eliding decades of their lives only to place them in the middle of new adventures. *The Witches of Eastwick* (1984; film 1987), about a coven of witches, was followed by *The Widows of Eastwick* (2008), which trails the women into old age. *Bech: A Book* (1970), *Bech Is Back* (1982), and

*John Updike, 1994.* Michael Brennan/Hulton Archive/Getty Images

*Bech at Bay* (1998) humorously trace the tribulations of a Jewish writer.

Updike's several collections of short stories include *The Same Door* (1959), *Pigeon Feathers* (1962), *Museums and Women* (1972), *Problems* (1979), *Trust Me* (1987), and *My Father's Tears, and Other Stories* (2009), which was published posthumously. He also wrote nonfiction and criticism, much of it appearing in *The New Yorker*. It has been collected in *Assorted Prose* (1965), *Picked-Up Pieces* (1975), *Hugging the Shore* (1983), and *Odd Jobs* (1991). *Still Looking: Essays on American Art* (2005) examines both art and its cultural presentation, and *Due Considerations* (2007) collects later commentary spanning art, sexuality, and literature. Updike also continued to write poetry, usually light verse. *Endpoint, and Other Poems*, published posthumously in 2009, collects poetry Updike had written between 2002 and a few weeks before he died; it takes his own death as its primary subject. *Higher Gossip*, a collection of commentaries, was released in 2011.

# *ATHOL FUGARD*

(b. June 11, 1932, Middleburg, South Africa)

The South African dramatist, actor, and director Athol Fugard became internationally known for his penetrating and pessimistic analyses of South African society during the apartheid period.

Fugard's earliest plays were *No-Good Friday* and *Nongogo* (both published in *Dimetos and Two Early Plays*, 1977), but it was *The Blood Knot* (1963), produced for stage (1961) and television (1967) in both London and New York City, that established his reputation. *The Blood Knot*, dealing with brothers who fall on opposite sides of the racial colour line, was the first in a sequence Fugard called "The Family Trilogy." The series continued with *Hello and Goodbye* (1965) and *Boesman and Lena* (1969) and was later published under the title *Three Port Elizabeth Plays* (1974). *Boesman and Lena*, filmed in 1973 with Fugard as Boesman, played to a wider audience than any previous South African play; another film adaptation was released in 2000.

Fugard's willingness to sacrifice character to symbolism caused some critics to question his commitment. Provoked by such criticism, Fugard began to question the nature of his art and his emulation of European dramatists. He began a more imagist approach to drama, not using any prior script but merely giving actors what he called "a mandate" to work around "a cluster of images."

*Athol Fugard (centre) with actors John Kani (left) and Winston Ntshona, 1973.* James Jackson/Hulton Archive/Getty Images

From this technique derived the imaginative if shapeless drama of *Orestes* (published in *Theatre One: New South African Drama*, 1978), and the documentary expressiveness of *Siswe Bansi Is Dead*, *The Island*, and *Statements After an Arrest Under the Immorality Act* (all published in *Statements: Three Plays*, 1974).

A much more traditionally structured play, *Dimetos* (1977), was performed at the 1975 Edinburgh Festival. *A Lesson from Aloes* (published 1981) and *"Master Harold"...and the Boys* (1982) were performed to much acclaim in London and New York City, as was *The Road to Mecca* (1985; film 1992), the story of an eccentric older woman about to be confined against her will in a nursing home. Throughout the 1970s and '80s Fugard worked to create and sustain theatre groups that, despite South African drama's particular vulnerability to censorship, produced plays defiantly indicting the country's apartheid policy.

After the dismantling of apartheid laws in 1990–91, Fugard's focus turned increasingly to his personal history. In 1994 he published the memoir *Cousins*, and throughout the 1990s he wrote plays—including *Playland* (1992), *Valley Song* (1996), and *The Captain's Tiger* (1997)—that have strong autobiographical elements. Subsequent plays include *Sorrows and Rejoicings* (2002), about a poet who returns to South Africa after years of exile; *Victory* (2009), a stark examination of postapartheid South Africa; and *The Train Driver* (2010), an allegorical meditation on white South Africans' collective guilt about apartheid.

Films in which Fugard acted include *Marigolds in August* (1980; written with Ross Devenish) and *The Killing Fields* (1984). Fugard also wrote the novel *Tsotsi* (1980; film 2005). *Notebooks, 1960–1977* (1983) collects selections from Fugard's journals, and *Karoo, and Other Stories* (2005) is a compilation of short stories and journal extracts. In 2011 Fugard received a Tony Award for lifetime achievement.

# *Sir V.S. Naipaul*

(b. August 17, 1932, Trinidad)

The Trinidadian writer of Indian descent Sir Vidiadhar Surajprasad Naipaul is known for his pessimistic novels set in developing countries. For these revelations of what the Swedish Academy called "suppressed histories," Naipaul won the Nobel Prize for Literature in 2001.

Descended from Hindu Indians who had immigrated to Trinidad as indentured servants, Naipaul left Trinidad to attend the University of Oxford in 1950. He subsequently settled in England, although he traveled extensively thereafter. His earliest books (*The Mystic Masseur*, 1957; *The Suffrage of Elvira*, 1958; and *Miguel Street*, 1959) are ironic and satirical accounts of life in the Caribbean. His fourth novel, *A House for Mr. Biswas* (1961), also set in Trinidad, was a much more important work and won him major recognition. It centres on the main character's attempt to assert his personal identity and establish his independence as symbolized by owning his own house. Naipaul's subsequent novels used other national settings but continued to explore the personal and collective alienation experienced in new nations that were struggling to integrate their native and Western-colonial heritages. The three stories in *In a Free State* (1971), which won Britain's Booker Prize, are set in various countries; *Guerrillas* (1975) is a despairing look at an abortive uprising on a Caribbean island; and *A Bend in the River* (1979) cynically examines the uncertain future of a newly independent state in Central Africa. *A Way in the World* (1994) is an essaylike novel examining how history forms individuals' characters. Naipaul's other novels include *The Mimic Men* (1967) and *The Enigma of Arrival* (1987).

Among Naipaul's nonfiction works are three studies of India, *An Area of Darkness* (1965), *India: A Wounded Civilization* (1977), and *India: A Million Mutinies Now* (1990); *The Five Societies—British, French, and Dutch—in the West Indies* (1963); and *Among the Believers: An Islamic Journey* (1981). Naipaul was knighted in 1989.

In 1998 he published *Beyond Belief: Islamic Excursions Among the Converted Peoples*, a portrayal of the Islamic faith in the lives of ordinary people in Iran, Pakistan, Indonesia, and Malaysia. *Half a Life* (2001) is a novel about an Indian immigrant to England and then Africa. He becomes "half a person," as Naipaul has said, "living a borrowed life." Released the year that Naipaul received the Nobel Prize,

*Half a Life* was considered by many critics to illustrate beautifully the reasons that he won the prize. Subsequent works include *The Writer and the World* (2002) and *Literary Occasions* (2003), both collections of previously published essays. The novel *Magic Seeds* (2004) is a sequel to *Half a Life*. In *The Masque of Africa* (2010)—which was based on his travels in Côte d'Ivoire, Gabon, Ghana, Nigeria, Uganda, and South Africa—Naipaul returned to his exploration of religion, focusing on African beliefs.

# SHEL SILVERSTEIN

(b. September 25, 1932, Chicago, Illinois, U.S.—
d. May 10, 1999, Key West, Florida)

Shel Silverstein was an American cartoonist, children's author, poet, songwriter, and playwright best known for his light verse and quirky cartoons.

In the 1950s Silverstein drew for the military magazine *Stars and Stripes* while serving in Japan and Korea, and he also contributed to *Playboy*. He created the adult book of drawings *Now Here's My Plan: A Book of Futilities* (1960) before turning to works for children. His first efforts, written under the name Uncle Shelby, included *Uncle Shelby's ABZ Book: A Primer for Tender Young Minds* (1961) and *Who Wants a Cheap Rhinoceros* (1964). Among his memorable characters were the protagonist in *Uncle Shelby's Story of Lafcadio, the Lion Who Shot Back* (1963); the boy-man and tree in *The Giving Tree* (1964), his most famous prose work; and the partial circle in *The Missing Piece* (1976). Silverstein's last illustrated collection, *Falling Up*, was published in 1996.

Silverstein, who was often compared to Dr. Seuss, used such locales as the land of Listentoemholler and the castle

*Shel Silverstein*, c. *1968*. Alice Ochs/Michael Ochs Archive/ Getty Images

Now. His first major poetry collection, *Where the Sidewalk Ends* (1974), featured the popular title verse:

> *There is a place where the sidewalk ends*
> *And before the street begins,*
> *And there the grass grows soft and white,*
> *And there the sun burns crimson bright,*
> *And there the moon-bird rests from his flight*
> *To cool in the peppermint wind.*

His pictures more than complemented his words. Accompanying "The Edge of the World" is the drawing of a small girl peering over the edge of a ledge so thin that a fire hydrant, a dog, a signpost, and a worm protrude halfway through. The cover of *A Light in the Attic* (1981) shows a boy with a windowed attic forming the top of his head. The words of another poem form the neck of a giraffe.

Silverstein often eschewed happy endings because children, he said, might otherwise wonder why they themselves were not comparably happy. He was credited for helping young readers develop an appreciation of poetry, and his serious verse reveals an understanding of common childhood anxieties and wishes. Silverstein also wrote one-act plays, sometimes working with David Mamet, and songs.

## SYLVIA PLATH

(b. October 27, 1932, Boston, Massachusetts, U.S.—
d. February 11, 1963, London, England)

Sylvia Plath was an American poet and novelist whose best-known works are preoccupied with alienation, death, and self-destruction.

Plath published her first poem at age eight. She entered and won many literary contests and while still in high school sold her first poem to *The Christian Science Monitor* and her first short story to *Seventeen* magazine. She entered Smith College on a scholarship in 1951 and was a cowinner of the *Mademoiselle* magazine fiction contest in 1952. Plath enjoyed remarkable artistic, academic, and social success at Smith, but she also suffered from severe depression and underwent a period of psychiatric hospitalization. She graduated from Smith with highest honours in 1955 and went on to Newnham College in Cambridge, England, on a Fulbright fellowship. In 1956 she married the English poet Ted Hughes. For the following two years she was an instructor in English at Smith College.

In 1960, shortly after Plath and her husband returned to England, her first collection of poems appeared as *The Colossus*. Her novel, *The Bell Jar*, was published in 1963 under the pseudonym "Victoria Lucas." Strongly autobiographical, the book describes the mental break-down, attempted suicide, and eventual recovery of a young college girl and parallels Plath's own breakdown and hospitalization in 1953. In 1962 Plath and Hughes separated.

During her last three years Plath abandoned the restraints and conventions that had bound much of her early work. She wrote with great speed, produc-ing poems of stark self-revelation and confession. The anxiety, confusion, and doubt that haunted her were transmuted into verses of great power and pathos borne on flashes of incisive wit. Several poems, including the well-known "Daddy," explore her conflicted relation-ship with her father, Otto Plath, who died when she was age eight. In 1963, after this burst of productivity, Plath took her own life.

*Ariel* (1965), a collection of her later poems, helped spark the growth of a devoted and enthusiastic following of readers and scholars. The reissue of *The Bell Jar* under her own name in 1966 and the appearance of small collections of previously unpublished poems, including *Crossing the Water* (1971) and *Winter Trees* (1971), were welcomed by critics and the public alike. *Johnny Panic and the Bible of Dreams*, a book of short stories and prose, was published in 1977. *The Collected Poems*, which includes many previously unpublished poems, appeared in 1981 and received the 1982 Pulitzer Prize, making Plath the first to receive the honour posthumously. Plath had kept a journal for much of her life, and in 2000 *The Unabridged Journals of Sylvia Plath*, covering the years from 1950 to 1962, was published. A biographical film of Plath starring Gwyneth Paltrow (*Sylvia*) appeared in 2003. In 2009 Plath's radio play *Three Women* (1962) was staged professionally for the first time.

Many of Plath's posthumous publications were compiled by Hughes, who became the executor of her estate. However, controversy surrounded his editing practices, especially when he revealed that he had destroyed the last journals written prior to her suicide.

# PHILIP ROTH

(b. March 19, 1933, Newark, New Jersey, U.S.)

The American novelist and short-story writer Philip Roth produced works that are characterized by an acute ear for dialogue, a concern with Jewish middle-class life, and the painful entanglements of sexual and familial love. In Roth's later years his writings were informed by an increasingly naked preoccupation with mortality and with the failure of the aging body and mind.

Roth received an M.A. from the University of Chicago and taught there and elsewhere. He first achieved fame with *Goodbye, Columbus* (1959; film 1969), whose title story candidly depicts the boorish materialism of a wealthy Jewish suburban family. Roth's first novel, *Letting Go* (1962), was followed in 1967 by *When She Was Good*, but he did not recapture the success of his first book until *Portnoy's Complaint* (1969; film 1972), an audacious satirical portrait of a contemporary Jewish male at odds with his domineering mother and obsessed with sexual experience.

Several minor works, including *The Breast* (1972), *My Life As a Man* (1974), and *The Professor of Desire* (1977), were followed by one of Roth's most important novels, *The Ghost Writer* (1979), which introduced an aspiring young writer named Nathan Zuckerman. Roth's two subsequent novels, *Zuckerman Unbound* (1981) and *The Anatomy Lesson* (1983), trace his writer-protagonist's subsequent life and career and constitute Roth's first Zuckerman trilogy. These three novels were republished together with the novella *The Prague Orgy* under the title *Zuckerman Bound* (1985). A fourth Zuckerman novel, *The Counterlife*, appeared in 1993.

Roth was awarded a Pulitzer Prize for *American Pastoral* (1997), a novel about a middle-class couple whose daughter becomes a terrorist. It is the first novel of a second Zuckerman trilogy, completed by *I Married a Communist* (1998) and *The Human Stain* (2000; film 2003). In *The Dying Animal* (2001; filmed as *Elegy*, 2008), an aging literary professor reflects on a life of emotional isolation. *The Plot Against America* (2004) tells a counterhistorical story of fascism in the United States during World War II.

With *Everyman* (2006), a novel that explores illness and death, Roth became the first three-time winner of the PEN/Faulkner Award for Fiction, which he had won previously for *Operation Shylock* (1993) and *The Human Stain*. *Everyman* also marked the start of a period during which

Roth produced relatively brief novels, all focused on issues of mortality. *Exit Ghost* (2007) revisits Zuckerman, who has been reawoken to life's possibilities after more than a decade of self-imposed exile in the Berkshire Mountains. *Indignation* (2008) is narrated from the after-life by a man who died at age 19. *The Humbling* (2009) revisits *Everyman*'s mortality-obsessed terrain, this time through the lens of an aging actor who, realizing that he has lost his talent, finds himself unable to work. A polio epidemic is at the centre of *Nemesis* (2010), set in Newark, New Jersey, in 1944. In 2011 Roth won the Man Booker International Prize.

# ANDREY VOZNESENSKY

(b. May 12, 1933, Moscow, Russia, U.S.S.R. —
d. June 1, 2010, Moscow, Russia)

Andrey Voznesensky was a Russian poet who was one of the most prominent of the generation of writers that emerged in the Soviet Union after the Stalinist era.

Voznesensky spent his early childhood in the city of Vladimir. In 1941 he moved with his mother and sister to Kurgan, in the Ural Mountains, while his father assisted in the evacuation of factories from besieged Leningrad. The profound effects of the war on his developing psyche later found vivid expression in his poetry.

After the war the family returned to Moscow, and Voznesensky pursued his education. While still a student at Moscow Architectural Institute, from which he graduated in 1957, he sent some of his own verses to the renowned author Boris Pasternak, who encouraged him and became his model and tutor for the next three years.

Voznesensky's first published poems, which appeared in 1958, are experimental works marked by changing metres and rhythms, a distinctive use of assonance and sound associations, and a passionate but intellectually subtle moral fervour. His important early works include the long narrative poem *Mastera* (1959; "The Masters") and two poetry collections, *Mozaika* (1960; "Mosaic") and *Parabola* (1960).

During the late 1950s and early '60s, Soviet poets staged a creative renaissance. Poetry readings became so popular that they sometimes were held in sports arenas in order to accommodate thousands of listeners. Along with his contemporary Yevgeny Yevtushenko, the charismatic Voznesensky became a star attraction at these events. The readings came to a sudden halt in 1963, however, when Soviet artists and writers working in "excessively experimental" styles were subjected to an official campaign of condemnation. Along with his fellow poets outside the approved school of Socialist Realism, Voznesensky suffered seven months of official criticism; he was returned to partial favour only after writing an ironic recantation in the government newspaper *Pravda*. Charges of obscurity, experimentation, and "ideological immaturity" continued to be periodically leveled against Voznesensky and his peers throughout the 1960s and '70s. Despite frequent criticism of his work, Voznesensky retained his position as an "official" writer (he received the State Prize in 1978, for instance), which was a result of his ability to produce works on strategic themes when necessary. He was therefore able to act in ways otherwise dangerous for a Soviet author: he wrote letters that condemned the occupation of Czechoslovakia and defended the novelist Aleksandr Solzhenitsyn, and he collaborated on the underground magazine *Metropol*.

In what is perhaps his best-known poem, "Goya" (1960), the author uses a series of powerful metaphors to express the horrors of war. "Akhillesovo serdtse" ("My Achilles Heart") and "Avtoportret" ("Self-Portrait") tell of his suffering and anger during the 1963 crackdown. His later works include the volumes *Sorok liricheskikh otstupleny iz poemy "Treugolnaya grusha"* (1962; "Forty Lyric Digressions from the Poem 'Triangular Pear'"), *Antimiry* (1964; *Antiworlds*), *Vypusti ptitsu!* (1974; "Let the Bird Free!"), and *Soblazn* (1978; "Temptation"). On the whole, Voznesensky's works of the 1980s and '90s did not significantly change his reputation, notwithstanding his attempts to create new forms of poetry, including visual poetry. He also wrote a memoir, *Na virtualnom vetru* (1998; "Under the Virtual Wind").

# YEVGENY YEVTUSHENKO

(b. July 18, 1933, Zima, Irkutsk oblast, Russia, U.S.S.R.)

Yevgeny Yevtushenko (Evgenii Evtushenko) remains best known as a poet and a spokesman for the younger post-Stalin generation of Russian poets. His internationally publicized demands for greater artistic freedom and for a literature based on aesthetic rather than political standards signaled an easing of Soviet control over artists in the late 1950s and '60s.

A fourth-generation descendant of Ukrainians exiled to Siberia, Yevtushenko grew up in Moscow and the small town on the Trans-Siberian Railway line that is the setting of his first important narrative poem, *Stantsiya Zima* (1956; *Zima Junction*). He was invited to study at the Gorky Institute of World Literature in Moscow, and he gained popularity and official recognition after Joseph Stalin's death in 1953. Yevtushenko's gifts as an orator and publicist, his magnetic personality, and his fearless fight for a return to artistic honesty soon made him a leader of Soviet youth. He revived the brash, slangy, unpoetic language of the early Revolutionary poets Vladimir Mayakovsky and Sergey Yesenin and reintroduced such traditions as love lyrics and personal lyrics, which had been discouraged under Stalinism. His poem *Baby Yar* (1961), mourning the Nazi massacre of an estimated 34,000 Ukrainian Jews, was an attack on lingering Soviet anti-Semitism.

Yevtushenko's travels and poetry readings in the United States and Europe established cultural links with the West, but he fell into disfavour at home when he published his *Precocious Autobiography* in Paris in 1963. He was recalled and his privileges were withdrawn, but he was restored to favour when he published his most ambitious cycle of poems, *Bratsk Station* (1966; originally published in Russian), in which he contrasts the symbol of a Siberian power plant bringing light to Russia with the symbol of Siberia as a prison throughout Russian history.

Yevtushenko's play *Under the Skin of the Statue of Liberty*, which was composed of selections from his earlier poems about the United States, was produced in Moscow in 1972. His first novel, published in Russian in 1982, was translated and published in English as *Wild Berries* in 1984; that same year, a novella, *Ardabiola*, appeared in English translation. In 1978 he embarked on an acting career, and in 1981 a book of his photographs, *Invisible Threads*, was published. He published more poetry in *The Collected Poems, 1952–1990* (1991), *The Best of the Best: The Evening Rainbow* (1999; also published as *Evening Rainbow*), and *Walk on the Ledge: A New Book of Poetry in English and Russian* (2005). His autobiographical novel *Don't Die Before Your Death* (1994; also published as *Don't Die Before You're Dead*) treats the attempted coup against Mikhail Gorbachev in Soviet Russia in 1991.

# CORMAC MCCARTHY

(b. July 20, 1933, Providence, Rhode Island, U.S.)

Cormac McCarthy is an American writer in the Southern Gothic tradition whose novels about wayward characters in the rural American South and Southwest are noted for their dark violence, dense prose, and stylistic complexity.

McCarthy attended the University of Tennessee at Knoxville and served in the U.S. Air Force from 1953 to 1956. Readers were first introduced to McCarthy's difficult narrative style in the novel *The Orchard Keeper* (1965), about a Tennessee man and his two mentors. Social outcasts highlight such novels as *Outer Dark* (1968), about two incestuous siblings; *Child of God* (1974), about a lonely man's descent into depravity; and *Suttree* (1979), about a man who overcomes his fixation on death.

McCarthy's *Blood Meridian* (1985), a violent frontier tale, was a critical sensation, hailed as his masterpiece. *Blood Meridian* tells the story of 14-year-old boy who joins a gang of outlaws hunting Native Americans along the U.S.-Mexico border in the 1840s. The group is headed by a malevolent figure called the Judge, who leads the gang through a series of staggeringly amoral actions, through which McCarthy explores the nature of good and evil.

McCarthy achieved popular fame with *All the Pretty Horses* (1992; film 2000), winner of the National Book Award. The first volume of *The Border Trilogy,* it is the coming-of-age story of John Grady Cole, a Texan who travels to Mexico. The second installment, *The Crossing* (1994), set before and during World War II, follows the adventures of brothers Billy and Boyd Parham and centres around three round-trip passages that Billy makes between southwestern New Mexico and Mexico. The trilogy concludes with *Cities of the Plain* (1998), which interweaves the lives of John Grady Cole and Billy Parham through their employment on a ranch in New Mexico.

McCarthy's later works include *No Country for Old Men* (2005; film 2007), a modern, bloody western that opens with a drug deal gone bad. In the postapocalyptic *The Road* (2006; Pulitzer Prize; film 2009), a father and son struggle to survive after a disaster, left unspecified, that has all but destroyed the United States. McCarthy also wrote the plays *The Stonemason* (2001) and *The Sunset Limited* (2006; television movie 2011).

# Ko Un

(b. August 1, 1933, Kunsan, North Cholla province,
Japanese-occupied Korea [now South Korea])

The prolific Korean poet Ko Un gained an international readership with verse informed by both his political activism in Korea and his broader concern for humanity.

Ko was born in a farming village, and his schooling took place under Japanese authorities who were intent on suppressing Korean language and culture, especially during World War II. He began writing poetry in 1945. Physically slight and emotionally sensitive, Ko as a young adult endured the deadly struggle between the communists and nationalists and the viciousness of the ensuing Korean War (1950–53). He was traumatized by the all-pervasiveness of death and the loss of friends and family in the turmoil of the period, and he lost hearing in one ear as a result of a suicide attempt. In 1952 he sought solace by becoming a Son (Zen) Buddhist monk. He continued to write and published his first book of poetry, *Pian-gamseong* ("Transcendental Sensibility"), in 1960.

Ko's anomie became more pronounced after militarists under General Park Chung Hee seized power in South Korea in 1961. Ko left the monastic life in 1962, and in 1970 he attempted suicide a second time. Ko embraced Korean nationalism in the 1970s and became actively involved in social and political causes. His activism led to two arrests and short prison terms in the following six years. In 1980 he was given a 20-year sentence for antigovernment activities and was jailed in a military prison, where one of his fellow prisoners was opposition leader Kim Dae Jung, later president of South Korea and a Nobel Peace Prize laureate.

Often kept in total darkness in his cell, Ko later related that he began to envision personalities he had known in his life, from the time when he was a boy in the countryside to his days as a political activist in the capital, as well as figures from national history. He decided then to write a poem about every person he had known. The first three volumes of his Man'inbo ("Ten Thousand Lives") project were published in 1986 in Korean.

*Ko Un, 2006.* Sang Wha Lee

Ko was pardoned and released from prison in 1982, and in 1985 he married and moved to a village, Anseong, south of Seoul. In the much more liberal South Korean political climate that followed the democratic constitution of 1987, Ko flourished as a widely admired poet and leader in the Korean cultural scene. He was elected chairman of the Association of Korean Arts for 1989–90 and served as president of the Association of Writers for National Literature (1992–94). He accepted a resident professorship in the graduate school of Kyonggi University in Seoul. In 1998 and 1999 Ko was a visiting professor at the University of California, Berkeley, and at Harvard University's Harvard-Yenching Institute. A proponent of Korean reunification, Ko in 1998 led the first South Korean delegation to North Korea and recorded his observations in a book of poems, *Nam kwa puk* (2000; "South and North").

Ko's first volume of poetry in English translation, *The Sound of My Waves*, was published in 1992. His later books in English translation include *Beyond Self: 108 Korean Zen Poems* (1997); *Ten Thousand Lives* (2005), excerpts from the first 10 volumes of the Ten Thousand Lives project; and *The Tree Way Tavern* (2006). Ko's work drew the attention of prominent American poets, including Allen Ginsberg, Robert Hass, and Gary Snyder, all of whom contributed forewords to these books. Ko also published novels, drama, and literary criticism.

Despite Ko's career in political activism, his poetry is not didactic or shrill; rather, it reflects his study of the Chinese and Zen traditions and a concern with humanity that ran even deeper than his political beliefs. He began writing in a Modernist vein, but he soon turned out more-lively, passionate, and down-to-earth verses that were rooted in Korea's Chinese and Japanese legacies but that above all rejoiced in their Koreanness. His poetry is demotic and often brash, written to be read aloud, and its subjects are usually everyday people and commonplace occurrences. Ko's poems run the gamut from multivolume epics and the mammoth Ten Thousand Lives project to Zen-infused, seemingly simple images.

# WOLE SOYINKA

(b. July 13, 1934, Abeokuta, Nigeria)

The Nigerian playwright and political activist Akinwande Oluwole Soyinka received the Nobel Prize for Literature in 1986. He sometimes wrote of modern West Africa in a satirical style, but his serious intent and his belief in the evils inherent in the exercise of power usually was evident in his work as well.

A member of the Yoruba people, Soyinka attended Government College and University College in Ibadan before graduating in 1958 with a degree in English from the University of Leeds in England. Upon his return to Nigeria, he founded an acting company and wrote his first important play, *A Dance of the Forests* (produced 1960; published 1963), for the Nigerian independence celebrations. The play satirizes the fledgling nation by stripping it of romantic legend and by showing that the present is no more a golden age than was the past.

He wrote several plays in a lighter vein, making fun of pompous, Westernized schoolteachers in *The Lion and the Jewel* (first performed in Ibadan, 1959; published 1963) and mocking the clever preachers of upstart prayer-churches who grow fat on the credulity of their parishioners in *The Trials of Brother Jero* (performed 1960; published 1963) and *Jero's Metamorphosis* (1973). But his more serious plays, such as *The Strong Breed* (1963), *Kongi's Harvest* (opened the first Festival of Negro Arts in Dakar, 1966; published 1967),

*The Road* (1965), *From Zia, with Love* (1992), and even the parody *King Baabu* (performed 2001; published 2002), reveal his disregard for African authoritarian leadership and his disillusionment with Nigerian society as a whole.

Other notable plays include *Madmen and Specialists* (performed 1970; published 1971), *Death and the King's Horseman* (1975), and *The Beatification of Area Boy* (1995). In these and Soyinka's other dramas, Western elements are skillfully fused with subject matter and dramatic techniques deeply rooted in Yoruba folklore and religion. Symbolism, flashback, and ingenious plotting contribute to a rich dramatic structure. His best works exhibit humour and fine poetic style as well as a gift for irony and satire and for accurately matching the language of his complex characters to their social position and moral qualities.

From 1960 to 1964 Soyinka was coeditor of *Black Orpheus*, an important literary journal. From 1960 onward he taught literature and drama and headed theatre groups at various Nigerian universities, including those of Ibadan, Ife, and Lagos. After winning the Nobel Prize, he also was sought after as a lecturer, and many of his lectures were published—notably the Reith Lectures of 2004, as *Climate of Fear* (2004).

Though he considered himself primarily a playwright, Soyinka also wrote novels—*The Interpreters* (1965) and *Season of Anomy* (1973)—and several volumes of poetry. The latter include *Idanre, and Other Poems* (1967) and *Poems from Prison* (1969; republished as *A Shuttle in the Crypt*, 1972), published together as *Early Poems* (1998); *Mandela's Earth and Other Poems* (1988); and *Samarkand and Other Markets I Have Known* (2002). His verse is characterized by a precise command of language and a mastery of lyric, dramatic, and meditative poetic forms. He wrote a good deal of *Poems from Prison* while he was jailed in 1967–69 for speaking out against the war brought on by the attempted secession of Biafra from Nigeria. *The Man Died* (1972) is his prose account of his arrest and 22-month imprisonment. Soyinka's principal critical work is *Myth, Literature, and the African World* (1976), a collection of essays in which he examines the role of the artist in the light of Yoruba mythology and symbolism. *Art, Dialogue, and Outrage* (1988) is a work on similar themes of art, culture, and society. He continued to address Africa's ills and Western responsibility in *The Open Sore of a Continent* (1996) and *The Burden of Memory, the Muse of Forgiveness* (1999).

Soyinka was the first black African to be awarded the Nobel Prize for Literature. An autobiography, *Aké: The Years of Childhood*, was published in 1981 and followed by the companion pieces *Ìsarà: A Voyage Around Essay* (1989) and *Ibadan: The Penkelemes Years: A Memoir, 1946–1965* (1994). In 2006 he published another memoir, *You Must Set Forth at Dawn*. In 2005–06 Soyinka served on the Encyclopædia Britannica Editorial Board of Advisors.

Soyinka has long been a proponent of Nigerian democracy. His decades of political activism included periods of imprisonment and exile, and he has founded, headed, or participated in several political groups, including the National Democratic Organization, the National Liberation Council of Nigeria, and Pro-National Conference Organizations (PRONACO). In 2010 Soyinka founded the Democratic Front for a People's Federation and served as chairman of the party.

# ŌE KENZABURŌ

(b. January 31, 1935, Ehime prefecture, Shikoku, Japan)

A Japanese novelist whose works express the disillusionment and rebellion of his post–World War II generation, Ōe Kenzaburō was awarded the Nobel Prize for Literature in 1994.

Ōe came from a family of wealthy landowners, who lost most of their property with the occupation-imposed land reform following the war. He entered the University of Tokyo in 1954, graduating in 1959, and the brilliance of his writing while he was still a student caused him to be hailed the most promising young writer since Mishima Yukio.

Ōe first attracted attention on the literary scene with *Shisha no ogori* (1957; *Lavish Are the Dead*), published in the magazine *Bungakukai*. His literary output was, however, uneven. His first novel, *Memushiri kouchi* (1958; *Nip the Buds, Shoot the Kids*), was highly praised, and he won a major literary award, the Akutagawa Prize, for *Shiiku* (1958; *The Catch*). But his second novel, *Warera no jidai* (1959; "Our Age"), was poorly received, as his contemporaries felt that Ōe was becoming increasingly preoccupied with social and political criticism.

Ōe became deeply involved in the politics of the New Left. The murder in 1960 of Chairman Asanuma Inejirō of the Japanese Socialist Party by a right-wing youth inspired Ōe to write two short stories in 1961, "Sebuntin" ("Seventeen") and "Seiji shōnen shisu" ("A Political Youth Dies"), the latter of which drew heavy criticism from right-wing organizations.

Married in 1960, Ōe entered a further stage of development in his writing when his son was born in 1963 with an abnormality of the skull. This event inspired his finest novel, *Kojinteki-na taiken* (1964; *A Personal Matter*), a darkly humorous account of a new father's struggle to accept the birth of his brain-damaged child. A visit to Hiroshima resulted in the work *Hiroshima nōto* (1965; *Hiroshima Notes*), which deals with the survivors of the atomic bombing of that city. In the early 1970s Ōe's writing, particularly his essays, reflected a growing concern for power politics in the nuclear age and for questions involving the developing world.

Ōe continued to investigate the problems of characters who feel alienated from establishment conformity and the materialism of postwar Japan's consumer-oriented society. Among his later works were the novel *Man'en gannen no futtōbōru* (1967; *The Silent Cry*), a collection of short fiction entitled *Warera no kyōki o ikinobiru michi o oshieyo* (1969; *Teach Us to Outgrow Our Madness*), and the novels *Pinchi rannā chōsho* (1976; *The Pinch Runner Memorandum*) and *Dōjidai gēmu* (1979; "Coeval Games").

The novel *Atarashii hito yo meza meyo* (1983; *Rise Up O Young Men of the New Age!*) is distinguished by a highly sophisticated literary technique and by the author's

frankness in personal confession; it concerns the growing up of a mentally retarded boy and the tension and anxiety he arouses in his family. Ōe's *Jinsei no shinseki* (1989; *An Echo of Heaven*) uses the religious ideology of the American writer Flannery O'Connor as a means to explore the suffering and possible salvation of a woman beset by a number of

*Ōe Kenzaburō receiving the Legion of Honor at the French Embassy, Tokyo, May 22, 2002. The award, instituted by Napoleon Bonaparte, is the highest rank the French government conveys on civilians.* AFP/ Getty Images

personal tragedies. *Chenjiringu* (2000; *The Changeling*) tells the story of a writer who relives his personal history, often in a dreamlike and surreal manner, after he receives a collection of audiotapes from an estranged friend who appears to have recorded his own suicide.

# THOMAS KENEALLY

(b. October 7, 1935, Sydney, Australia)

Thomas Keneally is an Australian writer best known for his historical novels. Keneally's characters are gripped by their historical and personal past, and decent individuals are portrayed at odds with systems of authority.

At age 17 Keneally entered a Roman Catholic seminary, but he left before ordination; the experience influenced his early fiction, including *The Place at Whitton* (1964) and *Three Cheers for the Paraclete* (1968). His reputation as a historical novelist was established with *Bring Larks and Heroes* (1967), about Australia's early years as an English penal colony. *The Chant of Jimmie Blacksmith* (1972; film 1980) won Keneally international acclaim; it is based on the actual story of a half-caste Aboriginal who rebels against white racism by going on a murder spree. *The Great Shame* (1998), a work inspired by his own ancestry, details 80 years of Irish history from the perspective of Irish convicts sent to Australia in the 19th century.

Although Australia figures prominently in much of Keneally's work, his range is broad. His well-received *Gossip from the Forest* (1975) examines the World War I armistice through the eyes of a thoughtful, humane German negotiator. He is also praised for his treatment of the American Civil War in *Confederates* (1979). His later fiction includes *A Family Madness* (1985), *To Asmara* (1989), *Flying Hero Class* (1991), *Woman of the Inner Sea* (1992), *Jacko* (1993), *Homebush Boy* (1995), *Bettany's Book* (2000), *The Tyrant's Novel* (2003), *The Widow and Her Hero* (2007), and *The Daughters of Mars* (2012).

Keneally's best-known work, *Schindler's Ark* (1982; also published as *Schindler's List*; film 1993), tells the true story of Oskar Schindler, a German industrialist who saved more than 1,300 Jews from the Nazis. Like many of Keneally's protagonists, Schindler is a rather ordinary man who acts in accord with his conscience despite the evil around him. Controversy surrounded the book's receipt of the Booker Prize for fiction; detractors argued that the work was mere historical reporting.

# ISMAIL KADARE

(b. January 28, 1936, Gjirokastër, Albania)

Ismail Kadare is an Albanian novelist and poet whose work, which explores his country's history and culture, has gained an international readership.

Kadare, whose father was a post office employee, attended the University of Tirana. He later went to Moscow to study at the Gorky Institute of World Literature. Upon returning to Albania in 1960, he worked as a journalist and then embarked on a literary career. He endured periods of controversy in his native country during the long rule of Enver Hoxha, whose dictatorial government Kadare alternately praised and criticized. In 1990, feeling threatened by the government and fearing arrest, Kadare defected to France.

Kadare first attracted attention in Albania as a poet, but it was his prose works that brought him worldwide fame. *Gjenerali i ushtrisë së vdekur* (1963; *The General of the Dead Army*), his best-known novel, was his first to achieve an international audience. It tells the story of an Italian general on a grim mission to find and return to Italy the remains of his country's soldiers who died in Albania during World War II. Among Kadare's other novels dealing with Albanian history is *Kështjella* (1970; *The Castle* or *The Siege*), a recounting of the armed resistance of the Albanian people against the Ottoman Turks in the 15th century. The same theme of resistance, but in a political context, recurs in *Dimri i madh* (1977; "The Great Winter"), which depicts the events that produced the break between Albania and the Soviet Union in 1961.

The novel *Ura me tri harqe* (1978; *The Three-Arched Bridge*), set in medieval Albania, received wide critical acclaim. Kadare's subsequent works of fiction include *Nëpunësi i pallatit të ëndrrave* (1981; *The Palace of Dreams*), *Dosja H.* (1990; *The File on H.*), and *Piramida* (1995; *The Pyramid*). *Tri këngë zie për kosovën* (1999; *Three Elegies for Kosovo*, or *Elegy for Kosovo*) comprises three stories about a 14th-century battle between Balkan leaders and the Ottoman Empire. *Lulet e ftohta të marsit* (2000; *Spring Flowers, Spring Frost*) tells the story of a painter in post-communist Albania, and *Pasardhësi* (2003; *The Successor*) examines the fate of one of Hoxha's presumed successors. In *Aksidenti* (2010; *The Accident*), a researcher tries to shed light on the mysterious backgrounds of a couple killed in a car accident.

Among Kadare's nonfiction volumes are *Kronikë në gur* (1971; *Chronicle in Stone*), a work that is as much about his childhood in wartime Albania as about the town of Gjirokastër itself, and *Eskili, ky humbës i madh* (1988; "Aeschylus, This Great Loser"), which examines the affinity between Albanian and Greek cultures from antiquity to modern times. *Nga një dhjetor në tjetrin* (1991; "From

One December to Another"; Eng. trans. *Albanian Spring: The Anatomy of Tyranny*) expresses his views on Albanian politics and government between 1944 and 1990.

The themes of Kadare's works, which are often semi-autobiographical, include Albanian history, politics, and folklore, blood-feud tradition, and ethnicity. His fiction has elements of romanticism, realism, and surrealism. He has been likened to the Russian poet Yevgeny Yevtushenko for dissenting from state-imposed guidelines for literature and to the Colombian novelist Gabriel García Márquez, in part because of their common interest in the grotesque and the surreal. Kadare was granted membership in the French Academy in 1996 and was later made an officer of the French Legion of Honour. In 2005 he became the first winner of the Man Booker International Prize.

# GEORGES PEREC

(b. March 7, 1936, Paris, France — d. March 3, 1982, Ivry-sur-Seine)

The French writer Georges Perec is often called the greatest innovator of form of his generation.

Perec was orphaned at an early age: his father was killed in action in World War II, and his mother died in a concentration camp. He was reared by an aunt and uncle and eventually attended the Sorbonne for several years. His best-selling first novel, *Les Choses: une histoire des années soixante* (1965; *Things: A Story of the Sixties*), concerns a young Parisian couple whose personalities are consumed by their material goods. In 1967 he joined the Ouvroir de Littérature Potentielle (Workshop of Potential Literature). Known in short as Oulipo, the group dedicated itself to

*Georges Perec, 1982.* Louis Monier/Gamma-Rapho/Getty Images

the pursuit of new forms for literature and the revival of old ones, and it had a profound impact on the direction of Perec's writing.

Perec's novel *La Disparition* (1969; *A Void*) was written entirely without using the letter *e*, as was its translation. A companion piece of sorts appeared in 1972 with the novella *Les Revenentes* ("The Ghosts"; published in English as *The Exeter Text* [1996]), in which every word has only *e* as its vowel. *W; ou, le souvenir d'enfance* (1975; *W; or, The Memory of Childhood*) is considered a masterpiece of innovative autobiography, using alternating chapters to tell two stories that ultimately converge. By far his most ambitious and most critically acclaimed novel is *La Vie: mode d'emploi* (1978; *Life: A User's Manual*), which describes each unit in a large Parisian apartment building and relates the stories of its inhabitants.

Perec's work in other areas includes a highly acclaimed 1979 television film about Ellis Island. *Je me souviens* (1978; "I Remember"), a book of about 480 sentences all beginning with the phrase "I remember" and recording memories of life in the 1950s, was adapted for the stage. A number of his other audacious formal experiments appeared in collections from members of Oulipo, including a 399-line poem in which each line is an anagram of the poem's title and a text that consists solely of a 5,000-letter palindrome. At his death, Perec was working on a detective novel, which, edited by Harry Mathews and Jacques Roubaud, was published as *53 Jours* (1989; *53 Days*). A collection of essays, *Penser/Classer* (1985; "To Think, to Classify"), was published posthumously, as was *Art et la manière d'aborder son chef de service pour lui demander une augmentation* (2008; *The Art and Craft of Approaching Your Head of Department to Submit a Request for a Raise*), a novella made up of one long sentence that Perec wrote in an effort to mimic a computer's method of interacting with data.

# MARIO VARGAS LLOSA

(b. March 28, 1936, Arequipa, Peru)

Jorge Mario Pedro Vargas Llosa is a Peruvian writer whose commitment to social change is evident in his novels, plays, and essays. In 1990 he was an unsuccessful candidate for president of Peru. Vargas Llosa was awarded the 2010 Nobel Prize in Literature "for his cartography of structures of power and his trenchant images of the individual's resistance, revolt, and defeat."

Vargas Llosa received his early education in Cochabamba, Bolivia, where his grandfather was the Peruvian consul. He attended a series of schools in Peru before entering a military school, Leoncio Prado, in Lima in 1950; he later attended the University of San Marcos in Lima. His first published work was *La huida del Inca* (1952; "The Escape of the Inca"), a three-act play. Thereafter his stories began to appear in Peruvian literary reviews, and he coedited *Cuadernos de composición* (1956–57; "Composition Books") and *Literatura* (1958–59). He worked as a journalist and broadcaster and attended the University of Madrid. In 1959 he moved to Paris, where he lived until 1966 in a Latin American expatriate community that included Argentine Julio Cortázar and Chilean Jorge Edwards. He later set his novel *Travesuras de la niña mala* (2006; *The Bad Girl*) in Paris during this period, its plot a reflection of Vargas Llosa's lifelong appreciation of Gustave Flaubert's *Madame Bovary* (1857).

Vargas Llosa's first novel, *La ciudad y los perros* (1963; "The City and the Dogs," filmed in Spanish, 1985; Eng. trans. *The Time of the Hero*), was widely acclaimed. Translated into more than a dozen languages, this novel, set in the Leoncio Prado, describes adolescents striving for survival in a hostile and violent environment. The corruption of the military school reflects the larger malaise afflicting Peru. The book was filmed twice, in Spanish (1985) and in Russian (1986), the second time as *Yaguar*.

The novel *La casa verde* (1966; *The Green House*), set in the Peruvian jungle, combines mythical, popular, and heroic elements to capture the sordid, tragic, and fragmented reality of its characters. *Los jefes* (1967; *The Cubs and Other Stories*, filmed as *The Cubs*, 1973) is a psychoanalytic portrayal of an adolescent who has been accidentally castrated. *Conversación en la catedral* (1969; *Conversation in the Cathedral*) deals with Manuel Odría's regime (1948–56). The novel *Pantaleón y las visitadoras* (1973; "Pantaleón and the Visitors," filmed in Spanish, 1975; Eng. trans. *Captain Pantoja and the Special Services*, film 2000) is a satire of the Peruvian military and religious fanaticism. His semiautobiographical novel *La tía Julia y el escribidor* (1977; *Aunt Julia and the Scriptwriter*, filmed 1990 as *Tune in Tomorrow*) combines two distinct narrative points of view to produce a contrapuntal effect.

Vargas Llosa also wrote a critical study of the fiction of Gabriel García Márquez in *García Márquez: Historia de un deicidio* (1971; "García Márquez: Story of a God-Killer"), a study of Gustave Flaubert in *La orgía perpetua: Flaubert y "Madame Bovary"* (1975; *The Perpetual Orgy: Flaubert and Madame Bovary*), and a study of the works of Jean-Paul Sartre and Albert Camus in *Entre Sartre y Camus* (1981; "Between Sartre and Camus").

After living three years in London, he was a writer-in-residence at Washington State University in 1969. In 1970 he settled in Barcelona. He returned to Lima in 1974 and lectured and taught widely throughout the world. A collection of his critical essays in English translation was published in 1978. *La guerra del fin del mundo* (1981; *The War of the End of the World*), an account of the 19th-century political conflicts in Brazil, became a best-seller in Spanish-speaking countries. Three of his plays—*La señorita de Tacna* (1981; *The Young Lady of Tacna*), *Kathie y el hipopotamo* (1983; *Kathie and the Hippopotamus*), and *La chunga* (1986; "The Jest"; Eng. trans. *La chunga*)—were published in *Three Plays* (1990).

In 1990 Vargas Llosa lost his bid for the presidency of Peru in a runoff against Alberto Fujimori, an agricultural engineer and the son of Japanese immigrants. Vargas Llosa wrote about this experience in *El pez en el agua: memorias* (1993; *A Fish in the Water: A Memoir*). He became a citizen of Spain in 1993 and was awarded the Cervantes Prize in 1994. Despite his new nationality, he continued to write about Peru in such novels as *Los cuadernos de don Rigoberto* (1997; *The Notebooks of Don Rigoberto*). His later works include the novels *La fiesta del chivo* (2000; *The Feast of the Goat*, film 2005), *El paraíso en la otra esquina* (2003; *The Way to Paradise*), *Travesuras de la niña mala* (2006; *The Bad Girl*), and *El sueño del celta* (2010; *The Dream of the Celt*), as well as the nonfiction *Cartas a un joven novelista* (1997; *Letters to a Young Novelist*), *El lenguaje de la pasión* (2001; *The Language of Passion*), and *La civilización del espectáculo* (2012; "The Civilization of Entertainment").

# DON DELILLO

(b. November 20, 1936, New York, New York, U.S.)

The American novelist Don DeLillo is a writer of postmodernist works that portray the anomie of an America cosseted by material excess and stupefied by empty mass culture and politics.

After his graduation from Fordham University, New York City (1958), DeLillo worked for several years as a copywriter at an advertising agency. DeLillo's first novel, *Americana* (1971), is the story of a network television executive in search of the "real" America. It was followed by *End Zone* (1972) and *Great Jones Street* (1973). *Ratner's Star* (1976) attracted critical attention with its baroque comic sense and verbal facility.

Beginning with *Players* (1977), DeLillo's vision turned darker, and his characters became more willful in their destructiveness and ignorance. Critics found little to like in the novel's protagonists but much to admire in DeLillo's elliptical prose. The thrillers *Running Dog* (1978) and *The Names* (1982), which was set mostly in Greece, followed. *White Noise* (1985), which won the National Book Award for fiction, tells of a professor of Hitler studies who is exposed to an "airborne toxic event"; he discovers that his wife is taking an experimental substance said to combat the fear of death, and he vows to obtain the drug for himself at any cost. In *Libra* (1988) DeLillo presented a fictional portrayal of Lee Harvey Oswald, the assassin of Pres. John F. Kennedy. *Mao II* (1991) opens with a mass wedding officiated by cult leader Sun Myung Moon and tells the story of a reclusive writer who becomes enmeshed in a world of political violence.

DeLillo received significant acclaim for the sprawling novel *Underworld* (1997), which provides a commentary on American history and culture in the Cold War era, in part by tracing the imagined journeys of the baseball that New York Giants outfielder Bobby Thomson hit for a pennant-winning home run in 1951. DeLillo's subsequent works of fiction include *The Body Artist* (2001), about the supernatural experiences of a recent widow; *Cosmopolis* (2003; film 2012), set largely in a billionaire's limousine as it moves across Manhattan; *Falling Man* (2007), which tells the story of a survivor of the September 11 attacks in 2001; and *Point Omega* (2010), a meditation on time.

In addition to his novels, DeLillo wrote several plays, the screenplay to the independent film *Game 6* (2005), and the short-story collection *The Angel Esmeralda: Nine Stories* (2011).

# THOMAS PYNCHON

(b. May 8, 1937, Glen Cove, Long Island, New York, U.S.)

T homas Pynchon is an American novelist and short-story writer whose works combine black humour and fantasy to depict human alienation in the chaos of modern society.

After earning his B.A. in English from Cornell University in 1958, Pynchon spent a year in Greenwich Village writing short stories and working on a novel. In 1960 he was hired as a technical writer for Boeing Aircraft Corporation in Seattle. Two years later he decided to leave the company and write full-time. In 1963 Pynchon won the Faulkner Foundation Award for his first novel, *V.* (1963), a whimsical, cynically absurd tale of a middle-aged Englishman's search for "V," an elusive, supernatural adventuress appearing in various guises at critical periods in European history. In his next book, *The Crying of Lot 49* (1966), Pynchon described a woman's strange quest to discover the mysterious, conspiratorial Tristero System in a futuristic world of closed societies. The novel serves as a condemnation of modern industrialization.

Pynchon's *Gravity's Rainbow* (1973) is a tour de force in 20th-century literature. In exploring the dilemmas of human beings in the modern world, the story, which is set in an area of post-World War II Germany called "the

Zone," centres on the wanderings of an American soldier who is one of many odd characters looking for a secret V-2 rocket that will supposedly break through the Earth's gravitational barrier when launched. The narrative is filled with descriptions of obsessive and paranoid fantasies, ridiculous and grotesque imagery, and esoteric mathematical and scientific language. For his efforts Pynchon received the National Book Award, and many critics deemed *Gravity's Rainbow* a visionary, apocalyptic masterpiece. Pynchon's next novel, *Vineland*—which begins in 1984 in California—was not published until 1990. Two vast, complex historical novels followed: in *Mason & Dixon* (1997), set in the 18th century, Pynchon took the English surveyors Charles Mason and Jeremiah Dixon as his subject, while *Against the Day* (2006) moves from the World's Columbian Exposition of 1893 through World War I. *Inherent Vice* (2009), Pynchon's rambling take on the detective novel, returns to the California counterculture milieu of *Vineland*.

Of his few short stories, most notable are "Entropy" (1960), a neatly structured tale in which Pynchon first uses extensive technical language and scientific metaphors, and "The Secret Integration" (1964), a story in which Pynchon explores small-town bigotry and racism. The collection *Slow Learner* (1984) contains "The Secret Integration."

# SIR TOM STOPPARD

(b. July 3, 1937, Zlín, Czechoslovakia [now in the Czech Republic])

The Czech-born British playwright Sir Tom Stoppard (born Tomas Straussler) created work that is marked by verbal brilliance, ingenious action, and structural dexterity.

His father was working in Singapore in 1938/39. After the Japanese invasion, his father stayed on (and was killed), but Stoppard's mother and her two sons escaped to India, where in 1946 she married a British officer, Kenneth Stoppard. Soon afterward the family went to live in England. Tom Stoppard (he had assumed his stepfather's surname) quit school and started his career as a journalist in Bristol in 1954. He began to write plays in 1960 after moving to London.

His first play, *A Walk on the Water* (1960), was televised in 1963; the stage version, with some additions and the new title *Enter a Free Man*, reached London in 1968. His play *Rosencrantz and Guildenstern Are Dead* (1964–65) was performed at the Edinburgh Festival in 1966. That same year his only novel, *Lord Malquist & Mr. Moon*, was published. His play was the greater success: it entered the repertory of Britain's National Theatre in 1967 and rapidly became internationally renowned. The irony and brilliance of this work derive from Stoppard's placing two minor characters of Shakespeare's *Hamlet* into the centre of the dramatic action.

A number of successes followed. Among the most notable stage plays were *The Real Inspector Hound* (1968), *Jumpers* (1972), *Travesties* (1974), *Every Good Boy Deserves Favour* (1978), *Night and Day* (1978), *Undiscovered Country* (1980, adapted from a play by Arthur Schnitzler), and *On the Razzle* (1981, adapted from a play by Johann Nestroy). *The Real Thing* (1982), Stoppard's first romantic comedy, deals with art and reality and features a playwright as a protagonist. *Arcadia*, which juxtaposes 19th-century Romanticism and 20th-century chaos theory and is set in a Derbyshire country house, premiered in 1993, and *The Invention of Love*, about A.E. Housman, was first staged in 1997. The trilogy *The Coast of Utopia* (*Voyage*, *Shipwreck*, and *Salvage*), first performed in 2002, explores the lives and debates of a circle of 19th-century Russian émigré intellectuals. *Rock 'n' Roll* (2006) jumps between England and Czechoslovakia during the period 1968–90.

Stoppard wrote a number of radio plays, including *In the Native State* (1991), which was reworked as the stage play *Indian Ink* (1995). He also wrote a number of notable television plays, such as *Professional Foul* (1977). Among his screenplays are *The Romantic Englishwoman* (1975), *Despair* (1978), and *Brazil* (1985). He directed the film version of *Rosencrantz and Guildenstern Are Dead* (1991), for which he also wrote the screenplay. In 1998 the screenplay for *Shakespeare in Love*, cowritten by Stoppard and Marc Norman, won an Academy Award. Stoppard also adapted the French screenplay for the English-language film *Vatel* (2000), about a 17th-century chef, and wrote the screenplay for *Enigma* (2001), which chronicles the English effort to break the German Enigma code. He later penned the script for a lavish miniseries (2012) based on novelist Ford Madox Ford's tetralogy *Parade's End* (1924–28), which centres on the decay of the Edwardian milieu during and after World War I.

His numerous other honours include the Japan Art Association's Praemium Imperiale prize for theatre/film (2009). Stoppard was knighted in 1997.

# Hunter S. Thompson

(b. July 18, 1937, Louisville, Kentucky, U.S.—
d. February 20, 2005, Woody Creek, Colorado)

Hunter Stockton Thompson was an American journalist and author who created the genre known as gonzo journalism, a highly personal style of reporting that made Thompson a counterculture icon.

Thompson, who had a number of run-ins with the law as a young man, joined the U.S. Air Force in 1956. He served as a sports editor for a base newspaper and continued his journalism career after being discharged in 1957. In the following years he also wrote two autobiographical novels, but both were initially rejected by publishing houses; *The Rum Diary* eventually saw publication in 1998 (film 2011). In 1965 Thompson infiltrated the Hell's Angels motorcycle gang, an experience he recounted in *Hell's Angels* (1967). The book led to writing assignments for *Esquire, Harper's, Rolling Stone*, and other magazines. In addition to his irreverent political and cultural criticism, Thompson also began to attract attention for his larger-than-life persona, which was highlighted by drug- and alcohol-fueled adventures and a distaste for authority.

In 1970 Thompson introduced his subjective style of reporting with the article *The Kentucky Derby Is Decadent and Depraved,* in which he was a central part of the story. A 1971 assignment for *Sports Illustrated* to cover a motorcycle race in Nevada resulted in perhaps his best-known work, *Fear and Loathing in Las Vegas: A Savage Journey to the Heart of the American Dream* (1972; film 1998), which became a contemporary classic and established the genre of gonzo journalism. First serialized in *Rolling Stone*, it documents the drug-addled road trip taken by Thompson (as his alter ego Raoul Duke) and his lawyer (Dr. Gonzo) while also discussing the end of the 1960s counterculture. The book featured frenetic artwork by Ralph Steadman, who illustrated many of Thompson's works. In *Fear and Loathing: On the Campaign Trail '72* (1973), Thompson chronicled the 1972 presidential campaigns of George McGovern and Richard Nixon. Later works include *The Great Shark Hunt* (1979), *Better Than Sex* (1994), and *Kingdom of Fear* (2003). Thompson died of a self-inflicted gunshot wound.

# ℵGUGI WA THIONG'O

(b. January 5, 1938, Limuru, Kenya)

Ngugi wa Thiong'o is East Africa's leading novelist, whose popular *Weep Not, Child* (1964) was the first major novel in English by an East African. As he became sensitized to the effects of colonialism in Africa, he adopted his traditional name and wrote in the Bantu language of Kenya's Kikuyu people.

Born James Thiong'o Ngugi, he received bachelor's degrees from Makerere University, Kampala, Uganda, in 1963 and from Leeds University, Yorkshire, England, in 1964. After doing graduate work at Leeds, he served as a lecturer in English at University College, Nairobi, Kenya, and as a visiting professor of English at Northwestern University, Evanston, Illinois, U.S. From 1972 to 1977 he was senior lecturer and chairman of the department of literature at the University of Nairobi.

The prizewinning *Weep Not, Child* is the story of a Kikuyu family drawn into the struggle for Kenyan independence during the state of emergency and the Mau Mau rebellion. *A Grain of Wheat* (1967), generally held to be artistically more mature, focuses on the many social, moral, and racial issues of the struggle for independence and its aftermath. A third novel, *The River Between* (1965), which was actually written before the others, tells of lovers kept apart by the conflict between Christianity and traditional ways and beliefs and suggests that efforts to reunite a culturally divided community by means of Western education are doomed to failure. *Petals of Blood* (1977) deals with social and economic problems in East Africa after independence, particularly the continued exploitation of peasants and workers by foreign business interests and a greedy indigenous bourgeoisie. In a novel written in Kikuyu and English versions, *Caitaani Mutharaba-ini* (1980; *Devil on the Cross*), Ngugi presented these ideas in an allegorical form. Written in a manner meant to recall traditional ballad singers, the novel is a partly realistic, partly fantastical account of a meeting between the Devil and various villains who exploit the poor. *Mūrogi was Kagogo* (2004; *Wizard of the Crow*) brings the dual lenses of fantasy and satire to bear upon the legacy of colonialism not only as it is perpetuated by a native dictatorship but also as it is ingrained in an ostensibly decolonized culture itself.

The *Black Hermit* (1968; produced 1962) was the first of several plays, of which *The Trial of Dedan Kimathi* (1976; produced 1974), cowritten with Micere Githae Mugo, is considered by some critics to be his best. He was also coauthor, with Ngugi wa Mirii, of a play first written in Kikuyu, *Ngaahika Ndeenda* (1977; *I Will Marry When I Want*), the performance of which led to his detention for a year without trial by the Kenyan government. (His book *Detained: A Writer's Prison Diary*, which was published in 1981, describes his ordeal.) The play attacks capitalism, religious hypocrisy, and corruption among the new economic elite of Kenya. *Matigari ma Njiruungi* (1986; *Matigari*) is a novel in the same vein.

Ngugi presented his ideas on literature, culture, and politics in numerous essays and lectures, which were collected in *Homecoming* (1972), *Writers in Politics* (1981), *Barrel of a Pen* (1983), *Moving the Centre* (1993), and *Penpoints, Gunpoints, and Dreams* (1998). In *Decolonising the Mind: The Politics of Language in African Literature* (1986), Ngugi argued for African-language literature as the only authentic voice for Africans and stated his own intention of writing only in Kikuyu or Kiswahili from that point on. Such works earned him a reputation as one of Africa's most articulate social critics. After a long exile from Kenya, Ngugi returned in 2004 with his wife to promote *Mŭrogi was Kagogo*. Several weeks later they were brutally assaulted in their home; the attack was believed by some to be politically motivated. After their recovery, the couple continued to publicize the book abroad. In 2010 Ngugi published *Dreams in a Time of War*, a memoir of his childhood in Kenya.

# RAYMOND CARVER

(b. May 25, 1938, Clatskanie, Oregon, U.S.—
d. August 2, 1988, Port Angeles, Washington)

Raymond Carver was an American short-story writer and poet whose realistic writings about the working poor mirrored his own life.

Carver was the son of a sawmill worker. He married a year after finishing high school and supported his wife and two children by working as a janitor, gas-station attendant, and delivery man. He became seriously interested in a writing career after taking a creative-writing course at Chico State College (now California State University, Chico) in 1958. His short stories began to appear in magazines while he studied at Humboldt State College (now Humboldt State University) in Arcata, California (B.A., 1963). Carver's first success as a writer came in 1967 with the story "Will You Please Be Quiet, Please?," and he began writing full-time after losing his job as a textbook editor in 1970. The highly successful short-story collection *Will You Please Be Quiet, Please?* (1976) established his reputation.

Carver began drinking heavily in 1967 and was repeatedly hospitalized for alcoholism in the 1970s, while continuing to turn out short stories. After conquering his drinking problem in the late 1970s, he taught for several years at the University of Texas at El Paso and at Syracuse University, and in 1983 he won a literary award whose generous annual stipend freed him to again concentrate on his writing full-time. His later short-story collections were *What We Talk About When We Talk About Love* (1981), *Cathedral* (1984), and *Where I'm Calling From* (1988). While his short stories were what made his critical reputation, he was also an accomplished poet in the realist tradition of Robert Frost. Carver's poetry collections include *At Night the Salmon Move* (1976), *Where Water Comes Together with Other Water* (1985), and *Ultramarine* (1986). He died of lung cancer at age 50.

In his short stories Carver chronicled the everyday lives and problems of the working poor in the Pacific Northwest. His blue-collar characters are crushed by broken marriages, financial problems, and failed careers, but they are often unable to understand or even articulate their own anguish. Carver's stripped-down, minimalist prose style is remarkable for its honesty and power. He is credited with helping revitalize the genre of the English-language short story in the late 20th century.

However, controversy arose over the nature of Carver's writing—and even his lasting literary reputation—in the early 21st century. It was revealed that his long-time editor, Gordon Lish, had drastically changed many of Carver's early stories. While Lish's significant involvement in Carver's writing had long been suspected, the extent of his editing became public knowledge when, in 2007, Carver's widow, the poet Tess Gallagher, announced that she was seeking to publish the original versions of the stories in *What We Talk About When We Talk About Love* (which appeared as *Beginners* in the U.K. and also as part of the Library of America's *Raymond Carver: Collected Stories* [both 2009]). Lish was shown to have changed characters' names, cut the length of many stories (over 75 percent of the text in two cases), and altered the endings of some stories. However, most of Carver's famously terse sentences were his own, as was the hallmark bleak working-class milieu of the short stories.

# *JOYCE CAROL OATES*

(b. June 16, 1938, Lockport, New York, U.S.)

The American novelist, short-story writer, and essayist Joyce Carol Oates is noted for her vast literary output in a variety of styles and genres. Particularly effective are her depictions of violence and evil in modern society.

Oates was born the daughter of a tool-and-die designer. She studied English at Syracuse University (B.A., 1960) and the University of Wisconsin (M.A., 1961). She taught English at the University of Detroit from 1961 to 1967 and at the University of Windsor in Ontario, Canada, from 1967 to 1978. From 1978 she taught at Princeton University. In 1961 she married Raymond J. Smith (died 2008), a fellow English student who himself became a professor and an editor. With him she published *The Ontario Review*, a literary magazine.

Early in her career Oates contributed short stories to a number of magazines and reviews, including the *Prairie Schooner*, *Literary Review*, *Southwest Review*, and *Epoch*, and in 1963 she published her first collection of short stories, *By the North Gate*. Her first novel, *With Shuddering Fall*, appeared in 1964 and was followed by a second short-story collection, *Upon the Sweeping Flood* (1965). She wrote prolifically thereafter, averaging about two books per year.

Her notable fiction works include *A Garden of Earthly Delights* (1967), *them* (1969; winner of a National Book Award), *Do with Me What You Will* (1973), *Black Water* (1992), *Foxfire: Confessions of a Girl Gang* (1993), *Zombie* (1995), *We Were the Mulvaneys* (1996), *Broke Heart Blues* (1999), *The Falls* (2004), *My Sister, My Love: The Intimate Story of Skyler Rampike* (2008), and *Mudwoman* (2012). Her forays into young adult fiction included *Big Mouth & Ugly Girl* (2002) and *Two or Three Things I Forgot to Tell You* (2012).

In 2001 she published the short-story collection *Faithless: Tales of Transgression*, "richly various" tales of sin. An extensive and mainly retrospective volume of her stories, *High Lonesome: New & Selected Stories, 1966–2006*, was published in 2006. *Wild Nights!: Stories About the Last Days of Poe, Dickinson, Twain, James, and Hemingway* (2008) featured fictionalized accounts of the final days of various iconic American writers. The stories in *Black Dahlia and White Rose* (2012) were threaded with menace and violence; the title piece fictionalized the sensational 1947 Black Dahlia murder in Los Angeles.

Oates also wrote mysteries (under the pseudonyms Rosamond Smith and Lauren Kelly), plays, essays, poetry, and literary criticism. Essays, reviews, and other prose pieces are included in *Where I've Been, and Where I'm Going* (1999) and *In Rough Country* (2010). In 2011 Oates published the memoir *A Widow's Story*, in which she mourned her husband's death.

Oates's novels encompass a variety of historical settings and literary genres. She typically portrays American individuals whose intensely experienced and obsessive lives end in bloodshed and self-destruction owing to larger forces beyond their control. Her books blend a realistic treatment of everyday life with horrific and even sensational depictions of violence.

# LES MURRAY

(b. October 17, 1938, Nabiac, New South Wales, Australia)

Les Murray is an Australian poet and essayist who in such meditative, lyrical poems as "Noonday Axeman" and "Sydney and the Bush" captured Australia's psychic and rural landscape as well as its mythic elements.

Murray grew up on a dairy farm and graduated from the University of Sydney (B.A., 1969). He worked as a writer in residence at several universities throughout the world and served as editor of *Poetry Australia* from 1973 to 1979. He also compiled and edited the *New Oxford Book of Australian Verse* (1986).

Murray's poetry celebrates a hoped-for fusion of the Aboriginal (which he called the "senior culture"), the rural, and the urban. The poem "The Buladelah-Taree Holiday Song Cycle," in the collection *Ethnic Radio* (1977), reflects his identification with Australia's Aboriginals; it uses Aboriginal narrative style to describe vacationing Australians. *The Boys Who Stole the Funeral* (1979) is a sequence of 140 sonnets about a pair of boys who surreptitiously remove a man's body from a Sydney funeral home for burial in his native Outback. Murray's poetry collections *Dog Fox Field* (1990), *The Rabbiter's Bounty* (1991), and *Translations from the Natural World* (1992) won him praise for his versatility and evocative descriptions of the Outback.

*Subhuman Redneck Poems* (1996) brings to the fore Murray's ever-present disdain for Western intellectual attitudes; many critics found his satirical assaults unbalanced. In *Fredy Neptune* (1999) Murray presented a verse narrative of the misfortunes of a German Australian sailor during World War I. Later collections such as *Learning Human, Selected Poems* (2001) and *The Biplane Houses* (2005) use forms ranging from folk ballads to limericks to express his appreciation for the natural world. His 2010 collection, *Taller When Prone*, celebrates ordinary Australians, often with a healthy dose of humour. In 2002 he published *The Full Dress*, which pairs poems with selections of art from the National Gallery of Australia, and *Poems the Size of Photographs*, a collection of short-form verse.

In addition to poetry, Murray also wrote several essay collections. *Peasant Mandarin* (1978) champions the antielitist vitality of "Australocentrism," at the same time demonstrating a high regard for a classical education and its traditions. The essays in *A Working Forest* (1997) indict academia for making poetry inaccessible to the average reader and give vent to Murray's dislike of modern poetic forms. Murray also presented the work of five leading but little-known Australian poets in *Fivefathers* (1995).

# SEAMUS HEANEY

(b. April 13, 1939, near Castledàwson, County Londonderry, Northern Ireland)

Seamus Heaney is an Irish poet whose work is notable for its evocation of Irish rural life and events in Irish history as well as for its allusions to Irish myth. He received the Nobel Prize for Literature in 1995.

After graduating from Queen's University, Belfast (B.A., 1961), Heaney taught secondary school for a year and then lectured in colleges and universities in Belfast and Dublin. He became a member of the Field Day Theatre Company in 1980, soon after its founding by playwright Brian Friel and actor Stephen Rea. In 1982 he joined the faculty of Harvard University as visiting professor and, in 1985, became full professor—a post he retained while teaching at the University of Oxford (1989–94).

Heaney's first poetry collection was the prizewinning *Death of a Naturalist* (1966). In this book and *Door into the Dark* (1969), he wrote in a traditional style about a passing way of life—that of domestic rural life in Northern Ireland. In *Wintering Out* (1972) and *North* (1975), he began to encompass such subjects as the violence in Northern Ireland and contemporary Irish experience, though he continued to view his subjects through a mythic and mystical filter. Among the later volumes that reflect Heaney's honed and deceptively simple style are *Field Work* (1979), *Station Island* (1984), *The Haw Lantern* (1987), and *Seeing Things* (1991). *The Spirit Level* (1996) concerns the notion of centredness and balance in both the natural and the spiritual senses. His *Opened Ground: Selected Poems, 1966–1996* was published in 1998. In *Electric Light* (2001) and *District and Circle* (2006), he returned to the Ireland of his youth. The poetry in *Human Chain* (2010) reflects on death, loss, regret, and memory.

Heaney wrote essays on poetry and on poets such as William Wordsworth, Gerard Manley Hopkins, and Elizabeth Bishop. Some of these essays have appeared in *Preoccupations: Selected Prose, 1968–1978* (1980) and *Finders Keepers: Selected Prose, 1971–2001* (2002). A collection of his lectures at Oxford was published as *The Redress of Poetry* (1995).

Heaney also produced translations, including *The Cure at Troy* (1991), which is Heaney's version of Sophocles's *Philoctetes*, and *The Midnight Verdict* (1993), which contains selections from Ovid's *Metamorphoses* and from *Cúirt an mheán oíche* (*The Midnight Court*), a work by the 18th-century Irish writer Brian Merriman. Heaney's translation of the Old English epic poem *Beowulf* (1999) became an unexpected international best-seller, while his *The Burial at Thebes* (2004) gave Sophocles' *Antigone* contemporary relevance.

# ᴇAMOS OZ

(b. May 4, 1939, Jerusalem)

The Israeli novelist, short-story writer, and essayist Amos Oz has produced works in which Israeli society is unapologetically scrutinized.

Born Amos Klausner, he was educated at the Hebrew University of Jerusalem and at the University of Oxford. He served in the Israeli army (1957–60, 1967, and 1973). After the Six-Day War in 1967, he became active in the Israeli peace movement and with organizations that advocated a two-state solution to the Israeli-Palestinian conflict. In addition to writing, he worked as a part-time schoolteacher and labourer.

Oz's symbolic, poetic novels reflect the splits and strains in Israeli culture. Locked in conflict are the traditions of intellect and the demands of the flesh, reality and fantasy, rural Zionism and the longing for European urbanity, and the values of the founding settlers and the perceptions of their skeptical offspring. Oz felt himself unable to share the optimistic outlook and ideological certainties of Israel's founding generation, and his writings present an ironic view of life in Israel.

His works of fiction include *Artsot ha-tan* (1965; *Where the Jackals Howl, and Other Stories*), *Mikha'el sheli* (1968; *My Michael*), *La-ga'at ba-mayim, la-ga'at ba-ruaḥ* (1973; *Touch the Water, Touch the Wind*), *Kufsah sheḥora* (1987; *Black Box*), and *Matsav ha-shelishi* (1991; *The Third State*). *Oto ha-yam* (1999; *The Same Sea*) is a novel in verse. The memoir *Sipur*

*Amos Oz, 2005.* © AP Images

'al ahavah ve-ḥoshekh (2002; *A Tale of Love and Darkness*) drew wide critical acclaim.

Oz was among the editors of *Siaḥ loḥamim* (1968; *The Seventh Day*), a collection of soldiers' reflections on the Six-Day War. His political essays are collected in such volumes as *Be-or ha-tekhelet ha-'azah* (1979; *Under This Blazing Light*) and *Be-'etsem yesh kan shete milḥamot* (2002; "But These Are Two Different Wars"). *How to Cure a Fanatic* (2006) is an English-language collection of two essays by Oz and an interview with him.

# MARGARET ATWOOD

(b. November 18, 1939, Ottawa, Ontario, Canada)

The Canadian writer Margaret Atwood is perhaps best known for her prose fiction and for her feminist perspective.

As an adolescent, Atwood divided her time between Toronto, her family's primary residence, and the sparsely settled bush country in northern Canada, where her father, an entomologist, conducted research. She began writing at age five and resumed her efforts, more seriously, a decade later. After completing her university studies at Victoria College at the University of Toronto, Atwood earned a master's degree in English literature from Radcliffe College, Cambridge, Massachusetts, in 1962.

In her early poetry collections, *Double Persephone* (1961), *The Circle Game* (1964, revised in 1966), and *The Animals in That Country* (1968), Atwood ponders human behaviour, celebrates the natural world, and condemns materialism. Role reversal and new beginnings are recurrent themes in her novels, all of them centred on women seeking their relationship to the world and the individuals around them. *The Handmaid's Tale* (1985; film 1990) is constructed around the written record of a woman living in sexual slavery in a repressive Christian theocracy of the future that has seized power in the wake of an ecological upheaval. The Booker Prize-winning *The Blind Assassin* (2000) is an intricately constructed narrative centring on the memoir of an elderly Canadian woman ostensibly writing in order to dispel confusion

*Dust jacket for the first American edition of* The Handmaid's Tale
*by Margaret Atwood, illustration by Fred Marcellino, published
by Houghton Mifflin Company, 1986.* **Between the Covers Rare
Books, Inc., Merchantville, N.J.**

about both her sister's suicide and her own role in the posthumous publication of a novel supposedly written by her sister.

Other novels by Atwood include the surreal *The Edible Woman* (1969); *Surfacing* (1972), an exploration of the relationship between nature and culture that centres on a woman's return to her childhood home in the northern wilderness of Quebec; *Lady Oracle* (1976); *Cat's Eye* (1988); *The Robber Bride* (1993; filmed for television 2007); and *Alias Grace* (1996), a fictionalized account of a real-life Canadian girl who was convicted of two murders in a sensationalist 1843 trial. In *Oryx and Crake* (2003), Atwood described a plague-induced apocalypse in the near future through the observations and flashbacks of a protagonist who is possibly the event's sole survivor. Her 2005 novel, *The Penelopiad: The Myth of Penelope and Odysseus*, was inspired by Homer's *Odyssey*. *The Year of the Flood* (2009) returns to the universe Atwood created in *Oryx and Crake*, using that book's minor characters in a retelling of the dystopic tale.

Atwood also wrote a number of short stories, collected in such volumes as *Dancing Girls* (1977), *Bluebeard's Egg* (1983), *Wilderness Tips* (1991), and *Moral Disorder* (2006). Her nonfiction includes *Negotiating with the Dead: A Writer on Writing* (2002), which grew out of a series of lectures she gave at University of Cambridge; *Payback* (2008), an impassioned essay that treats debt—both personal and governmental—as a cultural issue rather than as a political or economic one; and *In Other Worlds: SF and the Human Imagination* (2011), in which she illuminates her relationship to science fiction. In addition to writing, Atwood taught English literature at several Canadian and American universities.

# GAO XINGJIAN

(b. January 4, 1940, Ganzhou, Jiangxi province, China)

The Chinese émigré novelist, playwright, and critic Gao Xingjian (Kao Hsing-chien) was in 2000 awarded the Nobel Prize for Literature "for an oeuvre of universal validity, bitter insights and linguistic ingenuity." He is also renowned as a stage director and as an artist.

Gao was educated in state schools and from 1957 to 1962 attended the Beijing Foreign Languages Institute, where he earned a degree in French. Persecuted as an intellectual during the Cultural Revolution (the upheaval launched by Mao Zedong in an effort to renew the spirit of the Chinese Revolution), Gao was forced to destroy his early writings and was later sent to a reeducation camp, where he endured nearly six years of hard labour. Afterward he was assigned by the government to work at the Foreign Languages Press. He became a translator but was unable to publish his work or travel abroad until 1979.

Gao first gained critical recognition with the publication of the novella *Hanye zhong de xingchen* (1980; "Stars on a Cold Night"). In 1981 he became a resident playwright with the Beijing People's Art Theatre, and in 1982 his first play, *Juedui xinhao* (*Alarm Signal*), written in collaboration with Liu Huiyuan, was performed. His second and most celebrated play, *Chezhan* (1983; *Bus Stop*), incorporated various techniques of avant-garde European theatre. It was openly condemned by Communist Party officials. Gao continued to explore the boundaries of experimental drama with plays such as *Yeren* (1985; *Wild Man*) and, most notably, *Bi'an* (1986; *The Other Shore*), which was quickly banned by the authorities. Gao then embarked on a 10-month walking tour following the course of the

Yangtze River—a spiritual pilgrimage that became the basis for his first novel, *Lingshan* (1989; *Soul Mountain*). In 1987 he settled in France as a political refugee and subsequently became a French citizen.

Gao's play *Taowang* (1989; "Fugitives"), was set during the brutal 1989 suppression of student demonstrations in Tiananmen Square. Its publication angered the Chinese authorities, who banned Gao's works and declared him persona non grata. Gao wrote in both Chinese and French. Several of his plays have been published in *The Other Shore: Plays by Gao Xingjian* (1999).

# *J.M. COETZEE*

(b. February 9, 1940, Cape Town, South Africa)

The South African novelist, critic, and translator John Maxwell Coetzee is noted for his novels about the effects of colonization. In 2003 he won the Nobel Prize for Literature.

Coetzee was educated at the University of Cape Town (B.A., 1960; M.A., 1963) and the University of Texas (Ph.D., 1969). An opponent of apartheid, he nevertheless returned to live in South Africa, where he taught English at the University of Cape Town, translated works from the Dutch, and wrote literary criticism. He also held visiting professorships at a number of universities.

*Dusklands* (1974), Coetzee's first book, contains two novellas united in their exploration of colonization, *The Vietnam Project* (set in the United States in the late 20th century) and *The Narrative of Jacobus Coetzee* (set in 18th-century South Africa). *In the Heart of the Country* (1977; also published as *From the Heart of the Country*; filmed as *Dust*, 1986) is a stream-of-consciousness narrative of a Boer madwoman, and *Waiting for the Barbarians* (1980), set in some undefined borderland, is an examination of the ramifications of colonization. *Life & Times of Michael K* (1983), which won the Booker Prize, concerns the dilemma of a simple man beset by conditions he can neither comprehend nor control during a civil war in a future South Africa.

Coetzee continued to explore themes of the colonizer and the colonized in *Foe* (1986), his reworking of Daniel Defoe's *Robinson Crusoe*. Coetzee's female narrator comes to new conclusions about power and otherness and ultimately concludes that language can enslave as effectively as can chains. In *Age of Iron* (1990) Coetzee dealt directly with circumstances in contemporary South Africa, but in *The Master of Petersburg* (1994) he made reference to 19th-century Russia (particularly to Fyodor Dostoyevsky's work *The Devils*); both books treat the subject of literature in society. In 1999, with his novel *Disgrace*, Coetzee became the first writer to win the Booker Prize twice. After the novel's publication and an outcry in South Africa, he moved to Australia, where he was granted citizenship in 2006.

The structure of Coetzee's *Elizabeth Costello* (2003), a series of "lessons" (two of which had been published in an earlier volume) in which the eponymous narrator reflects on a variety of topics, puzzled many readers. One reviewer proposed that it be considered "non-nonfiction." Costello makes a surreal reappearance in Coetzee's *Slow Man* (2005), about a recent amputee's reluctance to accept his condition. *Diary of a Bad Year* (2007) employs a literally split narrative technique, with the text on the page divided into concurrent storylines, the main story being the musings of an aging South African writer modeled on Coetzee himself.

The notably reticent author's nonfiction books include *White Writing: On the Culture of Letters in South*

*Africa* (1988); *Doubling the Point: Essays and Interviews* (1992); *Giving Offense: Essays on Censorship* (1996); and the autobiographic trilogy *Boyhood: Scenes from Provincial Life* (1997), *Youth: Scenes from Provincial Life II* (2002), and *Summertime* (2009).

# JEAN-MARIE GUSTAVE LE CLÉZIO

(b. April 13, 1940, Nice, France)

The French author Jean-Marie Gustave Le Clézio is known for his intricate, seductive fiction and distinctive works of nonfiction that mediated between the past and the present, juxtaposing the modern world with a primordial landscape of ambiguity and mystery. He received the Nobel Prize for Literature in 2008.

Le Clézio was descended from a Breton family that had immigrated to the formerly French and subsequently British colony of Mauritius. Bilingual in French and English, he spent part of his childhood in Nigeria before completing his secondary education in France. After studying for a time in England, he returned to France, where he earned an undergraduate degree (1963) from the Institut d'Études Littéraires (now the University of Nice) and a master's degree (1964) from the University of Aix-en-Provence. In 1983 he completed a doctorate of letters at the University of Perpignan, France. Le Clézio traveled extensively and immersed himself in the study of other cultures, particularly those of the indigenous peoples of Mexico and Central America, which he wrote about in *Trois Villes saintes* (1980; "Three Holy Cities"), *Le Rêve mexicain; ou, la pensée interrompue* (1988; *The Mexican Dream; or, The Interrupted Thought of*

*Amerindian Civilizations*), and *La Fête chantée* (1997; "The Sung Feast").

Although he emerged within the French literary milieu dominated by writers of the nouveau roman (New Novel) such as Claude Simon, Alain Robbe-Grillet, and Marguerite Duras, Le Clézio developed independently from his contemporaries and established himself early in his career as an author of singular achievement and temperament. He made his debut as a novelist with the publication in 1963 of *Le Procès-verbal* (*The Interrogation*) and gained widespread acclaim as a young author when the book—which had been sent as an unsolicited manuscript to the prestigious Gallimard publishing house—was awarded the Prix Renaudot as the outstanding original novel of the year. Other publications that further enhanced Le Clézio's reputation in France and abroad included the short-story collection *La Fièvre* (1965; *Fever*) and the novels *Le Déluge* (1966; *The Flood*), *Terra amata* (1967; Eng. trans. *Terra Amata*), *La Guerre* (1970; *War*), and *Les Géants* (1973; *The Giants*). Le Clézio was drawn to the marginalized of society and offered a compassionate and evocative portrayal of the disenfranchised and displaced in search of meaning, identity, and reintegration. For example, Lalla, the protagonist of his acclaimed novel *Désert* (1980; *Desert*), is a North African Berber separated from her past and her cultural inheritance when she was forced to flee her desert homeland; she returns pregnant and resolved both to perpetuate her tribal inheritance and to embrace her legacy of memory and transcendence. *Désert* was awarded the Grand Prix Paul Morand by the French Academy.

Le Clézio's works also include essays, criticism, children's literature, and memoirs. Beginning with the publication in 1991 of *Onitsha* (Eng. trans. *Onitsha*), a semiautobiographical tale influenced by his childhood year in Nigeria, Le Clézio turned increasingly to semiautobiographical works such as the novels *La Quarantaine* (1995) and *Révolutions* (2003). In *L'Africain* (2004) Le Clézio recounted the childhood experience of being reunited with his father in the aftermath of World War II. Later works include *Ballaciner* (2007), a personal tribute to the art of filmmaking and its relationship to literature, and the novel *Ritournelle de la faim* (2008 "Ritornello of Hunger").

# JOSEPH BRODSKY

(b. May 24, 1940, Leningrad, Russia, U.S.S.R. [now St. Petersburg, Russia]—d. January 28, 1996, New York, New York, U.S.)

Joseph Brodsky was a Russian-born American poet who was awarded the Nobel Prize for Literature in 1987 for his important lyric and elegiac poems.

Brodsky left school at age 15 and thereafter began to write poetry while working at a wide variety of jobs. He began to earn a reputation in the Leningrad literary scene, but his independent spirit and his irregular work record led to his being charged with "social parasitism" by the Soviet authorities, who sentenced him in 1964 to five years of hard labour. The sentence was commuted in 1965 after prominent Soviet literary figures protested it. Exiled from the Soviet Union in 1972, Brodsky lived thereafter in the United States, becoming a naturalized U.S. citizen in 1977. He was a poet-in-residence intermittently at the University of Michigan, Ann Arbor, from 1972 to 1980, was a professor of literature at Mount Holyoke College (South Hadley, Massachusetts) from 1981 to 1996, and was a visiting professor at other schools. He received a MacArthur Foundation fellowship grant in 1981 and served as poet laureate of the United States in 1991–92.

Brodsky's poetry addresses personal themes and treats in a powerful, meditative fashion the universal concerns of life, death, and the meaning of existence. Despite what may be assumed from his exile, his writing was not overtly political but was instead unsettling to Soviet officials because of its overarching themes of antimaterialism and praise for individual freedom. His earlier works, written in Russian, include *Stikhotvoreniya i poemy* (1965; "Verses and Poems") and *Ostanovka v pustyne* (1970; "A Halt in the Wasteland"); these and other works were translated by George L. Kline in *Selected Poems* (1973), which includes the notable "Elegy for John Donne." His major works, in Russian and English, include the poetry collections *A Part of Speech* (1980), *History of the Twentieth Century* (1986), and *To Urania* (1988) and the essays in *Less Than One* (1986). His notable posthumous publications include the collections *So Forth* (1996) and *Nativity Poems* (2001) and the children's poem *Discovery* (1999).

# *Bharati Mukherjee*

(b. July 27, 1940, Calcutta, India)

Bharati Mukherjee is an Indian-born American novelist and short-story writer whose work reflects Indian culture and immigrant experience.

Mukherjee was born into a wealthy Calcutta family. She attended an anglicized Bengali school from 1944 to 1948. After three years abroad, the family returned to India. Mukherjee attended the University of Calcutta (B.A., 1959) and the University of Baroda (M.A., 1961). She then entered the University of Iowa Writers' Workshop, earning an M.F.A. in 1963 and a Ph.D. in 1969. From 1966 to 1980 she lived in Montreal, which she found provincial and racist. She then moved to the United States in 1980 and began teaching at the university level. She became a U.S. citizen in 1989 and that year accepted a position teaching postcolonial and world literature at the University of California at Berkeley.

Mukherjee's work features not only cultural clashes but undercurrents of violence. Her first novel, *The Tiger's Daughter* (1972), tells of a sheltered Indian woman jolted by immersion in American culture, then again shocked by her return to a violent Calcutta. *Wife* (1975) details the descent into madness of an Indian woman trapped in New York City by the fears and passivity resulting from her upbringing. In Mukherjee's first book of short fiction, *Darkness* (1985), many of the stories, including the acclaimed "The World According to Hsü," are not only indictments of Canadian racism and traditional Indian views of women but also sharp studies of the edgy inner lives of her characters. *The Middleman and Other Stories* (1988) centres on immigrants in the United States who are from developing countries, which is also the subject of two later novels, *Jasmine* (1989) and *The Holder of the World* (1993). The latter tells of a contemporary American woman drawn into the life of a Puritan ancestor who ran off with a Hindu raja.

Mukherjee's later works include *Wanting America: Selected Stories* (1995) and *Leave It to Me* (1997), which traces the journey of an American woman abandoned in India as a child and her return to her native land. *Desirable Daughters* (2002) attracted considerable acclaim for its intricate depictions of Indian caste relations and the immigrant experience of reconciling disparate worldviews. Mukherjee delved further into the family history of the characters from that novel in *The Tree Bride* (2004), broaching issues of the time-spanning ramifications of colonialism.

With her husband, Clark Blaise, Mukherjee wrote *Days and Nights in Calcutta* (1977), an account of their 14-month stay in India, and *The Sorrow and the Terror: The Haunting Legacy of the Air India Tragedy* (1987). Mukherjee also wrote several works of social analysis, including *Political Culture and Leadership in India* (1991), an assessment of leadership trends in West Bengal.

# JOHN IRVING

(b. March 2, 1942, Exeter, New Hampshire, U.S.)

The American novelist and short-story writer John Irving established his reputation with the novel *The World According to Garp* (1978; film 1982). As is characteristic of his other works, it is noted for its engaging story line, colourful characterizations, macabre humour, and examination of contemporary issues.

He was initially named after his father, John Blunt, but his mother changed his name following her divorce and subsequent remarriage. Irving attended Phillips Exeter Academy, where he took up wrestling—which would remain a lifelong passion and recurring theme in his writing—and struggled academically because of dyslexia. Following his graduation in 1962, he spent time at the Universities of Pittsburgh and Vienna before receiving a bachelor's degree in English from the University of New Hampshire (1965) and a master's degree in English from the University of Iowa (1967). From 1967 to 1978 Irving taught at a number of colleges and universities, including Windham College, the University of Iowa Writer's Workshop, Mount Holyoke College, and Brandeis University.

*Setting Free the Bears*, begun as his master's thesis, was published in 1968. The novel, a latter-day picaresque, charts the exploits of two college dropouts as they journey through Austria by motorcycle and plot the liberation of the titular bruins and other denizens of the Vienna Zoo. Both Irving's debut and the subsequent *The Water-Method Man* (1972) received enthusiastic notices; *The 158-Pound Marriage* (1974) was roundly panned. *The World According to Garp*, however, struck a chord with the international reading public. Infused with comedy and violence, Irving's breakthrough book chronicles the tragic life and death of the novelist T.S. Garp. Rife with his signature milieus and motifs—the rarefied universes of the New England private school and of Vienna, wrestling, infidelity, and absent fathers—the tragicomic novel won Irving a passionate following.

In *The Hotel New Hampshire* (1981; film 1984), concerning a family of unconventional personalities beset by tragedy, and *A Prayer for Owen Meany* (1989; adapted as the film *Simon Birch*, 1998), about the effects of a diminutive boy with messianic qualities on the life of the narrator, Irving continued to refine his use of hyperbole and the surreal to illuminate the human condition. *A Son of the Circus* (1994), an unevenly received amalgam of crime novel conceits and identity politics set in India, was followed by *A Widow for One Year* (1998; adapted as the film *The Door in the Floor*, 2008) and *The Fourth Hand* (2001).

Irving received an Academy Award for the screenplay of the 1999 film version of his novel *The Cider House Rules* (1985), which explores the ethical complexities of abortion. His collection *Trying to Save Piggy Sneed*—which includes short stories and essays—and his autobiography, *The Imaginary Girlfriend*, were both published in 1996. *My Movie Business* (1999) details Irving's experiences in adapting his novels to the screen. Later novels—in which the autobiographical threads present throughout his oeuvre become more pronounced—include *Until I Find You* (2005), which draws on elements of Irving's molestation at the hands of an older woman as a child, and *Last Night in Twisted River* (2009), which plots the bizarre course of a writer's path to success. Among his other novels are *In One Person* (2012), which examines sexual identity.

# MAHMOUD DARWISH

(b. March 13, 1942, Al-Birwa, Palestine [now El-Birwa, Israel]— d. August 9, 2008, Houston, Texas, U.S.)

Mahmoud Darwish (Maḥmūd Darwīsh) was a Palestinian poet who gave voice to the struggles of the Palestinian people.

After the establishment of the State of Israel in 1948, Darwish witnessed massacres that forced his family to escape to Lebanon. A year later their clandestine return to their homeland put them in limbo, as they were declared "present-absent aliens." Darwish left El-Birwa a second time in 1970 and traveled to the Soviet Union to complete his education in Moscow. He lived in Cairo, Beirut, London, and Paris, as well as Tunis, Tunisia, before returning in 1996 to live in Palestine, in the West Bank town of Ramallah. He was a member of the executive committee of the Palestine Liberation Organization (PLO) and wrote the declaration of independence issued by the Palestine National Council in 1988, but he resigned from the PLO in 1993 to protest the signing of the Oslo Accords by PLO chairman Yasīr 'Arafāt. In 2000 the Israeli education minister made plans to include Darwish's poems of reconciliation in the school curriculum, but Israeli Prime Minister Ehud Barak vetoed the plan.

Darwish authored several books of prose—including the memoirs *Yawmiyyāt al-ḥuzn al-ʿādī* (1973; *Journal of an Ordinary Grief*) and *Dhākirah lil-nisyān* (1987; *Memory for Forgetfulness*)—and more than 20 collections of poetry. From 1981 he also served as editor of the literary journal *Al-Karmel*. The power of his poetry could be explained by the sincerity of his emotions and the originality of his poetic images. He borrowed from the Hebrew Bible, the New Testament, classical Arabic literature, Arab Islamic history, and Greek and Roman mythology to construct his metaphors. It was Darwish's conviction that his life in exile inspired his creative work. He often personified Palestine itself as a mother or a cruel beloved. In his single-poem volume *Ḥālat ḥiṣār* (2002; "A State of Siege"), Darwish explored the multiple reoccupations of Ramallah and described the resulting sense of Palestinian isolation. However, he foresaw a future of peace and coexistence between Israelis and Palestinians that could be achieved through dialogue between cultures. Darwish diverged from the political in some of his poems, relying on symbolism to relate personal experience. He devoted an entire collection, *Jidāriyya* (2002; "Mural"), to his brush with death following heart surgery in 1998.

Darwish's work was translated into some two dozen languages. Collections of his poems in English translation include *The Adam of Two Edens* (2000), *Unfortunately, It Was Paradise* (2003), and *The Butterfly's Burden* (2007). Among his many international awards were the Lotus Prize (1969), the Lenin Peace Prize (1983), the French medal of Knight of Arts and Belles Letters (1997), the wiām (order) of intellectual merit from Moroccan King Muhammad VI in 2000, and the 2001 Lannan Foundation Prize for

Cultural Freedom. Darwish died after undergoing heart surgery in the United States.

## ISABEL ALLENDE

(b. August 2, 1942, Lima, Peru)

A Chilean American writer in the magic realist tradition, Isabel Allende is considered one of the first successful female novelists from Latin America.

Allende was born in Peru to Chilean parents. She worked as a journalist in Chile until she was forced to flee to Venezuela after the assassination (1973) of her uncle, Chilean Pres. Salvador Allende. In 1981 she began writing a letter to her terminally ill grandfather that evolved into her first novel, *La casa de los espíritus* (1982; *The House of the Spirits*). It was followed by the novels *De amor y de sombra* (1984; *Of Love and Shadows*), *Eva Luna* (1987), and *El plan infinito* (1991; *The Infinite Plan*) and the collection of stories *Cuentos de Eva Luna* (1990; *The Stories of Eva Luna*). All are examples of magic realism, in which realistic fiction is overlaid with elements of fantasy and myth. Her concern in many of these works is the portrayal of South American politics, and her first four works reflect her own experiences and examine the role of women in Latin America. *The Infinite Plan*, however, is set in the United States, and its protagonist is male.

Allende followed those works of fiction with the novels *Hija de la fortuna* (1999; *Daughter of Fortune*), about a Chilean woman who leaves her country for the California gold rush of 1848–49, and *Retrato en sepia* (2000; *Portrait in Sepia*), about a woman tracing the roots of her past. *El Zorro* (2005; *Zorro*) is a retelling of the well-known legend, and *Inés del alma mía* (2006; *Inés of My Soul*) tells the

fictionalized story of Inés Suárez, the mistress of con-
quistador Pedro de Valdivia. *La isla bajo el mar* (2009; *The
Island Beneath the Sea*) uses the 1791 slave revolt in Haiti as
a backdrop for a story about a mulatto slave who is forced
to become her owner's lover after his wife goes mad.

Allende's first nonfiction work, *Paula* (1994), was written as a letter to her daughter, who died of a hereditary
blood disease in 1992. A more lighthearted book, *Afrodita:
cuentos, recetas, y otros afrodisíacos* (1997; *Aphrodite: A Memoir
of the Senses*), shared her personal knowledge of aphrodisi-
acs and included family recipes. *Mi país inventado* (2003; *My
Invented Country*) recounted her self-imposed exile after
the September 11, 1973, revolution in Chile and her feelings about her adopted country, the United States—where
she has lived since the early 1990s—after the September 11
attacks of 2001. She published another memoir about her
extended family, *La suma de los dias* (*The Sum of Our Days*),
in 2007.

In 1996 Allende used the profits from *Paula* to fund
the Isabel Allende Foundation, which supports nonprofit
organizations targeting issues that women and girls in
Chile and the San Francisco Bay area face.

# SAM SHEPARD

(b. November 5, 1943, Fort Sheridan,
near Highland Park, Illinois, U.S.)

Sam Shepard is an American playwright and actor whose
plays adroitly blend images of the American West, Pop
motifs, science fiction, and other elements of popular and
youth culture.

As the son of a career army father, Shepard spent his
childhood on military bases across the United States and

in Guam before his family settled on a farm in Duarte, California. After a year of agricultural studies in college, he joined a touring company of actors and, in 1963, moved to New York City to pursue his theatrical interests. His earliest attempts at playwriting, a rapid succession of one-act plays, found a receptive audience in Off-Off-Broadway productions. In the 1965–66 season Shepard won Obie Awards (presented by the *Village Voice* newspaper) for his plays *Chicago*, *Icarus's Mother*, and *Red Cross*.

Shepard lived in England from 1971 to 1974, and several plays of this period—notably *The Tooth of Crime* (produced 1972) and *Geography of a Horse Dreamer* (produced 1974)—premiered in London. In late 1974 he became playwright-in-residence at the Magic Theatre in San Francisco, where most of his plays over the next decade were first produced.

Shepard's works of the mid-1970s showed a heightening of earlier techniques and themes. In *Killer's Head* (produced 1975), for example, the rambling monologue, a Shepard stock-in-trade, blends horror and banality in a murderer's last thoughts before electrocution; *Angel City* (produced 1976) depicts the destructive machinery of the Hollywood entertainment industry; and *Suicide in B-flat* (produced 1976) exploits the potentials of music as an expression of character.

Beginning in the late 1970s, Shepard applied his unconventional dramatic vision to a more conventional dramatic form, the family tragedy. *Curse of the Starving Class* (produced 1977; film 1994), the Pulitzer Prize-winning *Buried Child* (produced 1978), and *True West* (produced 1980) are linked thematically in their examination of troubled and tempestuous blood relationships in a fragmented society.

Shepard returned to acting in the late 1970s, winning critical accolades for his performances in such films as *Days of Heaven* (1978), *Resurrection* (1980), *The Right Stuff* (1983), and *Fool for Love* (1985), which was written by Shepard and based on his 1983 play of the same name. He also appeared in screen adaptations of other writers' novels, including *The Pelican Brief* (1993), *Snow Falling on Cedars* (1999), *All the Pretty Horses* (2000), and *The Notebook* (2004). Among his later films are *The Assassination of Jesse James by the Coward Robert Ford* (2007) and *Blackthorn* (2011), in which he portrayed the American outlaws Frank James and Butch Cassidy, respectively.

Shepard's other plays include *La Turista* (produced 1967), *The Unseen Hand* (produced 1969), *Operation Sidewinder* (produced 1970), *Seduced* (produced 1978), *A Lie of the Mind* (produced 1985), *Simpatico* (produced 1994; film 1999), *The God of Hell* (produced 2004), *Ages of the Moon* (produced 2009), and *Heartless* (produced 2012). In addition, he published several collections of short stories, such as *Days out of Days* (2010). In 1986 Shepard was elected to the American Academy of Arts and Letters.

# *TAHAR BEN JELLOUN*

(b. December 1, 1944, Fès, Morocco)

Tahar Ben Jelloun is a Moroccan-French novelist, poet, and essayist who has written expressively about Moroccan culture, the immigrant experience, human rights, and sexual identity.

While studying philosophy at Muḥammad V University in Rabat, Ben Jelloun began to write poems for the politically charged journal *Soufflés*. After publishing his first collection of poetry, *Hommes sous linceul de silence* (1971; "Men Under the Shroud of Silence"), he moved to France. There he continued to write poems, collected in *Cicatrices du soleil* (1972; "Scars of the Sun"), *Le Discours du chameau* (1974; "The Discourse of the Camel"), and *Grains de peau* (1974; "Particles of Skin"), but he started to focus on other forms of writing as well. His first novel was *Harrouda* (1973), an erotic poetic evocation of infancy, youth, and coming to manhood in Fès and Tangier.

In 1975 Ben Jelloun received a doctorate in social psychology from the University of Paris; his dissertation was published as *La Plus Haute des solitudes* (1977; "The Highest of Solitudes"). In 1976 he wrote a novel based on his research, *La Réclusion solitaire* (*Solitaire*), about the misery of the North African immigrant worker; it was also staged as a play, *Chronique d'une solitude* ("Chronicle of Loneliness"). In the same year, he published *Les Amandiers sont morts de leurs blessures* ("The Almond Trees Are Dead from Their Wounds")—poems and stories on his grandmother's death, the Palestinian question, North African immigration to France, love, and eroticism. A third novel, *Moha le fou, Moha le sage* (1978; "Moha the Fool, Moha the Wise"), is a satire of the modern North African state.

Much of Ben Jelloun's work in the early 1980s—notably the poetry collection *À l'insu du souvenir* (1980; "Unknown to Memory") and the semiautobiographical novel *L'Écrivain public* (1983; "The Public Writer")—was admired for its ability to evoke reality through fantasy, lyric, and metaphor and for its author's conviction that his art must express the struggle for human freedom. However, it was not until *L'Enfant de sable* (1985; *The Sand Child*), an imaginative, richly drawn novel that critiques gender roles in Arab society through the tale of a girl raised as a boy, that Ben Jelloun was accorded widespread praise and recognition. Its sequel, *La Nuit sacrée* (1987; *The Sacred Night*), won France's prestigious Prix Goncourt, a first for an African-born writer, and inspired a film adaptation (1993). The two books were eventually translated into more than 40 languages.

Later novels include *Jour de silence a Tanger* (1990; *Silent Day in Tangier*), a meditation on old age; *Les Yeux baissés* (1991; *With Downcast Eyes*), about an Amazigh (Berber) immigrant's struggle to reconcile her bifurcated identity; and *L'Homme rompu* (1994; *Corruption*), a gripping depiction of a moral quandary faced by a government employee. *Cette aveuglante absence de lumière* (2001; *This Blinding Absence of Light*), a harrowing account of the life of a Moroccan political prisoner that was partially inspired by Ben Jelloun's own 18-month detainment in an army camp in the late 1960s, won the International IMPAC Dublin Literary Award in 2004.

Ben Jelloun also received attention for his nonfiction, especially *Hospitalité francaise: racisme et immigration maghrebine* (1984; *French Hospitality: Racism and North African Immigrants*) and *Le Racisme expliqué à ma fille* (1998; *Racism Explained to My Daughter*), two provocative tracts that address the issue of xenophobia in France. The question-and-answer format of the latter was further employed in *L'Islam expliqué aux enfants* (2002; *Islam Explained*), written in response to the anti-Muslim sentiment that followed the September 11, 2001, attacks in the U.S. In addition, Ben Jelloun was a regular contributor to *Le Monde* and other periodicals. In 2008 he was made an officer of the Legion of Honour.

# *AUGUST WILSON*

(b. April 27, 1945, Pittsburgh, Pennsylvania, U.S.—
d. October 2, 2005, Seattle, Washington)

August Wilson was an American playwright best known as the author of a cycle of plays, each set in a different decade of the 20th century, about black

American life. He won Pulitzer Prizes for *Fences* (1986) and *The Piano Lesson* (1990).

Originally named Frederick August Kittel for his father, a white German immigrant who was largely absent from the family, he later adopted his mother's last name. Wilson's early years were spent in the Hill District of Pittsburgh, a poor but lively neighbourhood that became the setting for most of his plays. Primarily self-educated, he quit school at age 15 after being accused of having plagiarized a paper. He later joined the Black Arts movement in the late 1960s, became the cofounder and director of Black Horizons Theatre in Pittsburgh (1968), and published poetry in such journals as *Black World* (1971) and *Black Lines* (1972).

In 1978 Wilson moved to St. Paul, Minnesota, and by the early 1980s he wrote several plays, including *Jitney* (1979, revised in 2000; first produced 1982). Focused on cab drivers in the 1970s, it underwent subsequent revisions as part of his historical cycle. His first major play, *Ma Rainey's Black Bottom*, opened on Broadway in 1984 and was a critical and financial success. Set in Chicago in 1927, the play centres on a verbally abusive blues singer, her fellow black musicians, and their white manager. *Fences*, first produced in 1985, is about a conflict between a father and son in the 1950s; it received a Tony Award for best play. Wilson's chronicle of the black American experience continued with *Joe Turner's Come and Gone* (1988), a play about the lives of residents of a boardinghouse in 1911; *The Piano Lesson*, set in the 1930s and concerning a family's ambivalence about selling an heirloom; and *Two Trains Running* (1992), whose action takes place in a coffeehouse in the 1960s. *Seven Guitars* (1996), the seventh play of the cycle, is set among a group of friends who reunite in 1948 following the death of a local blues guitarist.

*August Wilson, 2003.* © AP Images

Subsequent plays in the series are *King Hedley II* (2005; first produced 1999), an account of an ex-con's efforts to rebuild his life in the 1980s, and *Gem of the Ocean* (first produced 2003), which takes place in 1904 and centres on Aunt Ester, a 287-year-old spiritual healer mentioned in previous plays, and a man who seeks her help. Wilson completed the cycle with *Radio Golf* (first produced 2005). Set in the 1990s, the play concerns the fate of Aunt Ester's house, which is slated to be torn down by real-estate developers. Music, particularly jazz and blues, is a recurrent theme in Wilson's works, and its cadence is echoed in the lyrical, vernacular nature of his dialogue.

Wilson received numerous honours during his career, including seven New York Drama Critics' Circle Awards for best play. He also held Guggenheim and Rockefeller fellowships. Shortly after his death, the Virginia Theater on Broadway was renamed in his honour.

# JOHN BANVILLE

(b. December 8, 1945, Wexford, Ireland)

John Banville is an Irish novelist and journalist whose fiction is known for being referential, paradoxical, and complex.

Banville attended St. Peter's College in Wexford. He began working in Dublin as a copy editor for the *Irish Press* (1969–83). He was later a copy editor (1986–88) and literary editor (1988–99) for the *Irish Times*.

His first piece of fiction, *Long Lankin* (1970), is a series of nine episodic short stories. This work was followed by two novels: *Nightspawn* (1971), an intentionally ambiguous narrative, and *Birchwood* (1973), the story of a decaying Irish family. *Doctor Copernicus* (1976), *Kepler* (1981), and *The Newton Letter: An Interlude* (1982) are fictional biographies based on the lives of noted scientists. These three works use scientific exploration as a metaphor to question perceptions of fiction and reality. *Mefisto* (1986) is written from the point of view of a character obsessed with numbers.

*The Book of Evidence* (1989) is a murder mystery and the first of a trilogy centred on the character Freddie Montgomery. *Ghosts* (1993) and *Athena* (1995) completed the trilogy. *The Untouchable* (1997), along with *Eclipse* (2000) and its sequel, *Shroud* (2002), are novels that tell more stories of conflicted individuals. *The Sea* (2005), a novel that was awarded the Booker Prize, tells the story of a widowed art historian who revisits a childhood destination on the sea. *The Infinities* (2009) is an eccentric work that relates a domestic drama that takes place in a parallel reality through the narrative of the Greek god Hermes, and *Ancient Light* (2012) uses characters that previously appeared in *Eclipse* and *Shroud* to recount an elderly man's vivid recollection of his earliest love as a means of coping with his daughter's suicide. Banville first used the pseudonym Benjamin Black for his crime novel *Christine Falls* (2006) and then in a number of subsequent detective potboilers, including *Silver Swan* (2007), *The Lemur* (2008), *A Death in Summer* (2011), and *Vengeance* (2012).

Banville's writing is experimental, challenging the conventional form of the novel. Common themes throughout his work include loss, obsession, destructive love, and the pain that accompanies freedom.

# ELFRIEDE JELINEK

(b. October 20, 1946, Mürzzuschlag, Austria)

The Austrian novelist and playwright Elfriede Jelinek is noted for her controversial works on gender relations, female sexuality, and popular culture. She was awarded the Nobel Prize for Literature in 2004.

Jelinek received her education in Vienna, where the combination of her academic studies with a rigorous program of musical training at the Vienna Conservatory contributed in part to her emotional breakdown at age 17. It was during her recovery that Jelinek turned to writing as a form of self-expression and introspection. After attending the University of Vienna, she made her literary debut with a collection of poems, *Lisas Schatten* (1967; "Lisa's Shadow"), and followed with her first published novel, *Wir sind Lockvögel Baby!* (1970; "We're Decoys, Baby!"). Using

*Elfriede Jelinek, 2000.* AFP/ Getty Images

language and the structural interplay of class consciousness as a means to explore the social and cultural parameters of dependency and authority, she earned critical recognition for *Michael: Ein Jugendbuch für die Infantilgeselleschaft* (1972; "Michael: A Young Person's Guide to Infantile Society").

A polemical feminist, Jelinek often wrote about gender oppression and female sexuality. In the satiric *Die Liebhaberinnen* (1975; *Women as Lovers*, 1994), she described the entrapment and victimization of women within a dehumanizing and patriarchal society. Her semiautobiographical novel *Die Klavierspielerin* (1983; *The Piano Teacher*, 1988) addressed issues of sexual repression; it was adapted for the screen in 2001. In her writings, Jelinek rejected the conventions of traditional literary technique in favour of linguistic and thematic experimentation.

Jelinek's significant novels include the satiric *Die Ausgesperrten* (1980; *Wonderful, Wonderful Times*, 1990), *Lust* (1989; *Lust*, 1992), and *Gier* (2000; *Greed*, 2006). Her most notable plays include *Was geschah, nachdem Nora ihren Mann verlassen hatte oder Stützen der Gesellschaften* (1980; *What Happened After Nora Left Her Husband; or, Pillars of Society*, 1994), which she wrote as a sequel to Henrik Ibsen's *A Doll's House*; *Clara S.: musikalische Tragödie* (1984; *Clara S.*, 1997); and *Bambiland* (2003).

# SIR SALMAN RUSHDIE

(b. June 19, 1947, Bombay [now Mumbai], India)

Sir Ahmed Salman Rushdie is an Anglo-Indian writer whose allegorical novels examine historical and philosophical issues by means of surreal characters, brooding humour, and an effusive and melodramatic prose style. His treatment of sensitive religious and political subjects made him a controversial figure.

Rushdie was the son of a prosperous Muslim businessman in India. He was educated at Rugby School and the University of Cambridge, receiving an M.A. degree in history in 1968. Throughout most of the 1970s he worked in London as an advertising copywriter, and his first published novel, *Grimus*, appeared in 1975. His next novel, *Midnight's Children* (1981), a fable about modern India, was an unexpected critical and popular success that won him international recognition.

The novel *Shame* (1983), based on contemporary politics in Pakistan, was also popular, but Rushdie's fourth novel, *The Satanic Verses*, encountered a different reception. Some of the adventures in this book depict a character modeled on the Prophet Muhammad and portray both him and his transcription of the Qur'ān in a manner that, after the novel's publication in the summer of 1988, drew criticism from Muslim community leaders in Britain, who denounced the novel as blasphemous. Public demonstrations against the book spread to Pakistan in January 1989. On February 14 the spiritual leader of revolutionary Iran,

Ayatollah Ruhollah Khomeini, publicly condemned the book and issued a fatwā (legal opinion) against Rushdie; a bounty was offered to anyone who would execute him. He went into hiding under the protection of Scotland Yard, and—although he occasionally emerged unexpectedly, sometimes in other countries—he was compelled to restrict his movements. Despite the standing death threat, Rushdie continued to write, producing *Imaginary Homelands* (1991), a collection of essays and criticism; the children's novel *Haroun and the Sea of Stories* (1990); the short-story collection *East, West* (1994); and the novel *The Moor's Last Sigh* (1995). In 1998, after nearly a decade, the Iranian government announced that it would no longer seek to enforce its fatwā against Rushdie. He later recounted his experience in the third-person memoir *Joseph Anton* (2012); its title refers to an alias he adopted while in seclusion.

Following his return to public life, Rushdie published the novels *The Ground Beneath Her Feet* (1999) and *Fury* (2001). *Step Across This Line*, a collection of essays he wrote between 1992 and 2002 on subjects from the September 11 attacks to *The Wizard of Oz*, was issued in 2002. Rushdie's subsequent novels include *Shalimar the Clown* (2005), an examination of terrorism that was set primarily in the disputed Kashmir region of the Indian subcontinent, and *The Enchantress of Florence* (2008), based on a fictionalized account of the Mughal emperor Akbar. The children's book *Luka and the Fire of Life* (2010) centres on the efforts of Luka—younger brother to the protagonist of *Haroun and the Sea of Stories*—to locate the titular fire and revive his ailing father.

Rushdie received the Booker Prize in 1981 for *Midnight's Children*. He subsequently won the Booker of Bookers (1993) and the Best of the Booker (2008). These special prizes were voted on by the public in honour of the prize's 25th and 40th anniversaries, respectively. Rushdie was knighted in 2007, an honour criticized by the Iranian government and Pakistan's parliament.

# OCTAVIA E. BUTLER

(b. June 22, 1947, Pasadena, California, U.S.—
d. February 24, 2006, Seattle, Washington)

Octavia Estelle Butler was an African American author chiefly noted for her science-fiction novels about future societies and superhuman powers. They are noteworthy for their unique synthesis of science fiction, mysticism, mythology, and African American spiritualism.

Butler was educated at Pasadena City College (A.A., 1968), California State University, and the University of California at Los Angeles. Encouraged by American science-fiction writer Harlan Ellison, she began her writing career in 1970. The first of her novels, *Patternmaster* (1976), was the beginning of her five-volume Patternist series about an elite group of mentally linked telepaths ruled by Doro, a 4,000-year-old immortal African. Other novels in the series are *Mind of My Mind* (1977), *Survivor* (1978), *Wild Seed* (1980), and *Clay's Ark* (1984).

In *Kindred* (1979) a contemporary black woman is sent back in time to a pre-Civil War plantation, becomes a slave, and rescues her white, slave-owning ancestor. Her later novels include the Xenogenesis trilogy—*Dawn: Xenogenesis* (1987), *Adulthood Rites* (1988), and *Imago* (1989)—and *The Parable of the Sower* (1993), *The Parable of the Talents* (1998), and *Fledgling* (2005). Butler's short story *Speech Sounds* won a Hugo Award in 1984, and her story *Bloodchild*, about human male slaves who incubate their alien masters' eggs, won both Hugo and Nebula awards.

Her collection *Bloodchild and Other Stories* was published in 1995. That same year Butler became the first science-fiction writer to be awarded a MacArthur Foundation fellowship, and in 2000 she received a PEN Award for lifetime achievement.

# STEPHEN KING

(b. September 21, 1947, Portland, Maine, U.S.)

Stephen King is an American novelist and short-story writer whose books were credited with reviving the genre of horror fiction in the late 20th century.

King graduated from the University of Maine in 1970 with a bachelor's degree in English. While writing short stories he supported himself by teaching and working as a janitor, among other jobs. His first published novel, *Carrie* (film 1976), about a tormented teenage girl gifted with telekinetic powers, appeared in 1974 and was an immediate popular success. *Carrie* was the first of many novels in which King blended horror, the macabre, fantasy, and science fiction. Among such works were *'Salem's Lot* (1975; film 2004), *The Shining* (1977; film 1980), *The Stand* (1978), *The Dead Zone* (1979; film 1983), *Firestarter* (1980; film 1984), *Cujo* (1981; film 1983), *The Running Man* (1982; film 1987), *Christine* (1983; film 1983), *Thinner* (1984; film 1996), *Misery* (1987; film 1990), *The Tommyknockers* (1987; film 1993), *The Dark Half* (1989; film 1993), *Needful Things* (1991; film 1993), *Dolores Claiborne* (1993; film 1995), *Dreamcatcher* (2001; film 2003), *Cell* and *Lisey's Story* (both 2006), *Duma Key* (2008), *Under the Dome* (2009), and *11/22/63* (2011). King published several of these works, including *The Dead Zone* and *The Running Man*, under the pseudonym Richard Bachman. A collection of the first four Bachman novels, *The Bachman*

*Books* (1985), contains the essay *Why I Was Bachman*. King also wrote a serial novel, *The Dark Tower*, whose first installment, *The Gunslinger*, appeared in 1982; an eighth volume was published in 2012.

In his books King explores almost every terror-producing theme imaginable, from vampires, rabid dogs, deranged killers, and a pyromaniac to ghosts, extrasensory perception and telekinesis, biological warfare, and even a malevolent automobile. In his later fiction, exemplified by *Dolores Claiborne*, King departed from the horror genre to provide sharply detailed psychological portraits of his protagonists, many of them women, who confront difficult and challenging circumstances. Though his work was sometimes disparaged as undisciplined and inelegant, King is a talented storyteller whose books gained their effect from realistic detail, forceful plotting, and the author's undoubted ability to involve and scare the reader. His work has consistently addressed such themes as the potential for politics and technology to disrupt or even destroy an individual human life. Obsession, the forms it can assume, and its power to wreck individuals, families, and whole communities are a recurring theme in King's fiction, driving the narratives of *Christine*, *Misery*, and *Needful Things*.

By the early 1990s King's books had sold more than 100 million copies worldwide, and his name had become synonymous with the genre of horror fiction. He also wrote short stories collected in such volumes as *Night Shift* (1978) and *Just After Sunset* (2008). He wrote several novellas and motion-picture screenplays. Some of his novels were adapted for the screen by such directors as John Carpenter, David Cronenberg, Brian De Palma, Stanley Kubrick, and Rob Reiner. King explored both his own career and the craft of writing in *On Writing* (2000), a book he completed as he was recovering from severe injuries received after being struck by a car. King experimented with different forms of book distribution: *The Plant: Zenith Rising* was released in 2000 solely as an e-book, distributed via the Internet, with readers asked but not required to pay for it, while the novella *UR* was made available in 2009 only to users of the Kindle electronic reading device.

# DAVID MAMET

(b. November 30, 1947, Chicago, Illinois, U.S.)

The American playwright, director, and screenwriter David Mamet is noted for his often desperate working-class characters and for his distinctive, colloquial, and frequently profane dialogue.

Mamet began writing plays while attending Goddard College, Plainfield, Vermont (B.A. 1969). Returning to Chicago, where many of his plays were first staged, he worked at various factory jobs, at a real-estate agency, and as a taxi driver; all these experiences provided background for his plays. In 1973 he cofounded a theatre company in Chicago. He also taught drama at several American colleges and universities.

Mamet's early plays include *Duck Variations* (produced 1972), in which two elderly Jewish men sit on a park bench and trade misinformation on various subjects. In *Sexual Perversity in Chicago* (produced 1974; filmed as *About Last Night...* [1986]), a couple's budding sexual and emotional relationship is destroyed by their friends' interference. *American Buffalo* (1976; film 1996) concerns dishonest business practices; *A Life in the Theatre* (1977) explores the teacher-student relationship; and *Speed-the-Plow* (1987) is a black comedy about avaricious Hollywood scriptwriters.

*Glengarry Glen Ross* (1983; film 1992), a drama of desperate real-estate salesmen, won the 1984 Pulitzer Prize for drama. *Oleanna* (1992; film 1994) probes the definition of sexual harassment through the interactions between a professor and his female student. Mamet attempted to address the accusations of chauvinism frequently directed at his work with *Boston Marriage* (1999), a drawing-room comedy about two lesbians. *Dr. Faustus* (2004) puts a contemporary spin on the German Faust legend, and *Romance* (2005) comically skewers the prejudices of a Jewish man and his Protestant lawyer. Later plays include *November* (2008), a farcical portrait of a U.S. president running for reelection; *Race* (2009), a legal drama that explores racial attitudes and tensions; and *The Anarchist* (2012), a two-woman drama about a prisoner and her warden. In all these works, Mamet used the rhythms and rhetoric of everyday speech to delineate character, describe intricate relationships, and drive dramatic development.

Mamet wrote screenplays for a number of motion pictures, including *The Postman Always Rings Twice* (1981); *The Verdict* (1982), for which he received an Academy Award nomination; *Rising Sun* (1993); *Wag the Dog* (1997), for which he received another Academy Award nomination; and *Hannibal* (2001), all adaptations of novels. He both wrote and directed the motion pictures *House of Games* (1987), *Homicide* (1991), and *The Spanish Prisoner* (1998). In 1999 he directed *The Winslow Boy*, which he had adapted from a play by Terence Rattigan. *State and Main* (2000), a well-received ensemble piece written and directed by Mamet, depicts the trials and tribulations of a film crew shooting in a small town. He also applied his dual talents to *Heist* (2001), a crime thriller, and *Redbelt* (2008), a latter-day samurai film about the misadventures of a martial arts instructor. Mamet created and wrote *The*

*Unit*, a television drama that premiered in 2006, which centred on the activities of a secret U.S. Army unit.

Mamet also wrote fiction, including *The Village* (1994); *The Old Religion* (1997), a novelization of an actual anti-Semitic lynching in the American South; and *Wilson: A Consideration of the Sources* (2000), which speculates on the havoc that might be caused by a crash of the Internet. He published several volumes articulating his stance on various aspects of theatre and film, including *On Directing Film* (1992), *Three Uses of the Knife* (1996), and *True and False: Heresy and Common Sense for the Actor* (1999). Compilations of his essays and experiences include *Writing in Restaurants* (1987), *Make-Believe Town* (1996), and *Bambi vs. Godzilla: On the Nature, Purpose, and Practice of the Movie Business* (2007). Mamet addressed the topic of anti-Semitism in *The Wicked Son: Anti-Semitism, Self-Hatred, and the Jews* (2006) and challenged American liberal orthodoxy in *The Secret Knowledge: The Dismantling of American Culture* (2011). He wrote several plays for children as well.

# ART SPIEGELMAN

(b. February 15, 1948, Stockholm, Sweden)

Art Spiegelman is an American author and illustrator whose Holocaust narratives *Maus I: A Survivor's Tale: My Father Bleeds History* (1986) and *Maus II: A Survivor's Tale: And Here My Troubles Began* (1991) helped to establish comic storytelling as a sophisticated adult literary medium.

Spiegelman immigrated to the United States with his parents in 1951. The family settled in Queens, New York, and Spiegelman, inspired by the clever artwork and subversive humour of *Mad* magazine, studied cartooning. As a teenager, he attended Manhattan's High School of Art and Design, and he embarked on a career as a professional artist, selling illustrations to the *Long Island Post*. He also began a two-decade run as a contributing artist and designer for Topps Chewing Gum, during which he helped develop the wildly successful Garbage Pail Kids and Wacky Packages trading cards. Spiegelman attended the State University of New York at Binghamton from 1965 to 1968, and he explored the alternative comics scene—most notably, the work of counterculture icon R. Crumb. After his mother's suicide in 1968, Spiegelman left college without obtaining a degree, and he spent the early 1970s contributing to the flourishing comics underground. In 1972 he published two strips that represented a break from his previous work. The first was *Maus*, originally a three-page story

*Art Spiegelman, 2008.* Nadja Spiegelman

that appeared in cartoonist Justin Green's *Funny Animals* anthology. The second, *Prisoner on the Hell Planet*, was an attempt to understand his mother's suicide through panels that evoked the bold intensity of German Expressionist woodcuts. These strips, along with other works, were collected in *Breakdowns* (1977).

In 1980 he cofounded *Raw*, an underground comic and graphics anthology, with his wife, Françoise Mouly. In it the pair sought to present graphic novels and "comix" (comics written for a mature audience) to a wider public. Recognized as the leading avant-garde comix journal of its era, *Raw* featured strips by European artists as well as previewed Spiegelman's own work. Beginning in *Raw*'s second issue (December 1980), Spiegelman resumed the story of *Maus*, in which he related the wartime experiences of his parents, Vladek and Anja, both survivors of the Auschwitz death camp. Compelling in

its ironic anthropomorphic animal depictions—the Jews and Nazis are drawn with the faces of mice and cats, respectively—its historical veracity, and its personal accounts, the story is made more complex by its contemporary framework. Spiegelman portrays himself as the adult Artie Spiegelman, who is attempting to understand and reconstruct his parents' past while coping with

*Cover of Art Spiegelman's* The Complete Maus *(1996). Courtesy of Random House*

the legacy of his mother's death, his aging and often difficult father, and his own sense of guilt. The literary quality of *Raw* and *Maus* pushed comix into the mainstream, and their success led to Spiegelman working as a *New York Times* illustrator, a *Playboy* cartoonist, and a staff artist and writer for *The New Yorker*.

The commercial and critical success of *Maus* earned Spiegelman a "Special Award" Pulitzer Prize in 1992 and a solo exhibit at New York City's Museum of Modern Art. In addition, *Maus II* became a *New York Times* best-seller. Initially appearing on the fiction list, it was moved to non-fiction after Spiegelman appealed for the transfer on the basis of the book's carefully researched factual scenes. The two *Maus* volumes were translated into more than 20 languages, and they were published together as *The Complete Maus* in 1996.

In 2000 Spiegelman and Mouly launched *Little Lit*, a comics anthology for children that collected work from comics creators Chris Ware, Neil Gaiman, and Daniel Clowes, children's authors Maurice Sendak and Lemony Snicket, and humorist David Sedaris, among others. Although Spiegelman achieved success with lighthearted fare for young readers—his *Open Me...I'm a Dog!* (1997) was well received—he was inspired by the events of September 11, 2001, to return to the comix format. Stating that "disaster is my muse," Spiegelman published *In the Shadow of No Towers* (2004), a collection of broadsheet-sized meditations on mortality and the far-reaching consequences of that day. In 2008 he released *Breakdowns: Portrait of the Artist as a Young %@&\*!*, which repackaged his long out-of-print *Breakdowns* collection as part of a longer graphic memoir. Spiegelman was made a Chevalier de l'Ordre des Arts et des Lettres in 2005.

# WILLIAM GIBSON

(b. March 17, 1948, Conway, South Carolina, U.S.)

The American-Canadian writer of science fiction William Gibson is the leader of the genre's cyberpunk movement.

Gibson grew up in southwestern Virginia. After dropping out of high school in 1967, he traveled to Canada and eventually settled there, earning a B.A. (1977) from the University of British Columbia. Many of Gibson's early stories, including *Johnny Mnemonic* (1981; film 1995) and *Burning Chrome* (1982), were published in *Omni* magazine. With the publication of his first novel, *Neuromancer* (1984), Gibson emerged as a leading exponent of cyberpunk, a new school of science-fiction writing. Cyberpunk combines a cynical, tough "punk" sensibility with futuristic cybernetic (i.e., having to do with communication and control theory) technology. Gibson's creation of "cyberspace," a computer-simulated reality that shows the nature of information, foreshadowed virtual reality technology and is considered the author's major contribution to the genre.

*Neuromancer*, which won three major science-fiction awards (Nebula, Hugo, and Philip K. Dick), established Gibson's reputation. Its protagonist is a 22nd-century data thief who fights against the domination of a corporate-controlled society by breaking through the global computer network's cyberspace matrix. *Count Zero* (1986) was set in the same world as *Neuromancer* but seven years later. The characters of *Mona Lisa Overdrive* (1988) can "die" into computers, where they may support or sabotage outer reality. After collaborating with writer Bruce Sterling on *The Difference Engine* (1990), a story set in Victorian England, Gibson returned to the subject of cyberspace in *Virtual Light* (1993). His *Idoru* (1996), set in 21st-century Tokyo, focuses on the media and virtual celebrities of the future. *All Tomorrow's Parties* (1999) concerns a clairvoyant cyberpunk who labours to keep a villain from dominating the world. *Pattern Recognition* (2003) follows a marketing consultant who is hired to track down the origins of a mysterious Internet video. In *Spook Country* (2007), characters navigate a world filled with spies, ghosts, and other nefarious unseen agents. *Zero History* (2010), which completed a trilogy that includes his previous two novels, reveals hidden governmental conspiracies through a search for a missing fashion designer. In 2012 Gibson published a collection of nonfiction, *Distrust That Particular Flavor*.

# MURAKAMI HARUKI

(b. January 12, 1949, Kyōto, Japan)

Murakami Haruki is the most widely translated Japanese novelist of his generation.

Murakami's first novel, *Kaze no uta o kike* (1979; *Hear the Wind Sing*; film 1980), won a prize for best fiction by a new writer. From the start his writing was characterized by images and events that the author himself found difficult to explain but which seemed to come from the inner recesses of his memory. Some argued that this ambiguity, far from being off-putting, was one reason for his popularity with readers, especially young ones, who were bored with the self-confessions that formed the mainstream of contemporary Japanese literature. His perceived lack of a political or intellectual stance irritated "serious" authors (such as Ōe Kenzaburō), who dismissed his early writings as being no more than entertainment.

Murakami's first major international success came with *Hitsuji o meguru bōken* (1982; *A Wild Sheep Chase*), a novel that acquires an eerie quality from the mysterious sheep that comes to possess the narrator's friend, known as "the Rat." The narrator and the Rat reappeared in Murakami's next important novel, *Sekai no owari to hādoboirudo wandārando* (1985; *Hard-Boiled Wonderland and the End of the World*), a fantasy that was successful with the public and won the prestigious Tanizaki Prize. Murakami adopted a more straightforward style for the coming-of-age novel *Noruwei no mori* (1987; *Norwegian Wood*; film 2010), which sold millions of copies in Japan and firmly established him as a literary celebrity.

Disaffected by the social climate in Japan and by his growing fame, Murakami sojourned in Europe for several years in the late 1980s, and in 1991 he moved to the United States. While teaching at Princeton University (1991–93) and Tufts University (1993–95), Murakami wrote one of his most ambitious novels, *Nejimaki-dori kuronikuru* (1994–95; *The Wind-Up Bird Chronicle*). The narrative represents a departure from his usual themes: it is devoted in part to depicting Japanese militarism on the Asian continent as a nightmare.

In 1995 Murakami returned to Japan, prompted by the Kōbe earthquake and by the sarin gas attack carried out by the AUM Shinrikyo religious sect on a Tokyo subway. The two deadly events subsequently served as inspiration for his work. *Andāguraundo* (1997; *Underground*) is a nonfiction account of the subway attack, and *Kami no kodomo-tachi wa mina odoru* (2000; *After the Quake*) is a collection of six short stories that explores the psychological effects of the earthquake on residents of Japan.

The novel *Supūtoniku no koibito* (1999; *Sputnik Sweetheart*) probes the nature of love as it tells the story of the disappearance of Sumire, a young novelist. Subsequent novels include *Umibe no Kafuka* (2002; *Kafka on the Shore*) and *Afutā dāku* (2004; *After Dark*). *1Q84* (2009), its title a reference to George Orwell's *Nineteen Eighty-four* (1949), shifts between two characters as they navigate an alternate reality of their own making; the book's dystopian themes range from the September 11 attacks to vigilante justice.

The short-story collections *The Elephant Vanishes* (1993) and *Blind Willow, Sleeping Woman* (2006) translate Murakami's stories into English. His memoir, *Hashiru koto ni tsuite kataru toki ni boku no kataru koto* (2007; *What I Talk About When I Talk About Running*), centres on his love for marathon running. An experienced translator of American literature, Murakami also published editions in Japanese of works by Raymond Carver, Paul Theroux, Truman Capote, Ursula K. Le Guin, and J.D. Salinger.

# MARTIN AMIS

(b. August 25, 1949, Oxford, Oxfordshire, England)

The English satirist Martin Amis is known for his virtuoso storytelling technique and his dark views of contemporary English society.

As a youth, Amis, the son of the novelist Kingsley Amis, thrived literarily on a permissive home atmosphere and a "passionate street life." He graduated from Exeter College, Oxford, in 1971 with first-class honours in English and worked for several years as an editor on such publications as the *Times Literary Supplement* and the *New Statesman*.

Amis's first novel was *The Rachel Papers* (1973), the tale of a young antihero preoccupied with his health, his sex life, and his efforts to get into Oxford. His first major critical success was *Money* (1984), a savagely comic satire of the conspicuous consumerism of the 1980s. *London Fields* (1989) is an ambitious novel set in 1999 in which a number of small-scale interpersonal relationships take place amid a society on the verge of apocalyptic collapse. His other major work of this period is *Time's Arrow* (1991), which inverts traditional narrative order from end to beginning to describe the life of a Nazi war criminal from death to birth. In Amis's works, according to one critic, "morality is nudged toward bankruptcy by 'market forces.'" Other novels of the first decades of his literary career include *Dead Babies* (1974), *Success* (1978), *Other People* (1981), *The Information* (1995), and *Night Train* (1997).

His short-story collection *Einstein's Monsters* (1987) finds stupidity and horror in a world filled with nuclear weapons. The forced-labour camps under Soviet leader Joseph Stalin are the subject of both the nonfiction *Koba the Dread* (2002) and the novel *House of Meetings* (2006). In his novel *The Pregnant Widow* (2010), Amis examined the sexual revolution of the 1970s and its repercussions on a group of friends who lived through it. The pop culture indictment *Lionel Asbo: State of England* (2012) chronicles the vicissitudes of a fictional small-time criminal and his upstanding nephew after the former wins the lottery and becomes a fixture in the tabloid press.

Amis was one of the most well-known public intellectuals of the late 20th and early 21st centuries. He was a frequent guest on television programs, and his decades-long friendship with British American author, critic, and intellectual Christopher Hitchens was arguably the most prominent and productive literary relationship of his era. Among Amis's volumes of essays are *The Moronic Inferno and Other Visits to America* (1986), *Visiting Mrs. Nabokov, and Other Excursions* (1993), and *The War Against Cliché* (2001). *Experience* (2000), an autobiography that often focuses on his father, was acclaimed for an emotional depth and profundity that some reviewers had found lacking in his novels.

# ORHAN PAMUK

(b. June 7, 1952, Istanbul, Turkey)

The Turkish novelist Orhan Pamuk is best known for works that probe Turkish identity and history. He was awarded the Nobel Prize for Literature in 2006.

Raised in a wealthy and Western-oriented family, Pamuk attended Robert College, an American school in Istanbul, and went on to study architecture at Istanbul Technical University. After three years he dropped out and devoted himself full-time to writing. In 1977 he graduated from the University of Istanbul with a degree in journalism. From 1985 to 1988 he lived in the United States and was a visiting scholar at Columbia University in New York and the University of Iowa.

Pamuk began writing seriously in 1974 and eight years later published his first novel, *Cevdet Bey ve oğulları* ("Cevdet Bey and His Sons"), a sweeping history of an Istanbul family during and after the establishment of the Turkish republic. He followed it with *Sessiz ev* (1983; *Silent House*), relying on multiple narrators to shape the story of a family gathering on the eve of the Turkish military coup of 1980. Pamuk first achieved international fame with *Beyaz kale* (1985; *The White Castle*), his third novel, which explores the nature of identity through the story of a learned young Italian captured and made a slave to a scholar in 17th-century Istanbul. His subsequent novels, which were widely translated, include *Kara kitap* (1990; *The Black Book*), a dense depiction of Istanbul, and the mysteries *Yeni hayat* (1996; *The New Life*) and *Benim adım kırmızı* (1998; *My Name Is Red*).

In *Kar* (2002; *Snow*) a Turkish poet living in exile in Germany faces the tensions between East and West when he travels to a poor town in a remote area of Turkey. *Masumiyet müzesi* (2008; *The Museum of Innocence*) investigates the relationship between an older man and his second cousin. Thwarted in his attempts to marry her, the man begins to collect objects that she has touched. Pamuk replicated the titular museum in reality, using a house in Istanbul to display a range of items amassed while plotting the story; it opened to the public in 2012, accompanied by the catalogue *Şeylerin masumiyeti* (*The Innocence of Objects*). Among Pamuk's other works are *İstanbul: hatıralar ve şehir* (2004; *Istanbul: Memories and the City*, also published as *Istanbul: Memories of a City*), a partly fictionalized memoir, and *The Naive and Sentimental Novelist* (2010), in which he explicated his theories on the novel as a literary form.

Many of Pamuk's novels, often autobiographical and intricately plotted, show an understanding of traditional Turkish Islamic culture tempered by a belief that Turkey's future lies in the West. Pamuk drew criticism from some in Turkey for advocating the country's integration into Europe and its accession to the European Union. In 2005, after a Swiss newspaper published an interview in which he repeated claims that Turks had deliberately killed a million Armenians in 1915 and 30,000 Kurds more recently, Pamuk was charged with "denigrating Turkishness" and put on trial in Turkey in December. The charges, which produced international controversy, were later dropped.

# HILARY MANTEL

(b. July 6, 1952, Hadfield, Derbyshire, England)

The English writer Hilary Mantel is known for her bleakly comic, socially probing novels set in a wide range of contemporary and historical milieus.

Born into a working-class Roman Catholic family, Mantel attended convent school before embarking on a law degree at the London School of Economics. She finished her studies at the University of Sheffield in 1973 and found work first as a social worker and then as a store assistant. After moving to Botswana with her husband, a geologist, Mantel turned her attention to creating fiction, driven to write by the cultural isolation she experienced in Africa as well as by the inactivity imposed on her by a chronic medical condition, later diagnosed as endometriosis. In 1983 she and her husband relocated to Jiddah, Saudi Arabia, where she completed her first novel, *Every Day Is Mother's Day* (1985), before eventually moving back to England.

The book, a dark comedy about a social worker's involvement with an emotionally unbalanced woman and her autistic daughter, established Mantel's talent for vivid characterization and sharp social criticism, and she capitalized on its success a year later with a sequel, *Vacant Possession*. In 1987 Mantel wrote an essay for the British magazine *The Spectator* about her experiences in Jiddah, and she subsequently served (1987–91) as a film and book reviewer for the publication. Jiddah also provided the backdrop for her next novel, *Eight Months on Ghazzah Street* (1988), a political thriller charged with a sense of profound cultural conflict. Demonstrating her versatility, Mantel followed that book with a fanciful religious mystery set in 1950s England, *Fludd* (1989).

Mantel's reputation was further enhanced with the publication of the novel *A Place of Greater Safety* (1992), a richly detailed chronicle of the French Revolution as seen through the eyes of three of its central participants. She drew on her years in Botswana to write the novel *A Change of Climate* (1994), about British missionaries in South Africa, and on her own straitened adolescence for the clear-eyed coming-of-age novel *An Experiment in Love* (1995). Three years later she returned to historical fiction with *The Giant, O'Brien*, which imaginatively explores and contrasts the lives of two real 18th-century figures—a freakishly tall side-show performer steeped in the Irish oral tradition and a Scottish surgeon in thrall to modern science.

Mantel took a break from novels to write *Giving Up the Ghost* (2003), a memoir that depicts her anxiety-ridden childhood and her later struggle with illness. That same year she produced a collection of loosely autobiographical short stories, *Learning to Talk*. Additional recognition came for *Beyond Black* (2005), a wryly humourous novel about a psychic, which was short-listed for the Orange Prize for Fiction, but it was her next book that set the literary world abuzz. A voluminous fictional narrative depicting the rise of Thomas Cromwell to become the principal adviser to King Henry VIII of England, *Wolf Hall* (2009) was lauded for its impressive scope and complex portrayal of its subject. It was honoured with the Booker Prize as well as the National Book Critics Circle Award, and it became an international best-seller. A sequel, *Bring Up the Bodies* (2012), which focused more narrowly on Cromwell's role in the downfall of Anne Boleyn, also won the Booker Prize. Mantel was made CBE (Commander of the Order of the British Empire) in 2006.

# SIR ANDREW MOTION

(b. October 26, 1952, London, England)

The British poet, biographer, and novelist Sir Andrew Motion is especially noted for his narrative poetry. He was poet laureate of England from 1999 to 2009.

Motion attended Radley College and University College, Oxford (B.A., 1974; M.Litt., 1977), where he was a student of poet John Fuller. From 1976 to 1980 he taught at the University of Hull and from 1995 at the University of East Anglia in Norwich. In the interim between these teaching positions, he was the editor of *Poetry Review* (1980–83) and worked in a variety of editorial capacities for two London publishing houses.

Motion's first verse collection, *The Pleasure Steamers*, was published in 1978. It contains "Inland," which describes the fear and helplessness of 17th-century villagers who must abandon their homeland following a devastating flood; the poem received the Newdigate Prize in 1975. Noted for his insight and empathy, Motion frequently wrote about isolation and loss. Much influenced by the poets Edward Thomas and Philip Larkin—whose low-key poetic voices often caused their work to be overlooked and undervalued—Motion wrote critical works on both men, *The Poetry of Edward Thomas* (1980) and *Philip Larkin* (1982), as well as a biography of Larkin (*Philip Larkin: A Writer's Life*, 1993). He also produced a biography of poet John Keats (*Keats*, 1997) and his biography of the talented Lambert family, *The Lamberts: George, Constant & Kit* (1986), earned him the Somerset Maugham Award (established by Somerset Maugham to enable writers under age 35 to travel to "enrich their writing") in 1987.

Motion's later collections of poetry include *Secret Narratives* (1983), *Dangerous Play: Poems, 1974–84* (1984), *Natural Causes* (1987), *Love in a Life* (1991), *The Price of Everything* (1994), *Salt Water* (1997), *Public Property* (2002), and *The Cinder Path* (2009). Among his works of fiction are *The Pale Companion* (1989); *Famous for the Creatures* (1991); *Wainewright the Poisoner* (2000), a "fictional confession" by 19th-century painter, essayist, and alleged murderer Thomas Griffiths Wainewright; *The Invention of Dr. Cake* (2003), a fictional biography of the obscure poet-doctor William Tabor; and *Silver: Return to Treasure Island* (2012), a sequel to Robert Louis Stevenson's popular adventure novel. In 2006 Motion published a memoir, *In the Blood*, and in 2008 he released a collection of essays titled *Ways of Life: On Places, Painters, and Poets*.

As poet laureate, Motion sought to make poetry accessible to a wider audience. He especially targeted younger people, encouraging schools to teach poetry regularly. He was the first laureate to serve a fixed, 10-year term; previous laureates had received a lifetime appointment. Motion was knighted in 2009.

# ROBERTO BOLAÑO

(b. April 28, 1953, Santiago, Chile—d. July 15, 2003, Barcelona, Spain)

The Chilean author Roberto Bolaño Ávalos was one of the leading South American literary figures at the turn of the 21st century.

Bolaño's family moved throughout Chile at the behest of his truck-driver father until 1968, when they settled in Mexico City. A voracious reader who was also dyslexic, Bolaño was a middling student. He dropped out of high school shortly after moving to Mexico City and dedicated himself to poetry and leftist political causes. By his own account, Bolaño returned to Santiago in 1973 to take part in a socialist revolution that many Chileans presumed was impending; while there he was captured by the forces of Augusto Pinochet but was saved from possible death by a former schoolmate who happened to be his prison guard, leading to his release and return to Mexico. However, some of his contemporaries deny this account and insist that he never went to Chile. That one of the signal moments of Bolaño's life—which was relayed only through his own accounts—is so fraught with uncertainty reflects the central feature of his writing: almost all of the prose he produced was in some way a fictionalized version of his own life history. As such, the line between his biography and his fiction is perpetually blurred.

Bolaño's literary career began when he published a poetry collection while living in Mexico. In 1977 he left Mexico to travel the world and eventually settled in Spain, where he married and held a series of low-paying jobs while still working on his craft. He turned to prose after the birth of his son in 1990, believing that fiction would be more remunerative than poetry. After producing a series of short stories, he published the novel *La pista de hielo* (*The Skating Rink*) in 1993, which he followed with *La literatura nazi en América* (1996; *Nazi Literature in the Americas*) and *Estrella distante* (1996; *Distant Star*).

Bolaño's breakthrough work was *Los detectives salvajes* (1998; *The Savage Detectives*), which tells the story of a circle of radical Mexican poets known as the "visceral realists." The book begins as a diary of a young poet new to the group, but it then telescopes into a chronicle of the adventures of the visceral realists' two founders on their search through Mexico for an elusive poet and their subsequent globe-trotting, as told from the perspectives of more than 50 narrators. The novel made Bolaño a literary star throughout Latin America and won the prestigious Rómulo Gallegos Prize (the Spanish-language equivalent of the Booker Prize). He continued his frenetic writing pace, publishing at least one new book each year, spurred in large part by a looming awareness of his impending death (he was diagnosed with a chronic liver ailment in 1992). Notable among the last volumes published during his lifetime is *Nocturno de Chile* (2000; *By Night in Chile*), the searing deathbed rant of a Chilean priest through which Bolaño chastised what he saw as the many failings of his native country, from the Roman Catholic Church to the Pinochet regime. Bolaño died while awaiting a liver transplant in a Barcelona hospital at age 50.

While he became a well-known and critically hailed author in Spanish-speaking countries following the publication of *Los detectives salvajes*, Bolaño was not widely translated until after his death. His worldwide literary reputation was made with the posthumous publication of his magnum opus, *2666* (2004). That massive novel is divided into five loosely connected sections, which Bolaño considered publishing separately. The book's most-acclaimed section, the fourth, details a series of gruesome murders of young women (loosely based on actual murders that took place in Juárez, Mexico, at the time of the novel's setting) through a series of sanitized investigative reports, taking the reader on an unflinching exploration of suffering and grief. After the publication of *2666*, nearly all of Bolaño's earlier Spanish writings were translated into English, and a number of additional works were posthumously printed, including the short-story collection *El secreto del mal* (2007; *The Secret of Evil*) and the novel *El tercer reich* (2010; *The Third Reich*).

# HERTA MÜLLER

(b. August 17, 1953, Nițchidorf, Romania)

Romanian-born German writer Herta Müller won the Nobel Prize for Literature in 2009 for her works revealing the harshness of life in Romania under the dictatorship of Nicolae Ceaușescu. The award cited Müller for depicting "the landscape of the dispossessed" with "the concentration of poetry and the frankness of prose."

Müller, of German Swabian descent, grew up in Banat, a German-speaking region of totalitarian Romania. She attended the University of Timișoara and, as a student, became involved with Aktionsgruppe Banat, a group of writers fighting for freedom of speech. After graduating, she worked from 1977 to 1979 as a translator at a machine factory, a job from which she was fired for refusing to cooperate with the Securitate, the notoriously vast and ruthless Romanian secret police. Her first book, a collection of short stories titled *Niederungen* (1982; *Nadirs*), was censored by the Romanian government, but she won a following in Germany when the complete version of the book was smuggled out of the country. After publishing a second book of stories, *Drückender Tango* (1984; "Oppressive Tango")—which, like her first collection, depicted frankly the general misery of life in a small Romanian village similar to her own German-speaking hometown—she was forbidden to publish again in Romania, and in 1987 she emigrated with her husband, Romanian-born German author Richard Wagner, and moved to Germany.

Her first novel, *Der Mensch ist ein grosser Fasan auf der Welt* (*The Passport*), was published in Germany in 1986.

Although her circumstances had changed, her work continued to present and examine the formative experiences of her life: themes such as totalitarianism and exile pervade her work. Her style was described by Romanian journalist Emil Hurezeanu as "lively, poetic, [and] corrosive." Among Müller's later novels were *Reisende auf einem Bein* (1989; *Traveling on One Leg*), *Der Fuchs war damals schon der Jäger* (1992; "Already Back Then, the Fox Was the Hunter"), *Herztier* (1994; *The Land of Green Plums*), and *Heute wär ich mir lieber nicht begegnet* (1997; *The Appointment*). In 1998 Müller received the International IMPAC Dublin Literary Award for *The Land of Green Plums*. In addition to fiction, she published volumes of poetry and essays, including in the latter category *Hunger und Seide* (1995; "Hunger and Silk") and *Der König verneigt sich und tötet* (2003; "The King Bows and Kills"). Her novel *Atemschaukel* ("Swinging Breath") was published in 2009.

# ALAN MOORE

(b. November 18, 1953, Northampton, England)

Alan Moore is a British writer whose works included some of the most influential books in comics history.

Moore entered the publishing industry in the early 1970s, working as a writer and artist for a number of independent magazines. He broke into the mainstream with stories for *Doctor Who Weekly* and the science-fiction anthology series *2000AD*, but his gift for deconstructing the superhero genre first appeared in 1982, when he resurrected the classic British hero Marvelman (called Miracleman in the United States) for the magazine *Warrior*. Moore imagined Marvelman as a middle-aged reporter who had forgotten his role as the world's preeminent superhero, and later stories examined how an individual with godlike powers would interact with human society.

Moore's next project, *V for Vendetta* (1982–86), turned the Marvelman narrative on its head, placing near-infinite power in the hands of a ruling political party (modeled on Britain's National Front) and casting an erudite terrorist as the protagonist. In 1983 DC Comics hired Moore to write *Swamp Thing*, a straightforward monster comic that Moore transformed into a monthly meditation on life and death. It pushed the boundaries of what could be done in a mainstream book, and his success with it led to *Watchmen*. Published serially from 1986 to 1987, *Watchmen* helped define the term *graphic novel* to many readers, and its mature story line, which sampled from the dystopian visions of both Marvelman and *V for Vendetta*, was unlike anything that had previously been seen in the superhero genre. *Watchmen*'s characters were morally complex, and the climax of the story is, fundamentally, a meditation on utilitarianism within a superheroic milieu.

Moore's work on Marvelman, which was later continued by fellow writer Neil Gaiman, would spend subsequent years in intellectual property limbo as various parties fought over who owned the rights to the original stories as well as the rights to the later tales by Moore and Gaiman. Moore's *From Hell* (originally published 1991–96), an atmospheric commentary on the declining British Empire as seen through the Jack the Ripper killings, was turned into a straightforward action film (2001) with an unlikely happy ending. This less-than-satisfactory experience with Hollywood would be repeated with *The League of Extraordinary Gentlemen* (first published in 1999), a clever tale that reimagined prominent literary characters of the Victorian era, such as *Dracula*'s Mina Murray and Dr. Jekyll's monstrous alter ego, Mr. Hyde, as British secret agents. The film version, released in 2003, was stripped of its literary sensibility, and new characters—including a crime-fighting Tom Sawyer—were added to appeal to an American audience.

Moore's later work continued to examine the psychology of the superhero, most notably in the Image Comics title *Supreme*. Moore launched his own publishing imprint, America's Best Comics, in 1999 with the flagship title *Promethea*. At first glance *Promethea* appeared to be a reimagining of Wonder Woman, but the book soon transformed into an exposition of Moore's beliefs about Kabbala, a form of Jewish mysticism that originated in the 12th century.

When film adaptations of *V for Vendetta* (2006) and *Watchmen* (2009) debuted in theatres, Moore's name was conspicuously absent from the credits. His previous ill-fated dealings with Hollywood had convinced him that his creations could best be served by remaining on the printed page, and he requested that his name not be associated with those films.

# STIEG LARSSON

(b. August 15, 1954, Skelleftehamn, Sweden—
d. November 9, 2004, Stockholm)

Karl Stig-Erland Larsson was a Swedish writer and activist whose posthumously published Millennium series of crime novels brought him international acclaim.

Larsson grew up with his maternal grandparents in northern Sweden until age nine, when he rejoined his parents in Stockholm. As a teenager he wrote obsessively and, inspired by his grandfather's ardent antifascist beliefs, developed an interest in radical leftist politics. Following a mandatory 14-month stint in the Swedish army, Larsson participated in rallies against the Vietnam War and became involved in a revolutionary communist group, through which he briefly edited a Trotskyist journal. In 1977, after traveling to Ethiopia to train Eritrean dissidents, he landed a job as a graphic designer for the Swedish news agency Tidningarnas Telegrambyrå (TT), where he later worked as a journalist as well and would remain for 22 years. He soon began to also pen articles for *Searchlight*, a British magazine that investigated and exposed fascism.

By the 1990s Larsson had become a respected muckraker and an expert on the activities of those involved in extreme right-wing movements in Sweden. In 1991 he cowrote (with Anna-Lena Lodenius) a book on the subject, *Extremhögern* ("The Extreme Right"). Four years later, in response to the rising tide of neo-Nazism in Sweden, he helped establish the Expo Foundation—an organization dedicated to studying antidemocratic tendencies in society in an effort to counteract them—and he served as editor in chief of its *Expo* magazine. As one of his country's most vocal opponents of hate groups, he became a frequent target of death threats.

Larsson started to write fiction in 2001 as a means of generating additional income. Influenced by the detective novels of English-language writers such as Elizabeth George and Sara Paretsky, he conceived a 10-volume series of thrillers in which a disgraced journalist (and seeming alter ego), Mikael Blomkvist, pairs with a young tech-savvy misfit, Lisbeth Salander, to uncover a host of crimes and conspiracies. When he contacted a publisher in 2003, he had already written two novels, and he later completed a third; the following year, however, he suffered a fatal heart attack. Though Larsson had lived with Eva Gabrielsson for three decades before his death, he had never married nor written a valid will, and so the rights to and control

*Stieg Larsson, 1998.* AP Images/Scanpix Sweden/Jan Collsioo

over his estate passed to his father and brother in what became, as his fame grew, a highly publicized and contentious affair.

The first book in the series, *Män som hatar kvinnor* (2005; "Men Who Hate Women"; Eng. trans. *The Girl with the Dragon Tattoo*), which tracked the mismatched protagonists' investigation into a decades-old disappearance, was swiftly met with praise in Sweden—in particular for Larsson's indelible characterization of Salander as a surly pixie with a troubled past. Its two sequels—*Flickan som lekte med elden* (2006; *The Girl Who Played with Fire*), which delved into the seedy world of sex trafficking, and *Luftslottet som sprängdes* (2007; "The Air Castle That Blew Up"; Eng trans. *The Girl Who Kicked the Hornets' Nest*), an adrenaline-fueled exploration of institutional corruption—earned similar acclaim. Though some critics charged that the novels' determined focus on systematic violence against women was complicated by overly graphic depictions of such violence, the trilogy became wildly popular both within and outside Sweden. Together, Larsson's novels were translated into more than 30 languages and sold tens of million copies worldwide. A Swedish film adaptation of the series was produced in 2009, and an English-language film of the first novel emerged two years later.

# KAZUO ISHIGURO

(b. November 8, 1954, Nagasaki, Japan)

The Japanese-born British novelist Kazuo Ishiguro is known for his lyrical tales of regret fused with subtle optimism.

In 1960 Ishiguro's family immigrated to Great Britain, where he attended the universities of Kent (B.A., 1978) and East Anglia (M.A., 1980). Upon graduation he worked at a homeless charity and began to write in his spare time. He initially gained literary notice when he contributed three short stories to the anthology *Introduction 7: Stories by New Writers* (1981).

Ishiguro's first novel, *A Pale View of Hills* (1982), details the postwar memories of Etsuko, a Japanese woman trying to deal with the suicide of her daughter Keiko. Set in an increasingly Westernized Japan following World War II, *An Artist of the Floating World* (1986) chronicles the life of elderly Masuji Ono, who reviews his past career as a political artist of imperialist propaganda. Ishiguro's Booker Prize-winning *The Remains of the Day* (1989; film 1993) is a first-person narrative, the reminiscences of Stevens, an elderly English butler whose prim mask of formality has shut him off from understanding and intimacy. With the publication of *The Remains of the Day*, Ishiguro became one of the best-known European novelists at just 35 years of age. His next novel, *The Unconsoled* (1995)—a radical stylistic departure from his early, conventional works that received passionately mixed reviews—focuses on lack of communication and absence of emotion as a concert pianist arrives in a European city to give a performance. *When We Were Orphans* (2000), an exercise in the crime-fiction genre set against the backdrop of the Sino-Japanese War in the 1930s, traces a British man's search for his parents, who disappeared during his childhood. In 2005 Ishiguro published *Never Let Me Go* (film 2010), which through the story of three human clones warns of the ethical quandries raised by genetic engineering. A short-story collection, *Nocturnes: Five Stories of Music and Nightfall*, was published in 2009. Ishiguro also wrote screenplays for British television as well as for the feature films *The Saddest Music in the World* (2003) and *The White Countess* (2005). He was appointed Officer of the Order of the British Empire (OBE) in 1995.

# *Mo Yan*

(b. February 17, 1955, Gaomi, Shandong province, China)

The Chinese novelist and short-story writer Mo Yan (Mo Yen, a pseudonym of Guan Moye) is renowned for his imaginative and humanistic fiction, which became popular in the 1980s. Mo was awarded the 2012 Nobel Prize in Literature.

Guan Moye attended a primary school in his hometown but dropped out in the fifth grade during the turmoil of the Cultural Revolution. He participated in farmwork for years before he started to work in a factory in 1973. He joined the People's Liberation Army (PLA) in 1976 and began writing stories in 1981 under the pseudonym Mo Yan, which means "Don't Speak."

While studying literature at the PLA Academy of Art from 1984 through 1986, he published stories such as *Touming de hongluobo* ("Transparent Red Radish") and *Baozha* ("Explosions"; Eng. trans. in *Explosions and Other Stories*). His romantic historical story *Honggaoliang* (1986; "Red Sorghum") was later published with four additional stories in *Honggaoliang jiazu* (1987; "Red Sorghum Family"; *Red Sorghum*); it won him widespread fame, especially after its adaptation into a film of the same name (1987). In his subsequent work he embraced various approaches, from myth to realism, from satire to love story, but his tales were always marked by an impassioned humanism. In 1989 his novel *Tiantang suantai zhi ge* (*The Garlic Ballads*) was published and in 1995 so, too, was the collection *Mo*

*Yan wenji* ("Collected Works of Mo Yan"). Of the stories contained in the latter book, Mo himself was most satisfied with *Jiuguo* (1992; Eng. trans. *The Republic of Wine*). The novel *Fengru feitun* (1995; *Big Breasts and Wide Hips*) caused some controversy, both for its sexual content and for its failure to depict class struggle according to the Chinese Communist Party line. Mo was forced by the PLA to write a self-criticism of the book and to withdraw it from publication (many pirated copies remained available, however).

Mo left his position in the PLA in 1997 and worked as a newspaper editor, but he continued writing fiction, with his rural hometown as the setting for his stories. He said that he had been greatly influenced by writers such as the American novelist William Faulkner and the Japanese novelists Minakami Tsutomu, Mishima Yukio, and Ōe Kenzaburō. His later works include the collection of eight stories *Shifu yue lai yue mo* (2000; *Shifu, You'll Do Anything for a Laugh*) and the novels *Tanxiang xing* (2001; "The Sandalwood Torture"), *Shengsi pilao* (2006; *Life and Death Are Wearing Me Out*), and *Wa* (2009; "Frog").

# MICHEL HOUELLEBECQ

(b. February 26, 1956 or 1958, Réunion, France)

Michel Houellebecq is a writer, satirist, and provocateur whose work exposes his sometimes darkly humorous, often offensive, and thoroughly misanthropic view of humanity and the world. He is one of the best-known, if not always the best-loved, French novelists of the early 21st century.

Born Michel Thomas, he was sent by his parents to live with his maternal grandparents when he was an infant. At age five or six he was transferred to the care of his paternal grandmother, whose maiden name he later adopted. His body of work gives evidence that the abandonment by and continued absence of his parents, who divorced when he was young, deeply scarred him. At the boarding school he attended, he became a well-read outcast. At 18 he enrolled in preparatory school. Though he studied the sciences, in which he excelled, Houellebecq was drawn to the company of writers in Paris and began to write poetry. His guardian grandmother died in 1978. In 1980 he took a degree in agronomy (a branch of agriculture), a field in which he rapidly lost interest.

Houellebecq submitted some poems for publication in *Nouvelle Revue de Paris*, and they were accepted. His editor there, Michel Bulteau, encouraged him to write for a series Bulteau had initiated at Éditions le Rocher publishing house. As a result of this connection, Houellebecq wrote *H.P. Lovecraft: contre le monde, contre la vie* (1991; *H.P. Lovecraft: Against the World, Against Life*), a biography and an appreciation of that American master of the macabre. The same year, Houellebecq published a collection of short prose meditations, *Rester vivant: méthode* (*To Stay Alive: A Method*), and his first book of poetry, *La Poursuite du bonheur* (*The Pursuit of Happiness*). In order to support himself in his nascent writing career, he worked as a computer programmer, a job that inspired his first novel; *Extension du domaine de la lutte* (1994; *Whatever*; film 1999) featured an unnamed computer technician. This book brought him a wider audience.

He gained his first real international attention only four years later with the publication of *Les Particules élémentaires* (1998; film 2006), published as *Atomised* in the

United Kingdom and as *The Elementary Particles* in the United States. In it he presented two half brothers who were abandoned by their parents in childhood. Bruno is driven by an insatiable sexual appetite, while Michel, a scientist, avoids the issue of any attachment whatsoever by focusing his attention on the cloning of human life. The book's combination of reactionary political views and pornographic passages, as well as its misogynistic plot and scathing indictment of the 1960s "free love" generation that produced these unhealthy human specimens, made it the source of much controversy. *New York Times* critic Michiko Kakutani considered it "a deeply repugnant read," but it won the 2002 IMPAC Dublin Literary Award.

As his award reveals, Houellebecq's dark perspective brought him many fans, but the author remained a figure of controversy for expressing publicly in interviews as well as in his works what some readers considered racist, sexist, and deeply cynical views. His later works include *Lanzarote* (2000; *Lanzarote*), an attack on the European vacation practices; *Plateforme* (2001; *Platform*), a consideration of sex tourism in which he drew a spiteful and savage portrait of his mother; and *La Possibilité d'une île* (2005; *The Possibility of an Island*, film 2008, directed by the author), a bleak futuristic tale about the implications and possibilities of reproduction by cloning. In 2008 *Ennemis publics* (*Public Enemies*) documented an exchange of opinions—via e-mail—between Houellebecq and French public intellectual Bernard-Henri Lévy on a variety of subjects, including what they considered undeserved criticism. Houellebecq's fifth novel, *La Carte et le territoire* (2010; *The Map and the Territory*), which featured a character by the name of Houellebecq, won the 2010 Prix Goncourt.

# TONY KUSHNER

(b. July 16, 1956, New York, New York, U.S.)

The American dramatist Tony Kushner became one of the most highly acclaimed playwrights of his generation after the debut of his two-part play *Angels in America* (1990, 1991).

Kushner grew up in Lake Charles, Louisiana, and attended Columbia University and New York University. His early plays include *La Fin de la Baleine: An Opera for the Apocalypse* (1983), *A Bright Room Called Day* (1985), *Yes, Yes, No, No* (1985), and *Stella* (1987). His major work, *Angels in America: A Gay Fantasia on National Themes*, consists of two lengthy plays that deal with political issues and the AIDS epidemic in the 1980s while meditating on change and loss—two prominent themes throughout Kushner's oeuvre. The first part, *Millennium Approaches* (1990), won a Pulitzer Prize and a Tony Award for best play; the second, *Perestroika* (1991), also won a Tony Award for best play. *Angels in America* proved to be extremely popular for a work of its imposing length (the two parts run seven hours in total), and it was adapted for an Emmy Award-winning television film in 2003.

Later plays include *Slavs!* (1994); *A Dybbuk; or, Between Two Worlds* (1995), an adaptation of S. Ansky's Yiddish classic *Der Dibek*; *Henry Box Brown; or, The Mirror of Slavery* (1998); and *Homebody/Kabul* (1999), which addresses the relationship between Afghanistan and the West. Kushner also wrote the book for the musical *Caroline, or Change* (1999). His unfinished *Only We Who Guard the Mystery Shall Be Unhappy*, written in response to the Iraq War, was performed in a number of readings in 2004. His translation of Bertolt Brecht's *Mother Courage and Her Children* was staged in New York City in 2006. Kushner's *The Intelligent Homosexual's Guide to Capitalism and Socialism with a Key to the Scriptures* (2009) is a naturalistic drama about an extended family of intellectuals dealing with their patriarch's desire to commit suicide.

In addition to his work for the stage, he cowrote (with Eric Roth) the screenplay for Stephen Spielberg's film *Munich* (2005) and wrote the screenplay for Spielberg's *Lincoln* (2012). Kushner also authored the children's book *Brundibar* (2003; illustrated by Maurice Sendak) and coedited (with Alisa Solomon) the essay collection *Wrestling with Zion: Progressive Jewish-American Responses to the Israeli-Palestinian Conflict* (2003).

# RODDY DOYLE

(b. May 8, 1958, Dublin, Ireland)

The Irish author Roddy Doyle is known for his unvarnished depiction of the working class in Ireland. Doyle's distinctively Irish settings, style, mood, and phrasing made him a favourite fiction writer in his own country as well as overseas.

After majoring in English and geography at University College, Dublin, Doyle taught those subjects for 14 years at Greendale Community School, a Dublin grade school. During the summer break of his third year of teaching, Doyle began writing seriously. In the early 1980s he wrote a heavily political satire, *Your Granny's a Hunger Striker*, but it was never published.

Doyle published the first editions of his comedy *The Commitments* (1987; film 1991) through his own company, King Farouk, until a London-based publisher took over. The work was the first installment of his internationally acclaimed Barrytown trilogy, which also included *The Snapper* (1990; film 1993) and *The Van* (1991; film 1996). The trilogy centres on the ups and downs of the never-say-die Rabbitte family, who temper the bleakness of life in an Irish slum with familial love and understanding.

Doyle's fourth novel, *Paddy Clarke Ha Ha Ha* (1993), won the 1993 Booker Prize. Set in the 1960s in a fictional working-class area of northern Dublin, the book examines the cruelty inflicted upon children by other children. The protagonist, 10-year-old Paddy Clarke, fears his classmates' ostracism, especially after the breakup of his parents' marriage. In mid-1994 Doyle launched the BBC miniseries *Family*, which generated heated controversy throughout conservative Ireland. The program shed harsh light on a family's struggle with domestic violence and alcoholism and portrayed the bleaker side of life in a housing project, the same venue he had used in his earlier, more comedic Barrytown trilogy.

Doyle later wrote *The Woman Who Walked into Doors* (1997), a novel about domestic abuse; *A Star Called Henry* (1999), about an Irish Republican Army (IRA) soldier named Henry Smart and his adventures during the Easter Rising; *Oh, Play That Thing* (2004), which follows Smart as he journeys through America; *The Deportees* (2007), a collection of short stories; and *The Dead Republic* (2010), the finale of the Henry Smart trilogy that shows him returning to Ireland and coming to grips with his troubling past in the IRA.

# DAVID FOSTER WALLACE

(b. February 21, 1962, Ithaca, New York, U.S.—
d. September 12, 2008, Claremont, California)

David Foster Wallace was an American novelist, short-story writer, and essayist whose dense works provide a dark, often satirical analysis of American culture.

Wallace was the son of a philosophy professor and an English teacher. He received a B.A. from Amherst College in 1985. He was completing a master's degree in creative writing at the University of Arizona when his highly regarded debut novel, *The Broom of the System* (1987), was

*David Foster Wallace.* Steve Liss/Time & Life Pictures/Getty Images

published. He later taught creative writing at Illinois State University and at Pomona College. He received a MacArthur Foundation fellowship grant in 1997.

Wallace became best known for his second novel, *Infinite Jest* (1996), a massive, multilayered novel that he wrote over the course of four years. In it appear a sweeping cast of postmodern characters that range from recovering alcoholics and foreign statesmen to residents of a halfway house and high-school tennis stars. Presenting a futuristic vision of a world in which advertising has become omnipresent and the populace is addicted to consumerism, *Infinite Jest* takes place during calendar years that have been named by companies that purchased the rights to promote their products. *Infinite Jest* was notably the first work of Wallace's to feature what was to become his stylistic hallmark: the prominent use of notes (endnotes, in this case), which were Wallace's attempt to reproduce the nonlinearity of human thought on the page. Critics, who found Wallace's self-conscious, meandering writing style variously exhilarating and maddening, compared *Infinite Jest* to the novels of Thomas Pynchon and Don DeLillo.

Wallace's short stories are collected in *Girl with Curious Hair* (1989), *Brief Interviews with Hideous Men* (1999), and *Oblivion* (2004). He was also an acclaimed nonfiction writer, using his signature digressive, foot-note-heavy prose to produce elaborate essays on such seemingly uncomplicated subjects as the Illinois state fair, talk radio, and luxury cruises. His essay collections include *A Supposedly Fun Thing I'll Never Do Again* (1997) and *Consider the Lobster, and Other Essays* (2005). *Everything and More: A Compact History of Infinity* (2003) is a survey of the mathematical concept of infinity. He also wrote, with Mark Costello, *Signifying Rappers: Rap and Race in the Urban Present* (1990; 2nd ed. 1997).

Wallace had suffered from depression since his early 20s, and, after numerous failed attempts to find an efficacious drug regimen, he took his own life. Three years after Wallace's death, another novel, *The Pale King* (2011), which the author had left unfinished, was released. The book was assembled by Michael Pietsch (who had long been Wallace's editor). It is set in an Internal Revenue Service office in Peoria, Illinois, U.S., during the late 20th century. Most of its characters are examiners of annual income tax returns, and the book's central theme is boredom—specifically, boredom as a potential means of attaining bliss and, as such, an alternative to the culture of overstimulation that was the main subject of *Infinite Jest*. A third collection of his nonfiction writing, *Both Flesh and Not* (2012), was also published posthumously.

# MICHAEL CHABON

(b. May 24, 1963, Washington, D.C., U.S.)

The American novelist and essayist Michael Chabon is known for his elegant deployment of figurative language and adventurous experiments with genre conceits.

Chabon was the elder of two children. His father, who was a pediatrician and hospital administrator, and mother, who became a lawyer following the couple's 1975 divorce, moved the family to the ostensibly utopian planned community of Columbia, Maryland, in 1969. Following high school, he enrolled briefly at Carnegie Mellon University (1980–81) before transferring to the University of Pittsburgh, where he earned a bachelor's degree in English in 1984. He then attended the University of California, Irvine, receiving a master's degree in English in 1987.

*Michael Chabon.* Ulf Andersen/Getty Images

Chabon's adviser submitted his master's thesis, a work of fiction, to a New York publisher without his knowledge. The volume, which related the sexual awakenings and existential meanderings of a gangster's son during his first summer out of college, earned Chabon a record advance and was published as *The Mysteries of Pittsburgh* (1988; film 2008). *A Model World and Other Stories* (1991) was a compilation of some of his short fiction. His next novel, *Wonder Boys* (1995; film 2000), centres on a weekend in the life of a stymied creative writing professor as he wrangles with his various personal and professional failures.

Another short-story collection, *Werewolves in Their Youth* (1999), assembled pieces originally published in magazines such as *The New Yorker* and *GQ.* Chabon's third novel, *The Amazing Adventures of Kavalier and Clay* (2000), is the sprawling tale of two Jewish cousins who, at the cusp of the comic book phenomenon that began in the mid-1930s, devise a superhero and shepherd him to fame in the pages of their own serial. In conveying the vagaries along their path to eventual happiness, Chabon liberally larded the tale with mythological references. The golem of Prague was central among them, serving as a metaphor for both rebirth and the process of generating a fictional character. The novel earned him the Pulitzer Prize in 2001. He followed with *Summerland* (2002), an expansive young adult novel that features a hero who must save his father (and the world) from the apocalypse by winning a game of baseball against a cast of tricksters drawn from American folklore.

*The Yiddish Policemen's Union* (2007), which speculatively situated the Jewish state in Sitka, Alaska, rather than Israel, deploys hard-boiled detective novel conventions in relating the resolution of a murder. The novel won a Hugo Award in 2008. *Gentlemen of the Road* (2007), a picaresque featuring medieval Jewish brigands, was serialized in *The New York Times* and then published as a novel. Chabon also penned the children's book *The Astonishing Secret of Awesome Man* (2011). He scrutinized the consequences of corporate domination and examined American race relations in the novel *Telegraph Avenue* (2012), which centres on the denizens of a small jazz and soul record shop threatened by the imminent incursion of a rival chain store.

*Maps and Legends: Reading and Writing Along the Borderlands* (2008) and *Manhood for Amateurs: The Pleasures and Regrets of a Husband, Father, and Son* (2009) are collections of essays ruminating on his obsession with the intersections of fiction genres and on domestic life, respectively. Chabon also ventured into screenwriting, penning a draft of the script for *Spider-Man 2* and collaborating on the script for *John Carter* (2012), adapted from an Edgar Rice Burroughs novel.

# J.K. ROWLING

(b. July 31, 1965, Chipping Sodbury, near Bristol, England)

The British author Joanne Kathleen Rowling is the creator of the popular and critically acclaimed Harry Potter series, about a young sorcerer in training.

After graduating from the University of Exeter in 1986, Rowling began working for Amnesty International in London, where she started to write the Harry Potter adventures. In the early 1990s she traveled to Portugal to teach English as a foreign language, but, after a brief marriage and the birth of her daughter, she returned to the United Kingdom, settling in Edinburgh. Living on public assistance between stints as a French teacher, she continued to write.

Rowling's first book in the series, *Harry Potter and the Philosopher's Stone* (1997; also published as *Harry Potter and the Sorcerer's Stone*), was an immediate success, appealing to both children (its intended audience) and adults. Featuring vivid descriptions and an imaginative story line, it followed the adventures of the unlikely hero Harry Potter, a lonely orphan who discovers that he is actually a wizard and enrolls in the Hogwarts School of Witchcraft and Wizardry. The book received numerous awards, including the British Book Award. Succeeding volumes—*Harry Potter and the Chamber of Secrets* (1998), *Harry Potter and the Prisoner of Azkaban* (1999), *Harry Potter and the Goblet of*

*Author J.K. Rowling and 12-year-old actor Daniel Radcliffe at the world film premiere of* Harry Potter and the Philosopher's Stone *in London, Nov. 4, 2001. (The movie was titled* Harry Potter and the Sorcerer's Stone *in the United States.)* Gareth Davies/Getty Images

*Fire* (2000), *Harry Potter and the Order of the Phoenix* (2003), and *Harry Potter and the Half-Blood Prince* (2005)—also were best-sellers, available in more than 200 countries and some 60 languages. The seventh and final installment in the series, *Harry Potter and the Deathly Hallows*, was released in 2007.

The Harry Potter series sparked great enthusiasm among children and was credited with generating a new interest in reading. Film versions of the books were released in 2001–11 and became some of the top-grossing movies in the world. In addition, Rowling wrote the companion volumes *Fantastic Beasts & Where to Find Them* (2001), *Quidditch Through the Ages* (2001), and *The Tales of Beedle the Bard* (2008), all of which originated as books read by Harry Potter and his friends within the fictional world of the series. Proceeds from their sales were donated to charity. Rowling made her first foray into adult fiction with *The Casual Vacancy* (2012), a contemporary social satire set in a small English town.

Rowling was appointed Officer of the Order of the British Empire (OBE) in 2001. In 2009 she was named a chevalier of the French Legion of Honour.

# DAVID MITCHELL

(b. January 12, 1969, Southport, Lancashire, England)

David Mitchell is an English author whose novels are noted for their lyrical prose style and complex structures.

Mitchell was raised in a small town in Worcestershire, Eng. He did not speak until age five and developed a stammer by age seven, both of which contributed to a boyhood spent in solitude that consequently involved a great deal of reading. He attended the University of Kent, from which he received a B.A. in English and American literature and an M.A. in comparative literature. In 1994 he began an eight-year sojourn in Japan, where he taught English as a second language and dedicated himself to his writing.

Mitchell's first published work was *Ghostwritten* (1999), a collection of interconnected narratives that take place in a variety of locations throughout the world. While criticized by some as derivative of the novels of Murakami Haruki, the book is nevertheless noteworthy for its plotting and realistic characterizations, which are unusually sophisticated for a first novel. *Ghostwritten* won the John Llewellyn Rhys Prize for the best work of fiction by a British author under 35 years of age. Mitchell's next book, *Number9dream* (2001), the story of a Japanese man searching for his missing father told in a manner that makes it unclear if the action takes place in reality or the narrator's mind, also won measured praise from critics.

Mitchell's third novel, *Cloud Atlas* (2004; film 2012), was his breakthrough work. Hailed by some reviewers as a modern masterpiece upon its publication, *Cloud Atlas* consists of a series of six interlinked stories—written in differing styles—through which Mitchell explores and critiques the seeming progress of the postindustrial age. In the first half of the book, the narratives progress chronologically from a 19th-century travel journal of an American notary to a postapocalyptic future where Western civilization has been nearly extinguished. The interrupted stories are then brought to their respective conclusions (in reverse chronological order) over the second half of the novel, which ultimately ends with the tale of the 19th-century notary.

Mitchell followed the audaciously structured *Cloud Atlas* with *Black Swan Green* (2006), a relatively straightforward bildungsroman that semiautobiographically follows a stammering 13-year-old growing up in Worcestershire in the 1980s. His fifth work, *The Thousand Autumns of Jacob de Zoet* (2010), is a historical novel centred on the former Japanese trading island of Dejima at the turn of the 18th century.

# DAVE EGGERS

(b. March 12, 1970, Boston, Massachusetts, U.S.)

Dave Eggers is an American author, publisher, and literacy advocate whose breakout memoir, *A Heartbreaking Work of Staggering Genius* (2000), was followed by other fiction and nonfiction successes. He also founded the publishing house McSweeney's in 1998.

Eggers grew up in Boston and in Illinois, and for a time he studied journalism at the University of Illinois at Urbana-Champaign. When he was 21, however, the death of both of his parents within a very brief period led him to drop his studies in order to help raise his 8-year-old brother, Christopher (Toph). The two moved to California, where Eggers cofounded the short-lived satiric *Might* magazine. Eggers was an editor at Salon.com and a writer for a number of publications, including *Esquire* magazine, before releasing *A Heartbreaking Work of Staggering Genius*. The memoir, which was enriched with postmodern writing techniques and fictionalized encounters, detailed Eggers's experiences raising Toph. It earned him instant acclaim and literary stardom, as well as a Pulitzer Prize nomination.

In an effort to create a platform for other young writers, Eggers founded McSweeney's publishing house, which started with the 1998 launch of the literary magazine *Timothy McSweeney's Quarterly Concern*. In 2003 it was joined by *The Believer*, a journal of literary reviews and interviews and other, often esoteric, pop-culture musings. McSweeney's also served as a book imprint and in 2005 originated the DVD "magazine" *Wholphin*, featuring new or underexposed short films.

The creation in 2002 of Eggers's nonprofit organization 826 Valencia, based in San Francisco, was a further foray into literary advocacy. It was a volunteer-based writing laboratory devoted to developing kids' creativity and love of books through programs that included free tutoring and writing workshops. Soon after, branches of 826 Valencia opened in other major cities, including Chicago, Seattle, and New York, and the organization became known as 826 National. Each branch was located behind a store that both generated revenue and served as a cheeky "front" for the education happening behind closed doors; i.e., 826 Valencia served also as a pirate supply store, and the front of 826 Chicago was a spy supply store masquerading as the Boring Store.

A number of fiction books followed Eggers's memoir, notably *What Is the What: The Autobiography of Valentino Achak Deng* (2006). The book chronicled the story of a South Sudanese man who had survived the destruction of his family's village during Sudan's civil war and made his way to the United States. In 2007 the Heinz Family Foundation made Eggers the youngest-ever recipient of its arts and humanities award, noting his contributions not only to literature but also to the writing community.

In 2009 the film version of Maurice Sendak's *Where the Wild Things Are* was released concurrently with Eggers's novelization of the screenplay, which he had cowritten with director Spike Jonze. The movie and book were loose adaptations of Sendak's original, inspired as much by its wistful beauty and loving approach to the child mind as by its story. That year Eggers also saw the film *Away We Go*, which he cowrote with his wife, Vendela Vida, appear on the big screen. His other books include *Zeitoun* (2009), a nonfiction account of a Syrian American man and his experiences in New Orleans following Hurricane Katrina, and

*Dave Eggers, 2004.* Stephen Lovekin/FilmMagic/Getty Images

the novel *A Hologram for the King* (2012), which reflected anxieties about globalization with its tale of a middle-aged American pursuing business in Saudi Arabia.

# ZADIE SMITH

(b. October 27, 1975, London, England)

The British author Zadie Smith is known for her treatment of race, religion, and cultural identity and for her novels' eccentric characters, savvy humour, and snappy dialogue. She became a sensation in the literary world with the publication of her first novel, *White Teeth*, in 2000.

Smith, the daughter of a Jamaican mother and an English father, changed the spelling of her first name from Sadie to Zadie at age 14. She began writing poems and stories as a child and later studied English literature at the University of Cambridge (B.A., 1998). While there, she began writing *White Teeth*, and at age 21 she submitted some 80 pages to an agent. A frenzied bidding war ensued, and the book eventually was sold to Hamish Hamilton. Smith took several more years to complete the novel, and in 2000 it was published to rave reviews. Set in the working-class suburb of Willesden in northwest London, *White Teeth* chronicled the lives of best friends Archie Jones, a down-on-his-luck Englishman whose failed suicide attempt opens the novel, and Samad Iqbal, a Bengali Muslim who struggles to fit into British society. Spanning some 50 years, the novel also detailed the trials and tribulations of their families, which prompted some critics to hail Smith as a modern-day Charles Dickens. The ambitious work won numerous awards, including the Whitbread First Novel Award (2000), and was a finalist for the National Book Critics Circle Award and the Orange Prize for Fiction.

Smith's second novel, *The Autograph Man*, was published in 2002. It centred on Alex-Li Tandem, a Chinese Jewish autograph trader who sets out to meet a reclusive 1950s starlet and in the process undertakes his own journey of self-discovery. *The Autograph Man*, which also addressed the public's obsession with celebrity and pop culture, received mostly positive reviews. Soon after the novel's publication, Smith became a fellow at Harvard University's Radcliffe Institute for Advanced Study.

*On Beauty*, published in 2005, further established Smith as one of the foremost British novelists of her day. The novel, heavily modeled on E.M. Forster's *Howards End*, chronicled the lives of two families in the fictional town of Wellington, Massachusetts, just outside Boston. A comic work studying the culture wars and racial and ethnic overlap in a liberal college town, *On Beauty* was praised for its acumen and scathing satire. The novel was a finalist for the Man Booker Prize and won the 2006 Orange Prize for fiction.

*NW* (2012) centres on two women whose friendship—tempered by their straitened upbringings in a gritty London council estate—is tested by their divergent paths in adulthood. Though lauded for its evocative sense of place and sharply observed characters, the novel was deemed plotless and confusing by some critics.

Smith also edited and contributed to the short-story collection *The Book of Other People* (2007) and published a collection of essays, *Changing My Mind* (2009).

# GLOSSARY

**acolyte** One who assists a member of the clergy in a liturgical service by performing minor duties.

**agitprop** political propaganda in the form of art, music, literature, film, etc.

**agronomy** The science of soil management and field-crop production.

**anglicize** To alter to a characteristic English form.

**anomie** The state of society or an individual in which normative standards of conduct and belief have weakened or disappeared. In individuals, the condition is commonly characterized by personal disorientation, anxiety, and social isolation.

**anthropomorphic** Ascribing human characteristics to nonhuman things.

**apocryphal** Of doubtful authorship or authenticity.

**argot** A special language that is particular to a certain group.

**assonance** A relatively close repetition of sounds, especially of vowels, or a repetition of vowels without repetition of consonants that is used as an alternative to rhyme in verse.

**attaché** A technical expert on a country's diplomatic staff at a foreign capital.

**autodidactic** Having the characteristics of one who is self-taught.

**Berber** A member of any of various peoples living in northern Africa west of Tripoli.

**bildungsroman** A novel showing the moral and psychological growth during the main character's formative years.

**bourgeoisie** The members of the middle class.

**bruin** A bear.

**cacophonous** Harsh- and loud-sounding.

**cangue** A heavy wooden device worn around the shoulders once used in China and other parts of Asia to punish and humiliate criminals.

**canon** Any comprehensive list of books within a field or genre.

**cartography** The process of mapmaking; also the construction, compilation, and design of a written work.

**chevalier** A member of any of various orders of knighthood or of merit (as the Legion of Honour).

**colloquial** A familiar, informal, and conversational style.

**colloquy** A high-level, serious conversation.

**Confabulario** A term invented by author Juan José Arreola, meaning a collection of fables.

**contrapuntal** Characterized by two or more independent melodies sounded together.

**corpus** The complete works of an author.

**cosset** Pamper.

**curmudgeon** A grumpy, and usually old, person.

**demotic** Of or relating to the people; popular; common.

**didactic** Designed or intended to teach.

**dithyramb** A song or poem honouring or praising a particular subject, often the god Dionysus.

**dystopia** An imaginary place that is depressingly wretched and whose people often have a fearful existence.

**elegiac** A metrical form of poetry that uses couplets and expresses sorrow or lamentation for something that has passed.

**elegize** To lament the death of someone in an elegy (a pensive, melancholy poem).

**elide** To suppress, alter, or omit.

**elliptical** Writing characterized by extreme economy of expression or omission of superfluous elements; concise.

**elope** To go away secretly to marry.

**emeritus** Retaining a title after honorably retiring from duties.

**entomology** The study of insects.

**epigram** A short poem often ending with a clever or witty expression.

**epistolary novel** A novel told through the medium of letters written by one or more of the characters.

**eponymous** Describing an object, such as a city or institution, that is named after a person.

**ethnology** The science that deals with the division of human beings into races and their origin, distribution, relations, and characteristics.

**excoriate** To denounce severely or berate.

**factotum** A general servant.

**fey** Quaintly unconventional; campy.

**flak** Antiaircraft guns.

**Gentile** A non-Jew, especially a Christian as distinguished from a Jew.

**ghazal** An Islamic lyric poem that begins with a rhymed couplet whose rhyme is repeated in all even lines and that is especially common in Persian literature.

**gonzo journalism** Highly personal, subjective, even eccentric, reporting created by Hunter S. Thompson.

**Igbo** A member of a people of the area around the lower Niger River in Africa.

**incantatory** Written or recited formula of words designed to produce a particular effect.

**Inquisition** Institution established by the Roman Catholic Church that swept over Europe in the 13th century, the purpose of which was to try persons accused of being heretics, that is, of revolting against religious authority. Punishment of those found to be guilty ranged from fines and excommunication to imprisonment for life or burning at the stake for incorrigible heretics.

**interlocutor** Someone who takes part in a conversation or debate.

**irascible** Hot-tempered; cranky.

**Jungian** Relating to, or characteristic of Carl Jung or his psychological doctrines, among them that the will to live is stronger than the sexual drive (contrasting with the theory of Sigmund Freud), and that personalities are classified in two types: introverts and extroverts.

**lagomorph** A rabbit, hare, or pika.

**libretto** The text of an opera, operetta, or other kind of musical theatre.

**metatextual** Referring to a form of written discourse in which one part of the text comments on another within the same work or another.

**mordant** Biting and caustic in thought, manner, or style.

**muckraker** Any of a group of American writers identified with pre–World War I reform and exposé literature.

**mulatto** A person of mixed white and black ancestry.

**Nō** A classic Japanese dance-drama having a heroic theme, a chorus, and highly stylized action, costuming, and scenery.

**oeuvre** An artist's complete body of work.

**Outback** The remote, predominantly undeveloped, rural area of Australia.

**partisan** A firm adherent to a party, faction, cause, or person, especially one exhibiting blind, prejudiced, and unreasoning allegiance.

**peregrination** A journey; travels.

**persona non grata** One who is unacceptable or unwelcome.

**picaresque** Describes a story that involves a rogue or adventurer surviving mainly by his or her wits in a treacherous society.

**polemic** A controversial discussion or argument; an aggressive attack on or the refutation of the opinions or principles of another.

**postmodernism** Various literary movements that originated in the second half of the 20th century and have in common a skepticism toward universal notions of truth and meaning.

**prosody** The study of poetic metre and versification.

**Rabelaisian** Characteristic of the works of Renaissance author François Rabelais, that is, marked by gross robust humour, satire, extravagance of caricature, and bold naturalism.

**reticence** Reluctance.

**sarin** A nerve gas.

**simulacrum** Superficial likeness; imitation.

**stipend** A fixed sum of money, typically modest in amount, that is paid periodically in compensation for services or to defray expenses.

**straitened** Characterized by financial hardship.

**sui generis** One of a kind; unique.

**sutra** In Buddhism, one of the narrative parts of the Buddhist religious literature.

**sybarite** One devoted to luxury and pleasure.

**titular** Relating to something mentioned in a title, specifically of a literary work.

**trenchant** Incisive; keen.

**trope** Any literary or rhetorical device using words in a way other than their literal sense; figurative use of language.

**White Russia** The former region of eastern Europe that is roughly coextensive with present-day Belarus. Belarus, formerly known as Belorussia, was the smallest of the three Slavic republics include in the Soviet Union (the larger two being Russia and Ukraine).

# BIBLIOGRAPHY

The authors in this volume are studied in such works as Judith Skelton Grant, *Robertson Davies: Man of Myth* (1994); Randi Birn and Karen Gould (eds.), *Orion Blinded: Essays on Claude Simon* (1981); Robert Weninger, *Framing a Novelist: Arno Schmidt Criticism 1970–1994* (1995); Alan Nadel, *Invisible Criticism: Ralph Ellison and the American Canon* (1988); José Quiroga, *Understanding Octavio Paz* (1999); Constantine FitzGibbon, *The Life of Dylan Thomas* (1965, reissued 1975), the official biography of the poet, commissioned by his trustees and approved by his widow; Gerhard Bach and Gloria L. Cronin (eds.), *Small Planets: Saul Bellow and the Art of Short Fiction* (2000); D.W. McPheeters, *Camilo José Cela* (1969), which discusses both the life and the literary output of the writer; Robert L. Nicholas, *The Tragic Stages of Antonio Buero Vallejo* (1972); Nancy B. Rich, *The Flowering Dream: The Historical Saga of Carson McCullers* (1999); Edward E. Ericson, Jr., *Solzhenitsyn and the Modern World* (1993); Earl E. Fitz, *Sexuality and Being in the Poststructuralist Universe of Clarice Lispector* (2001); Tim Hunt, *Kerouac's Crooked Road: The Development of a Fiction* (1981, reissued 1996), a pioneering critical study, the first to examine the relationships between the various versions and variations of *On the Road*; Neil Powell, *Amis & Son: Two Literary Generations* (2008); Timothy Ilse, *Abe Kōbō: An Exploration of His Prose, Drama, and Theatre* (2000); Horace A. Porter, *Stealing the Fire: The Art and Protest of James Baldwin* (1989); Brad Gooch, *Flannery: A Life of Flannery O'Connor* (2009); Tony Mitchell, *Dario Fo: People's Court Jester*, rev. and expanded ed. (1999); Harold

Bloom (ed.), *Gabriel García Márquez* (1989, reissued 1999); Anne Paolucci, *From Tension to Tonic: The Plays of Edward Albee* (1972, reissued 2000); Maarten Van Delden, *Carlos Fuentes, Mexico, and Modernity* (1998); Herbert Goldstone, *Coping with Vulnerability: The Achievement of John Osborne* (1982); Bruce King, *Derek Walcott: A Caribbean Life* (2000), the first authorized literary biography of the author; Jago Morrison, *The Fiction of Chinua Achebe* (2007); Patrick French, *The World Is What It Is: The Authorized Biography of V.S. Naipaul* (2008); Janet Malcolm, *The Silent Woman: Sylvia Plath & Ted Hughes* (1994); Barcley Owens, *Cormac McCarthy's Western Novels* (2000); Derek Wright, *Wole Soyinka Revisited* (1993), which discusses Soyinka's life and works; Susan J. Napier, *Escape from the Wasteland: Romanticism and Realism in the Fiction of Mishima Yukio and Oe Kenzaburo* (1991); Brenda Daly, *Lavish Self-Divisions: The Novels of Joyce Carol Oates* (1996); Henry Hart, *Seamus Heaney: Poet of Contrary Progressions* (1992); Reingard M. Nischik, *Engendering Genre: The Works of Margaret Atwood* (2009); Lev Loseff (Lev Losev), *Joseph Brodsky: A Literary Life*, trans. by Jane Ann Miller (2011; originally published in Russian, 2006); Stephen J. Bottoms, *Theatre of Sam Shepard: States of Crisis* (1998); Christopher Bigsby (ed.), *The Cambridge Companion to David Mamet* (2004), a collection of critical essays; and Marshall Boswell, *Understanding David Foster Wallace* (2003), a scholarly overview of Wallace's early novels and short stories.

# INDEX